SomeDay

INSIDE THE DREAM TOUR AND MICK FANNING'S 2007 CHAMPIONSHIP WIN

WILL SWANTON

ALLEN&UNWIN

First published in 2008

Allen & Unwin
83 Alexander Street
Crows Nest NSW 2065
Australia
Phone: (61 2) 8425 0100
Fax: (61 2) 9906 2218
Email: info@allenandunwin.com
Web: www.allenandunwin.com

The Cataloguing-in-Publication entry is
available from the National Library of Australia

   ISBN 978 1 74175 411 7.

All internal images copyright © Covered Images and
are reproduced with permission.
Images of the Fanning family are courtesy of Liz Osborne.

Set in 11.5/15 pt Fairfield by Bookhouse, Sydney
Printed and bound in Australia by Griffin Press

10 9 8 7 6 5 4 3 2 1

FSC
Mixed Sources
Product group from well-managed
forests and other controlled sources
Cert no. SCS-COC-001185
www.fsc.org
© 1996 Forest Stewardship Council

The paper this book is printed on is certified by
the © 1996 Forest Stewardship Council A.C.
(FSC). The printer holds FSC chain of custody
SCS-COC-001185. The FSC promotes environmentally
responsible, socially beneficial and economically
viable management of the world's forests.

Will Swanton has been a sports writer for a decade. He's covered the Australian Test cricket tours to England, India and the West Indies, plus the 2003 World Cup in South Africa. From swimming at the Olympic and Commonwealth Games, the Australian Open Golf tournament, Davis Cup tennis to State of Origin and Test rugby league, Will's seen Ian Thorpe win Olympic gold, Steve Waugh score Test centuries and Andrew Johns win rugby league premierships. But after five years following the World Surfing Tour, he's never seen anything like the Dream Tour.

Contents

Introduction

Mick and Sean Fanning used to talk about some day. They used to talk about how, when some day came, they would be on the world tour together. They used to talk about how, when *some day* came, one of them would be world champion. Well, check out Fanning's mood, speed, the unblinking look in his eyes. Check out the rest of the world's greatest boardriders stopping in their tracks to watch him free-surf and compete; one barn-burning wave after another. Check out the slack-jawed expressions on their faces: one part respect, one part awe, one part an increasing resignation to the fact that sometimes, when a man embarks upon a mission, he can become impossible to stop.

Some day may be just around the corner.

Mick still talks to Sean, but there's no guarantee anyone is listening. Sometimes, all you can do is hope and pray.

Four youths were in a car on the Gold Coast on 14 August, 1998. Control of the vehicle was lost. There was the panic-stricken acceleration and braking of the driver, gasps of disbelief from all four passengers, the turning of the night from fun to something more sinister. There was the screeching of tyres and a collision—an almighty collision. Two passengers were in the back of the car and they both died. One of them was Joel Green. The other was Sean Fanning.

Nobody on the Gold Coast saw Mick Fanning for a while after that. Not the real Mick Fanning.

Not all who wander are lost.

Tolkien

Do not ask—it is forbidden to know—what end the gods have in store for me and for you . . .

Horace (BC)

Surreal, so real. You sing.
It's a beautiful thing that can make a man sing.

1

Release the hounds

QUIKSILVER PRO
SNAPPER ROCKS, QUEENSLAND, AUSTRALIA

What happens when we die? Seriously, what happens? In this day and age, when we know everything about *everything*, isn't anyone trying to find out?

There's no way on Earth you're going to sit here and pretend you can truly comprehend the heartache Mick Fanning and the rest of his family have endured. And there's no way you can properly fathom the sheer physical pain Fanning experienced when he tore his hamstring clean off the bone. *Tore it clean off the bone*. But what you can do is make the following observation: Mick Fanning's quest to win this year's world championship will become an eight-month demonstration of the strength of the human spirit.

That may be a complete exaggeration of the facts. And that may be corny enough to make you want to hurl. But when you sift through all the bullshit of nonsensical judging, the fickleness of the ocean and the copious amounts of unexplained good fortune (dumb luck) required to survive an entire year of Heat Poker, that may be spot-on. There's just something about all this. Nobody will try harder. Nobody will be more meticulously prepared, or as relentlessly committed. Nobody will have a stare so laser-sharp it could cut you in half. Andy Irons is a competitive hard-arse but Fanning's game face will be so cold and piercing it could make Irons run home to mummy. The man formerly regarded as the most ferocious competitor on the planet will throw in the towel before the year is out.

'I was doing some stand-up paddle work in the flat water behind the Tweed,' says Australia's 1999 world champion, Mark Occhilupo. 'Mick was there. I watched him for a while. His coach was timing him over ten-second sprints. I couldn't believe it—they were just timing him paddling between two sticks. I'd never seen anyone do that. Doesn't sound like much, but I think it was. I was thinking, "If Mick is doing that, he's doing a whole bunch of stuff nobody knows about." He's super-fit, motivated and more professional than a lot of the guys out here. He has left no stone unturned.'

Fanning's mother, Liz Osborne, is proud of both her sons. The one on the tour living the dream; the one who is not. For the first time, you see a photo of Sean. It's Mick, with curly hair. You feel a chill.

You think of Sean and Liz—not Mick, for some reason, but Sean and Liz—when you buy a card. It's jet black. The print is purple, orange and blue. It says: *Live With Intention. Walk To The Edge. Listen Hard. Practise Wellness. Play With Abandon. Laugh. Choose With No Regret. Continue To Learn. Appreciate Your Friends. Do What You Love.* And then the big one, the one that makes you feel as though you'll never be able to do everything you want in this lifetime, the one that makes you realise that however much you do, you'll always have this overwhelming desire to do more. The one that makes you think that time is already running out. *Live As If This Is All There Is.* You read the card to your daughters and tell them what it means to live as if this is all there is and they get all excited and say, 'Yes, Daddy, let's do that!' But they're too young to understand.

Mick Fanning understands. He's seen the proof that tomorrow doesn't always come. Taj Burrow gets it, too. He's been going flat-chat for a decade. A man whose parents were magnificently free-spirited enough to spin a globe and head for wherever their fingers landed was in no danger of growing up to be a stiff. Vance and Nancy Burrow wanted to escape California. They could have pointed to anywhere on the planet with dud surf—England, the Gaza strip, Bondi—but they found Western Australia. 'Classic, eh?' Burrow says. 'So random. They went, "Yeah, how about Australia?" They came over in '72 and they loved it. They moved here for good in '74.' They had their only son four years later in the country town of Busselton. Burrow still lives at a far-flung place in the south of Western Australia called Yalingup. 'I had to surf when I was a kid,' he says. 'There was nothing else to do.'

Funny thing about Taj Burrow: he's never cared too much for the world title. Until now. Previously he'd been more devoted to the creation of his rip-roaring movies—*Sabotaj*, *Montaj* and *Fair Bits*. He had the misguided notion they would be his legacy. They will be *part* of his legacy. There's been a seismic change of heart. A little introspection. The realisation that he's sold himself short by basking in his globetrotting, surf-drenched lifestyle without muscling up for a proper crack at the crown and a suspicion that when he's 80 with no hair and no teeth and whittling sticks on his back porch on some remote property in Western Australia, he'll regret it. He will have movies and magazine covers and memories of the adulation but he won't have done himself justice. Conscience never fades.

'It used to be enough for me to be top five in the world every year, making money from doing what I loved and just living the dream, really,' Burrow says. 'But this year is different. I have a hunger for this. It's the most serious I've ever been. To be honest, I've never felt confident before that I was good enough to beat these guys. I'd watch Kelly and Andy and think, "How am I going to beat *that*?" I just couldn't keep my confidence up for a whole year. I'd have one event and feel invincible and I'd win it, but I just couldn't maintain the confidence. I'd get in these really bad frames of mind where I'd get down on myself and everyone would overtake me. But now I know I can mix it with anyone. I probably should have known it a lot sooner. I just try to tell myself at every event: "I can beat these guys". It's more of an internal thing for me. I started seeing people—who I knew I could beat—beat me and win contests. I just started thinking, "What am I doing? Why aren't I winning these events? Why isn't it me?" I want it to be me.'

Taj Burrow is 29. When did that happen? Clocks are ticking. He'll be put through the mill. There will be moments of immense personal satisfaction and triumph. But there will be periods of unbearable sadness and a need to fight like few people can. His body will fall apart but he will not surrender. There will be a time when he's as broken and vulnerable as an abandoned child, sleep-deprived and sobbing during one of the biggest contests of the year because the woman he loved has betrayed him in the worst possible fashion at the worst possible time. Lesser men would wilt, but Taj Burrow will not give up. This time, this year, he will not give up. He will expose himself to the intense highs and lows that come from dedicating yourself wholly to a burning ambition. The biggest battle can be to conquer yourself; the most intimidating stare from a mirror.

Spend five seconds with Taj Burrow and there are two recurring themes: his favourite sayings. The first is that he's stoked. This makes him stoked, that makes him stoked, in an ideal world everything would make him stoked. The second is his desire to nail everything. He goes to a bar and wants to nail the cocktail list. He goes surfing and wants to nail whatever high-voltage, gravity-defying manoeuvre he's attempting to pull off. He wants to nail his next heat; nail the next contest. When pedals are jammed to the metal for the start of what *Tracks* magazine will call 'the most bullshit year in pro surfing history', he is going to have much in common with Mick Fanning. Firstly, they've both reinvented themselves. Two irresistible forces are about to collide. Secondly, if they really are going to pull this off, if one of them really is going to become world champion, they're going to have to do something extraordinary. They're going to have to overcome the greatest surfer in history. They're going to have to nail Slater.

Kelly Slater is mobbed on arrival at Coolangatta airport. He walks into the Rainbow Bay Surf Club like he's walking onto a yacht. He's aloof. When she spots him, women's world champion Layne Beachley tells him he has enough world titles and he shoots back: 'What are you, my sister?' A wry smile. The women's tour has seven events and two of them overlap with the men's—here, and at Bells Beach. For the rest of the tour, when they leave Australia for Tahiti, Chile, South Africa, the US, France, Spain and Brazil, the men and women will go their separate ways. No-one will be too upset about this. The women don't like being at men's events because a) they are sent out in inferior conditions; b) they fear surfing some of the places the men do, such as the killing ground of Teahupo'o, where the less courageous femme fatales used to paddle onto the razor-sharp reef, sit petrified and motionless on their boards for half an hour before paddling back in without so much as having *tried* to catch a wave; and c) they don't get much respect from the men. The men don't like sharing contests with the women because a) they just don't. *Capisce?*

Slater looks a little uneasy. If you can look comfortably uneasy, that's him. He's been minding his own business in long shorts, T-shirt and sandals. Cameron Diaz is walking down the red carpet for the Oscars as Slater takes his seat on the balcony. He says hello, his handshake is firm. He'll talk about life, but not love. Any mention of Diaz, the Hollywood actress who may or may not be his latest flame, will result in him walking out the door, so conversation drifts towards the far end of the glamour spectrum: Joel Parkinson. No offence.

'I worry about a guy getting on a hot streak and I worry that if Joel can get himself on a hot streak at the start of the tour, he'll win the world title,' Slater says. 'I've got a funny feeling he'll get on that streak this year. Joel has that eye-of-the-tiger competitiveness about him but there's also such a relaxed flow about the way he surfs. When he starts winning, he's on auto-pilot. He can surf in his sleep and win. It's a remarkable thing to be able to look so relaxed on a wave. He's pushing hard on the inside but there's that calmness on the outside. Joel hasn't reached his potential yet.'

Maybe not, but he's reached the balcony. Why can't Australia win a men's world title, Joel? Why hasn't anyone done it since Occhilupo? Why can't you beat Slater? You scared of him? Overawed? What's your problem? 'I'm not the only Aussie on tour—go and get up the other blokes,' Parkinson says. He's grinning broadly. There won't be too many times this year when Joel Parkinson isn't grinning broadly. He's been described as being *as happy as a fucking clam* and that's an irresistibly accurate description. 'I'm going out there to do everything I possibly can,' a happy-as-a-fucking-clam Joel Parkinson says. 'You can't underestimate yourself. You've got to be positive and tell yourself you can do it. I'm telling myself it's possible.'

Robert Kelly Slater, 35, is from Cocoa Beach, Florida. He can be mentioned in the same breath as Tiger Woods and Roger Federer without it sounding foolish. He has eight world titles, including the last two. He won his eighth while barely getting his gloriously bald head wet. Every other pro on the tour stayed away from his victory party—except Fanning. Slater turns up at Conrad Jupiters casino for the ASP World Tour banquet in an Aston Martin and looks more like James Bond than James Bond does. He's a worldwide celebrity. He's rich. He's famous. He doesn't have to woo the world's most beautiful women because they woo him. Outwardly, he's got it all. Inwardly, what's going on?

'I practise in my mind,' he says. 'I look at a wave and I can imagine myself on that wave. I literally get the feeling in my body and in my muscles of how it's going to be when I ride that wave. I didn't surf a wave for three weeks before I got here, but I went out and it felt like I'd been surfing every day. It's a spiritual thing for me. It's just ingrained in my muscles and connected to my mind and somehow I feel like I can improve my surfing without even having to go in the water.'

Waves aren't always what a surfer is looking for. They're pushing and striving, but never quite arriving. 'I honestly don't know what my motivation is,' he says. 'I've put a lot of time into thinking about that the last few days. I think it's more about seeing the people around me achieve what they want to achieve. There are people whose lives I'm involved with and I want to make a difference to them. That's a higher goal for me than trying to win another contest. I want to see my mum have everything she wants in her life. And my brothers. And my competitors. I want to see everyone surfing at their peak. I'm trying to take a different path. When I first started on the tour, I was just so intensely focused on myself that people hated me. I'd win thirty thousand and not pay for dinner. I don't regret it, but I'm older now and trying to find something more important. Winning a world title isn't really that important any more. It's important in your career but in the big picture, it doesn't matter. It wasn't like I won a world title and thought, "Wow, I've found God". It wasn't that sort of feeling. There was a difference between what I'd achieved on paper and how I felt inside. I didn't feel that great inside. I was worried about the future, I was stressed out about the past. I had to get over a few bumps. It's just life. I go through bumps, you go through bumps, we all go through bumps. It's exciting, because you can look at your life and think, "There's so much more to come". Surfing isn't the biggest sport in the world but if I can use it to inspire people, then it becomes bigger than it is.'

Slater has an eleven-year-old daughter called Taylor. Her mother, Tamara, is one of Slater's ex-girlfriends. They had broken up before she found out she was pregnant. Slater is thankful for the miracle of a child even if he's not performing the kind of fatherhood role he envisaged. He's grateful that Tamara is a good mother—and that she doesn't judge too harshly his absences and chronic need for space. Like Fanning, Slater was raised in a broken home. What is it with a broken home? Perhaps you feel the overwhelming need to prove yourself. Perhaps it makes no difference. Slater says he was a normal kid with exceptional problems. His father was an alcoholic who unleashed tirades of abuse on his mother Judy before passing out drunk on the floor. Most nights, a young Kelly would sleep with a pillow over his head to drown out the screaming. One night, he slept outside on the driveway to escape the racket peeling paint from the walls. Slater was eleven when Judy kicked Steve out. He remembers the feeling of being able to breathe again. Three years earlier, the golden child had won his first contest while standing on a bodyboard and doing reverse 360s.

Slater distanced himself from his father and the resentment ran deep. But in 2000, Steve, a lifelong smoker, was diagnosed with throat cancer. His mother had died from the same disease when he was nineteen. The downside: Kelly Slater's father would die soon. The upside: there was a reconciliation with his son. Slater had a dream that Steve passed away without them having patched up their differences. So they succeeded in getting to know each other before it was too late. Steve watched Slater at the 2001 Pipeline Masters—then died the following May. Judy has since re-married. All she wants to do now is buy her dream home. Slater has two brothers, Stephen and Sean. *Another brother, another Sean.* All they want to do now is buy their dream homes—and go fishing. That's it. Simple pleasures. Slater travels the world following the sun and knows he has the most ridiculously idyllic existence anyone could possibly hope for, but then he goes back home to Florida where the waves suck and the attention is suffocating and he sees that all anyone really needs to be happy is their dream home— and a fishing rod.

'I had some really good years on tour when I first started but I was a competitive machine and everyone really did hate me,' he says. 'I didn't want that to continue.'

Slater was the world champion in 1992 and again from 1994 to 1998. Those five straight titles resulted from the most ruthless and vindictive assault in tour history, built primarily on anger and designed mainly to compensate for all the other problems in his life. He marched into events as though he was entering the Colosseum determined to *kill, kill, kill*. He would headbutt his board and scream, 'You stupid fuck!' or punch himself in the face. What a tragic thing that is, for such a tremendously gifted athlete and decent man to descend into moments of such self-disgust. Criticism or derogatory remarks were stored as ammunition. Losses gnawed in his gut until he had executed bloody revenge. Slater read a quote from Occhilupo—'It's time we get serious and stop these Seppo wankers'—and burned it into his brain. He attacked heats against Occhilupo like a hurricane and did not lose to him for a decade. Nothing mattered other than rankings, points, trophies, prize money and beating his opponents to a bloody pulp. But you can only stay pissed off for so long. By the end of '98, with six world titles, he wasn't angry anymore. He no longer *needed* competition. He likened it to having your heart broken by one girl, but mended by another. You feel better and you're eternally grateful to the second girl for helping you heal. But you just need a little time away to work out whether you truly love her—or not. Slater went off to clear his head. Straight after he won the '98 world title at Pipeline, right in the middle of his hedonistic celebrations, a two-year-old Taylor looked up at Slater and said she wanted him to help her build sand castles. The following night, he announced his retirement, effective immediately.

'It's great to win an event but if you don't feel really good inside, it's empty and meaningless,' he says. 'If surfing's gone, where am I? You have to keep looking around. You need to cover your bases. That's what excites me now. Where am I in my life? The surfing follows on from that.' All lives have a fork in the road. It's when you're young and dumb and you kiss the cute but evil girl you know you should not kiss. It's when you gamble the money you know you do not have. It's when you say the things you know should never be said. You know it's too late when the words are already coming out of your mouth. Slater's life has had two forks. One was repairing the relationship with his father. The other was breaking his foot during a free-surfing session in Tahiti. He was convinced he got what he deserved. Love, and you'll be loved in return. Hate, and you'll be hated back. Lie, cheat, steal, you'll get yours, buster. Lost a five-dollar note? There's another on the ground. Slater believes in karma. He was having beers before paddling onto the reef at Teahupo'o—not the right thing to do. He had flirted with a girl despite knowing she had a boyfriend—not the right thing to do. He fell on a wave and suffered a fractured foot—and that, in his fertile mind, was appropriate punishment. 'I thought about the things that were going on around the injury,' he says. 'The injury was symbolic.' He could have sulked and cursed his rotten luck and withdrawn from the contest because surfing Teahupo'o is dangerous enough when you're fully fit and focused let alone when you're doing it with a broken bone in your foot and searing pain shooting through your body every time you place a modicum of pressure on it, but Slater wanted to push himself. He wanted to start dealing with his problems. Maybe he wanted to punish himself some more. The bottom line was that he knew he wanted to change. Slater took painkillers and decided to fight. No more ill-timed beers, no more tempting a girl away from her boyfriend, no more bad karma. He won the final and it was another small step. 'There comes a time when you have to try to see the bigger picture,' he says. 'Not that it's always easy.'

Slater makes surfing truly global and the millions of dollars the big boys now earn are directly attributable to him. Got a big fat contract, pro? Thank Slater. But he's not one of the boys, nothing like it. Australia's Mick Lowe has been on the tour for a decade and admits he doesn't really know him. They all want Slater on tour, and even Irons admits the whole shebang would be hollow without him, but there's no interaction between Slater and the rest of the pros away from the contest zone. He doesn't travel with any of the other surfers, which is a rarity—but who cares? It's a free world. Fanning is about to take a leaf from his book. America's Taylor Knox is one of Slater's most staunch allies, having spent years hollering support when the rest of the pros are getting out their voodoo dolls and pinning Slater's eyes. The mantra: it doesn't matter who the other guy is, just so long as he wins and Slater loses. The other guy usually receives a pounding. Knox will sign with Rip Curl this year and spend large portions of his time travelling and staying far from Slater. They'll have the same pit boss at Rip Curl—Matt Griggs. They'll attend the same sponsorship functions. They'll be in the same hotels and reclining their seats on a lot of the same flights. Taylor Knox's new best mate is about to be Mick Fanning.

Slater lives in a different world. He's more likely to be hanging out with a Hollywood star. Matthew McConaughey is following him around Coolangatta like an obedient puppy dog. Jack Johnson's house at Pipeline is one of his homes away from home. Pearl Jam's Eddie Vedder is a close mate. At Waimea Bay in November 2006, after the Eddie Aikau big-wave contest, Slater was up on stage with Pearl Jam, arching his back and thrashing a black guitar with Quiksilver's SL8er slogan on it. It wasn't the first Quiksilver sticker you have ever seen, and it won't be the last. He's the face of the tour, face of this event, face of this rapidly expanding and increasingly professional sport. No-one, not even Irons, disputes it. 'Whether Andy Irons is winning world titles or not, Kelly sets the level of surfing with wherever he's at right now,' says world No.5 Bobby Martinez.

The flipside to Slater's total and utter domination of the sport is the kind of bitchiness shown by an anonymous rival being quoted in *Tracks* magazine as saying Slater is lucky to have eight world titles because he doesn't have a single friend. That is so fucking stupid, whoever said that is a coward. Anonymous quotes are pathetic. If you really believe something, if you really feel the need to slander someone like that, have the balls to put your name to it. And it's not even right. Slater has friends. You can be a drifter and still have friends. It's just that most of his are no longer on tour. And let's get real: it's virtually impossible for him to be too close to these blokes because at the end of the day, he's spent the best part of fifteen years thrashing the living daylights out of them. Humiliating them. Making them feel inept and inferior. For those five frenzied years in the 1990s, nothing mattered other than the savage beating of his opponents. Who's going to warm to that? In the movie *Flow*, he admits: 'I was so set and determined in my ways to win as much as I possibly could, but it became more of a complex sort of thing where, OK, now you have to deal with creating your own individuality. You have to be fine with beating guys you travel with. You need their mental and emotional support in some ways. It's sort of a complex issue when you just throw a bunch of guys together and travel around the world competing for everything from waves to girls to money. There were a lot of times travelling when I sort of felt like a loner. I was doing my own thing a bit, but I felt like I needed to distance myself to some degree to have the right mindset to accomplish what I was trying to do. Sometimes friendships and the closeness of people suffer because of that. You have to sit back and decide what actually is important in your life. Work out the one thing which is most important to you. At the time, that was the most important thing to me.'

Winning.

Slater is flying solo because his peers from the New School generation—Rob Machado, Ross Williams, Pat O'Connell and Shane Dorian—have long gone. Only Taylor Knox remains, without threatening for the world title. For Slater to be still towelling up these young punks at the age of 35 is extraordinary. As for Occhilupo still being on tour at 41—not relying on sponsors' invites, but being a fully fledged member without any favours—that defies description. When Slater was a rookie, the big kahunas were Occhilupo, Martin Potter and Tom Curren. They were ferocious and part of the clique. Now, it's just that his clique has fallen by the wayside.

Slater has a mortal enemy: Andy Irons. They have eleven world titles between them, and no time for each other whatsoever. They trade fuck-yous like other people swap phone numbers. They'll be at the same crowded table over dinner and when Slater leaves, there won't be so much as a nod in Irons' direction. Slater's constant protestations about wavering motivation drive the intense Irons up the fucking wall. He thinks Slater likes the limelight a little *too* much and detests all the umming and ahhing about Slater's retirement. Slater's indecisiveness is legendary. He's not even sure if he wants to sit on the fence. The most intriguing thing about his mind is that he can never make it up. You've seen the way Irons looks at Slater: respect for the surfer, condemnation of the man. And vice versa. They're not being cruel to be kind. They're being cruel because they hate each other's guts.

Slater feared for his sport when Irons was world champion. He views the No.1 ranking as a stewardship and doubted Irons was suitable for the role. You've seen Irons jeer Slater from the beach. They eyeball each other in practice sessions, sitting away from everyone else to engage in wave-by-wave combat. These are the best non-official heats you will ever see. Once, when Slater was looking for Knox at Pipeline, he ventured into the wrong house. 'There's nobody here you're looking for,' Irons barked. They are phenomenal surfers, behemoths of the modern age. Their 2006 Pipeline final may have been the greatest ever staged at the colloseum. Slater had Irons comboed; i.e., needing more than 10 points to win. Irons clawed his way back. He free-fell into a giant backdoor pit—and got a 10 to win. Andy Irons' last wave of the year was a 10 to beat Kelly Slater at Pipeline.

What hasn't been reported is the root of their problems: a boat trip in Fiji in 1998. Irons was the gung-ho rookie from the tough Hawaiian island of Kaui. A large gathering of pros left Tavarua to have a night out in Suva. On the way back, Irons and Slater started arguing. Witnesses say Irons wasn't showing the world champion a whole lot of respect. He grabbed Slater and put him in a headlock. It was a genuine physical altercation. Irons had his fist raised and was *this close* to throwing punches. That was the beginning of the end. In his quieter moments, Irons will confide in friends his belief that it's a great shame he and Slater have never overcome their rift. Slater holds no such concerns.

For everything Slater has done, for all the triumphs and world titles and moments of supreme brilliance, he says 'the most magical, most glorious moment of my career' was winning the final at Jeffreys Bay in 2005. Because he beat Irons. Slater was dead and buried with only a few minutes to go. He was exhausted and on the verge of giving up. J-Bay is filled with dolphins, sharks and whales and Slater saw a school of dolphins. Delirious from exhaustion, he followed them in the hope they would take him to a wave—and they did. Irons was on the sand. He was doing a Slater on Slater by coming in early with a commanding lead—the ultimate humiliation, toying with him and mocking him. Slater got to his feet. The hooter sounded, but his score would count because he was already standing. Slater reached that elevated plane where only the greats can go. He won by the skin of his teeth. He went running up the beach with his arm in the air in the most extravagant celebration of his career, having all but secured his first world title in seven years. Irons' three-year reign was over. It shattered him. Back then, Irons had three crowns and Slater had six. He was closing. He was hell-bent on surpassing Slater as the most successful surfer in history, but by the end of that year it was 7–3 and now it's 8–3 and that's all she wrote. Irons riles Slater. Otherwise patient men can become more furious than most. But the king keeps most of his emotions bubbling on the inside. In any argument about whether Irons deserves to be held in the same esteem as Slater, no more need be said than that: 8–3.

Irons is portrayed as a money-hungry villain in Jack McCoy's classic movie *Blue Horizon*. He can barely contain his rage when he says of Slater: 'My whole driving force right now is to take his pretty little picture and just crush it.' Irons remains highly offended by McCoy's portrayal of him. It may well have been a bit harsh. Andy Irons is volatile, but he is not a bad guy. Friends have told him that McCoy did him a great disservice. Others have suggested he look in the mirror. And they've suggested the mirror is *Blue Horizon*. You admit to a soft spot. He can be a prick, but mood swings are no crime. The best description you hear of him is this: 'Andy can wake up and feel great and it's ice-cream cones for everybody. But the next day he won't feel so good and nobody gets an ice-cream cone and you know what, you can pay him back for all the ice-cream cones he bought all you leaches yesterday.'

'Andy and I have had angry words,' Slater says. 'But that should be allowed to remain private.'

Slater turns up at the last minute for contests, or skips the first round altogether, with apologies more hollow than anything Teahupo'o has ever delivered. There have been times when he hasn't come at all, brushing off events when another world title has already been secured. He won the 2006 race at Mundaka in Spain, so didn't go to Brazil. Whatever his reasons, that's a slap in the face for the tour and everyone on it. He doesn't lack the most priceless attribute there is for a pro surfer: mongrel. He's made snide comments in the water, intimidated rookies, hassled and burned opponents, anything to win. He'll burn you in the same breath as he's saying I love you, without you knowing which signifies the real him. But another rub: when he does compete, he gives himself tirelessly to fans, media and sponsors. Slater knows his standing in the pantheon. He knows he's the king, and that the grommets idolise him. Every single time one of them holds out their autograph books and pens, he obliges long after the rest have gone home. Slater is good—brilliant—with the kids because he remembers being one of them. He still has these scribbled-on pieces of paper from when he was a little tacker. *To Kelly, Keep Surfing, Mark Richards. To Kelly, Best of Luck, Tom Curren. Kelly, See You On The Circuit Some Day, Tom Carroll.* Tens of thousands of children now have similar messages from him. Kelly Slater is no angel, but he's not the devil. He's just flesh and blood.

Irons is sitting two chairs down from Slater at a press conference on the eve of the Quiksilver Pro. The Rainbow Bay is overflowing with the world's surf media. Irons has the kind of flu which makes your bones creak. 'Kelly is pretty much the benchmark of surfing,' he says. 'He's surpassed every title—he's the man. To win a world title with him on tour, it makes it that much sweeter. Not having him here would definitely create a big hole, so I hope he stays around. It's definitely pushing my surfing, it's pushing everyone's surfing.' You hear the words and of course Irons means them because it's impossible not to pay homage to the deeds of Kelly Slater. Anything else would sound ridiculous. But you're looking at Irons from point-blank range and regardless of the fact he's ill and aching when he shuffles his feet under the table, you sense that crushing Slater's pretty little picture is still what he really wants to do.

'I don't know if I can commit myself to every event this year,' Slater says. 'I don't even know if I can commit myself to answering

that question. Last year I didn't know if I wanted to do the whole
tour and that was an honest feeling. I'm just going to go with the
flow. If I feel like I don't want to continue and would rather go
off in some other direction in my life, I'm fine with that. If I want
to do the tour again, I'll be fine with that, too. Last year I was on
the verge of not doing Bells. About two weeks before, I wasn't
going to go but I looked at the swell forecast and that put me over
the edge because the waves were going to be great. If it wasn't for
that swell, I probably wouldn't have done the tour at all and so I
wouldn't have been the world champion. It was some sort of godsend
that came my way.'

You remember the greatest single wave you have ever seen
anyone catch. It was at Jeffreys Bay in South Africa. He wore a
white wetsuit. It was eight foot and perfect. Blazing sunshine.
Corduroy lines licking the point. He had a fat little fishtail board.
He took off up the point at Boneyards, swooping and gliding down
the line, one beautiful long arc after another. There were no airs,
no floaters, no interest in getting vertical. He just kept making
these long swooping lines and you thought of Tolstoy's quote: 'One
of the first conditions of happiness is that the link between Man
and Nature shall not be broken.' Slater caressed the water with
the outstretched fingers of his right hand. The slightest of smiles
creased his tanned face, no stresses, no dramas, just a man at one
with the ocean.

It was poetry.

The handshake is again firm as Slater leaves the Rainbow Bay
Surf Club. Waves curl around the old lava rock, shhh, making that
noise, shhh. The following night, he strolls into the world tour's
launch party and mumbles about everyone being too intoxicated
for his liking. He leaves with Matthew McConaughey in tow. He
lives in a different world, mixes with different people. He spends
a lot of time alone. He'll set himself tasks like reading one novel
per week for a year. He's writing a book filled with his own theories

on surfing technique, scribbled on loose pieces of paper. It will be a timeless tome—*The Surf Lesson, by Kelly Slater*. His next career will be as a movie maker. His first documentary will be about the unadulterated magic and mystique of tube riding. He plays golf— the most solitary of sports—as often as he surfs. His handicap is 1.8. You've seen him sitting on a beach for hours, running his fingers through the sand, thinking. He collects shells. He wants to settle quietly in the hills of Hawaii, far from the madding crowd. He pines for an ordinary life, but loves the limelight. He doesn't want to be competitive, but can't help himself. You watch Kelly Slater leave—by himself. Everyone is so determined to work him out, but here's the thing about the greatest surfer in history... he hasn't even worked himself out yet.

LITTLE BLOODY SMART ARSE. Snapper Rocks is so freakin' crowded and then this hyped-up little punk comes zipping along and goes 'Oi' and you have to pull off your wave because if you don't, you know exactly what he'll do. He'll do what all these snotty-nosed little blond-haired clowns do when they don't get their way. He'll scream blue murder. Sure, he'll look all fresh-faced and innocent, but he'll start screaming with enough blood-curdling ferocity to wake the dead. Oi. The trumped-up little shit said 'Oi'. You're so fucking angry. Piss off, mate. Jesus H. Christ, just piss off. Surfing is supposed to be fun, but this ain't fun anymore. Look at all these people. WHY WON'T EVERYONE PISS OFF?

You can't even *think* about catching a wave on the Superbank without someone else thinking about it first. You can't even turn and start paddling for a wave without a dozen other people turning and trying to paddle over the top of you and abusing the hell out of you for committing no greater crime than what they're presently trying to do themselves. *Catch a damn wave.* Is that too much to ask? You return the abuse because every man has his pride, and now it's on for young and old and you'll be lucky to get out of here alive. You accidentally bump into another guy and he tells you to fuck off and you feel like cracking your board over the top of his head. You honestly want to kill him, or commit hari-kari, one of the two.

Everyone is abusing everyone else because everyone wants everyone else to piss off, just please piss off, but no-one is prepared to admit defeat and go in. The longer you're out there, the more you need that wave—that one face-melting wave—to prove all this bullshit is worthwhile. You know you have to get on the inside, so you get on the inside. You're so far on the inside that you're out behind the old lava rock and then . . . You're not entirely sure how this has happened, maybe the rip got 'em, maybe they've all caught waves, or the same wave, or maybe they really have all decided to just piss off . . . But there's no-one within 20 feet of you. Thank you, God. This is it. THIS IS IT. If a wave comes now, she's yours. Come on, come on, just one wave. And then you see her, your baby, your big green cathedral: the longest and sweetest crystal cylinder of your life and it's going to happen, it really is going to happen right now. She's yours. She's *all* yours. Nature is God, someone said. Man could never have created this. The sun on your back and face, the warm salt water on your skin and in your hair . . . Everything starts whispering that the world is a good and beautiful place. You'll howl with adrenaline. You'll realise that every problem you have—or thought you had—isn't really a problem at all. You'll feel the love and beauty, the beauty and flow; you'll feel *everything*. Nothing else will matter. You know what else you'll do? You'll endeavour to spread the love. You'll paddle back out and hug every one of the hombres still hassling each other out near the old lava rock. You'll tell them everything is alright. Don't you see? You two blokes over there, the one covered in tattoos and blood, the one beating the crap out of the other bloke who just dropped in on him . . . don't you halfwits see? It's all good. Release the eye gouge, my friend. Undo the headlock, brother. The waves, they love you. They just need a little time.

And here she comes, your wave. You love her, you honestly do. There's a full-blown rainbow in the wind-induced mist about 5 metres away, and you're quite sure this is heaven, and you're just as certain you're about to experience one of the greatest single moments of your life. You're laughing without knowing why. You're smiling, you can't help smiling while you're paddling because you've seen the light but then, right at the moment when you're about to take off, right at that climactic instant when you'll get to your feet on this high-voltage adventure of a lifetime—because that's what a wave at Snapper is, an adventure of a lifetime—this little fucking guy comes out of nowhere and goes 'Oi' in his pipsqueaky little voice and you have to abort the mission for fear of bawling. The rainbow is gone now. It's cold and dark and you're alone.

You watch the little shit rip down to Greenmount. That's what you were going to do. You watch him as you watch a loved one get on a train with no plans to come back. So sad. He throws enough spray to empty the ocean. You were going to do that. He gets air. You were going to do that. He flicks off the top of his stolen wave and starts hooting and hollering. You were going to do that. You think of all the ways you can wipe the cute little smile off his face when he returns, but he goes to shore and you're left out behind the old lava rock, paddling around in circles for another hour, thinking over and again until you just come straight out and say it: 'CAN EVERYONE JUST PLEASE PISS OFF?' Nobody does. You swear to God you'll rip that kid's head off if you ever see him again.

You're not paying much attention to the first-round heats. They're invariably as boring as batshit because they lack meaning. No consequences. No real losers. The winners of these three-man heats go straight to the third round. The losers go into the second round, so they get another chance. No-one can get knocked out and the atmosphere can be zzzz. Even if there's a massive boilover in round one, like, say, and this is just a hypothetical because it would never happen in real life, but just say eight-time world champion Kelly Slater has the stuffing kicked out of him by, say, and now we're *really* verging on the ridiculous because this would *never* happen in real life, that same little punk-pipsqueak who took your wave, it wouldn't matter too much because Slater would live to fight another day.

You're down the road from Snapper, not far from Mick Fanning's Rip Curl surf shop. Two pairs of rubber thongs cost $25. Bargain. They have bottle openers in the sole. Don't laugh. They've made him a fortune. Fanning's mother, Liz, doubles as his manager. She negotiated the shop into his contract. She used to be director of nursing at Brisbane Hospital, which seems a long way from the boardrooms of ruthless surfing companies, but underestimate Liz Osborne at your peril. 'Actually, I *do* have a background in all this,' she says. 'I have a Masters of Business. My clinical practice was mental health and mental health is all about negotiation. You learn how to engage people, get win-win situations. The guys at Rip Curl are great to Mick. We've had our moments, but that's my job. Rip Curl can think I'm pushing a bit hard, but it's my son we're talking about. They understand that. I don't have a problem standing up for him.'

Fanning smokes Jake Paterson and Adriano de Souza. Burrow loses to Trent Munro. Slater is about to face Danny Wills and Julian Someone. 'I'm excited to get in the water again,' he says. 'I'd just like to win this first contest.' Yesterday he didn't care about results, but now he does? 'That's how you win titles, just by winning the next heat, winning enough heats to win the next contest, winning enough contests so you win the title. You have to just get into the surf and the vibe here and not worry too much about the hoopla. I've got a bunch of new boards and I'm on a bit of a health kick right now—I'm juicing every morning and watching the surf. I feel really relaxed and in a good place.' You suspect Slater would be more dangerous if he was in a bad place. 'I'm just going to go with what I feel. I came close to not surfing a few times last year, but kept pushing through and it was magic in the end. I had to battle through some personal feelings with where I was with it. I guess I'm still unsure, but that's OK.'

You're wiping bits of hamburger from your face when a mate rings. You haven't watched Slater's first heat. Yes, what kind of half-arsed book is this. Slater has lost to Julian Someone. You sprint round to Snapper to interview the victor and sound the drums, blow the horns, can we get a hallelujah, it's that same little punk-pipsqueak smart-arse who stole your wave. You previously wanted to kill him. Now you're sticking a microphone under his nose and asking him to explain, please explain, how an eighteen-year-old having his first taste of the big time can beat Kelly Slater. Julian Someone speaks and you realise he's not a little punk at all. There's not even a pre-pubescent voice carrying so much as the hint of a pipsqueak. In fact, he's a good kid. But that's the thing: he's a kid.

Slater stands near the Rainbow Bay with the slightly bemused expression of a man who's just emerged from a plane wreck. He's not bleeding and nothing appears to be broken. But he just needs a moment to compose himself. 'Started out alright,' he says. 'I kind of sat there for a minute or two while they tried to get the heat started. I got cleaned up pretty good paddling out and I just felt that it wasn't going to go my way.'

The ASP re-seeds surfers for each of the first three rounds. The top seed is drawn against the lowest, the second highest against the second lowest, and so on. Slater is No.1. Dale Richards—the winner of the trials and the first Aboriginal surfer to make the main draw of a full-blown tour event—faces him in round two. He says matter-of-factly: 'I'm scared.' Slater's nostrils are filled with the smell of young meat. Get past Richards, and his next opponent will be . . . Julian Someone. They will dance again.

'Dale obviously knows the wave real well,' Slater says. 'But he hasn't had the chance to surf these events so much. We'll see if he can get himself real calm and just focused on what he's doing. If he doesn't get too distracted, he'll surf real good.' It's like someone telling you not to panic. Whatever you do, for the love of God, don't panic when I tell you this. So you're apoplectic with panic. Richards has only ever seen Slater in movies. He loses by the expected wide margin. *Back in your box.*

Walking up the beach, a mystery figure slaps a hat on Slater's head. He figures it's a representative of his major sponsor, Quiksilver. When the cameras are rolling, marketing types come from everywhere to place logo-heavy hats on the talent. There are few more intense corporate battles than the one staged between the heaviest corporate hitters in this multimillion-dollar industry: Quiksilver, Rip Curl and Billabong. Slater is with Quiksilver. Fanning is with Rip Curl. Burrow, Parkinson, Irons and Occhilupo are with Billabong. Every photo, every TV grab, every magazine shot and newspaper spread is a marketing victory of monumental proportions. It takes a while for Slater to realise this hat says, 'Go Dale.'

One certainty: Julian Someone is a dead man walking. No matter how much confidence he's derived from his first-up triumph over the king, no matter how many times his half-pissed mates on the beach tell him that if he can beat Slater once, he can beat him twice, no matter how much he tries to ignore the intimidating aura seeping from every pore of the most threatening presence on tour, there is nothing more certain in this life than his imminent burial in the sand. Put your house, children, wife/husband and any other item of value on Slater giving Julian Someone the mother of all hidings. He will not lose to him again.

It's a pummelling.

Some Day

Parkinson glides through the draw. Sharp as a butcher's knife. Why isn't *he* an eight-time world champion? Irons loses to Jake Paterson in the second round. Eliminated. It's the first sign of his mostly shithouse year to come. The Big Five—Fanning, Slater, Burrow, Parkinson and Irons—have become a Big Four. 'My goal was to knock out one of the title contenders, besides the Australians,' Paterson says. 'I want to see Australia bring home the title. I hope I helped the boys out.' Irons declines to comment in favour of the more cleansing act of retreating to the car park to smash his boards to smithereens. Fanning is marching around with the brooding intensity of a drill sergeant. One of The Big Five will win the world title. If you think differently, you think wrong. They will stalk each other with the intensity of the sheer bloody-minded. And you will watch them like a hawk. Most everybody else can get nicked.

Burrow has lost to Trent Munro, beaten Luke Munro and next faces Trent Munro again in what must be some sort of world record for the most times anyone has faced a Munro in the first three rounds of a professional sporting contest. Burrow can view Irons' angry loss in two ways. The Big Five has one less member and that's a good thing. But upsets have a habit of coming in clusters and that's a bad thing. Trent Munro has failed to requalify for the tour. Anyone outside the top 28 at the end of the year is booted back to the crapshoot otherwise known as the World Qualifying Series, but American Timmy Reyes has a savage knee injury so Munro has received a main-draw berth. He has 'dangerman' written all over him. He can beat anyone on his day and there's more than one casual observer backing him off the map when the crowd starts gathering on the old wooden boardwalk behind the rusted single shower. 'He's not the kind of guy who should be missing from the tour,' Burrow concedes. 'He's one of the best in the world. He should be in there with the rest of us. He's ripping.' Burrow is toast with a minute left on the black-and-white clock under the balcony of the Rainbow Bay. If he doesn't get a 7.5, we'll have a Big Three.

Burrow sneaks home and you think of Slater's belief in one manoeuvre being the difference between an ordinary year and world-title madness. 'I still feel a little uneasy,' he says. 'It kind of feels like I didn't make it.' He's as white as a ghost. 'I'm stoked.' And over the next few minutes, days, months and year, you have never heard anyone say the word stoked so much. 'I just tried to concentrate on that last wave and get the 7.5 and I only just scraped it in, so I'm *really* stoked.' Right, 'cause we thought you were only a little bit stoked. 'It was a stressful heat. I'm...' Stoked?

Fanning beats Danny Wills. Fanning's first board was a standard edition Wills. The man he beat in his first Bells final: Wills. One of the best blokes on tour: Wills. A man Fanning is inspired surfing against because he appreciates his rootsy, no-nonsense surfing: Wills. Someone Fanning looks up to: Wills. Someone Fanning has just caned: Wills. Something Fanning no longer gets swamped by: Awe.

'I've just got more experience now when I go against the older guys,' he says. 'I was really overwhelmed when I started on tour. It's hard to get used to sitting out there next to your favourite surfers. It was wild, so overwhelming, when I started. There were so many guys who I looked up to—Occ, Luke, Andy, Kelly, Taylor Knox, Willsy. It made my head spin. When you're only a young kid—I was twenty at the time—it's daunting. I still get a bit overwhelmed when I'm paddling out against those guys. I don't think that will ever change, but you just learn to... surf. You just go out there and surf and forget about whoever else is out there with you. But it's always in the back of your mind: "My god, I just beat Occy. I just beat Willsy". You're trying to act differently, but that's what you're thinking.'

The house Fanning shares with his fiancée, 22-year-old university student and catwalk model Karissa, is just five minutes away. First time he invited her to dinner, she thought he had given her the wrong address. *You said number two, right?* This veritable palace couldn't belong to a surfer. She was clueless about Fanning's achievements. She told a friend in 2005 that her new boyfriend surfed a bit and that he was going in something called the Quiksilver Pro. She asked how he might go. She was told that, yeah, he might go alright. Every year around Coolangatta, the spotlight is blinding. Every set of eyes tells him to *go, Mick, go*. His head is like chiselled stone. Every step is brisk and purposeful and when he takes off his shirt there is not one millimetre of body fat. But Fanning is an emotional soul beneath the wall. He needed to escape Coolangatta before this year's onslaught. Just as Slater and Burrow were packing their bags to go to the Gold Coast, he was leaving. If you'd pulled into the car park at Haleiwa in Hawaii a fortnight ago, you would have seen one surfer in the water in miserable rain and blasting wind and so-so waves. See the lonely surfer; a slave to the riding of the waves. It was Fanning, trying to get himself right. It's a noble pursuit, just trying to get yourself right.

Slater goes berserk against Julian Someone. He goes berserk in the way someone can go berserk with a sawn-off shotgun. Anyone and everything in their path is obliterated. It's an annihilation. His 19.83 points include the first perfect 10 of the year. He's mesmerising. He's masterful. You remember seeing Ian Thorpe winning the 400-metre freestyle at the Sydney Olympics and thinking that right there and then, right at that moment, he was doing exactly what he was born to do. You get the same feeling watching Fanning, Slater and Burrow. They don't look quite right on land. Fanning has bow legs, and a curvature of the spine. But in the water he seems part of the ocean. His legs lock into place. His back curls into the right shapes. 'Everything came together,' Slater says. 'That's the best heat I've had in a couple of years. Losses can be good for you. They can get you more focused. You go back, sort out what went wrong, work out where your head was at, and get back out there and fix it.'

Julian Someone—Julian *Wilson*—chuckles. 'I was expecting him to smash me. He kinda did.' Little bloody smartarse? No.

Fanning and Slater have been hurricanes, but Burrow limps through, doing just enough, but that's OK because you don't have to explain why you get through a heat, you don't have to draw diagrams, you don't have to prove whether you deserve to be there or not—you just have to get there. It's raining bullets, blowing a gale. The ocean is wild, savage. Young boys drape themselves in Australian flags. People hide under umbrellas. The Rainbow Bay Surf Club bursts at the seams and you fear the balcony will crash. Fanning is unshaven and rugged. His stare is so fierce you look twice. It's doubtful you have ever come across a more driven individual. Liz sits quietly. Matthew McConaughey and another piece of Hollywood, Kate Hudson, are Slater's support crew. McConaughey is wearing a blue bandana. First impression: what a dick. Don't tell him we said that. This is a private conversation and completely off the record. There are seven Australians in the last eight with Slater, ganging up on him, eyeing him off, circling like a pack of great whites. The first quarter-final is Parkinson and Bede Durbidge. You have to get this off your chest: it stinks to high heaven that Durbidge doesn't have a major sponsor. He has little ones—Mt Woodgee for his boards, free wax and other tidbits— but none of the other companies want him. Damn fools. Not long after beating Elvis at Graceland (Slater at Trestles), Durbidge went to Billabong HQ because his contract was up for renewal. Walking through the front door, he had no idea it was about to be up full stop. Not that Billabong didn't have their reasons. Business is business. It may sound idiotic to sack one of your most universally popular, divinely skilful and consistently successful team members, but they already had Burrow, Parkinson and Irons on their books, not to mention Occhilupo. Those four were sucking up a whole lot of cash. Something had to give, or someone, and it was Durbidge. He's peeved, but it's not in his nature to throw a chair through the window. Some moolah would be appreciated, though. It will cost him upwards of $70 000 to do the tour for the year, on top of the dastardly mortgage payments, the noose around too many people's necks, and that's with cattle-class seats and three-star hotels where the hot water runs out too soon and the air conditioning is on the blink. Durbidge will be digging into his own pockets unless Quiksilver or Rip Curl take him on. There's no shortage of motivation. 'Not to stick it to Billabong, really, but just for myself,' he says. 'I need to make as much money as I can in prize money.' The most common reaction to Durbidge being sponsorless: *he's fucking what-less?*

His plan of attack is go deep in the draw, gain reams of media exposure, beat a few of these superstars and prove he's marketable. He's been visualising the contest, and he can literally see himself standing on the stage with his completely blank and stickerless board—THIS SPACE FOR SALE—in one hand and the winner's trophy in the other. And the big fat cardboard cheque between his teeth. He really does imagine he's going to power his way into the final and in these carefully constructed day dreams, the man he will face in the decider is Fanning.

'Bede is easily the best unsponsored surfer in the world,' Slater says. 'Billabong, wake up. I don't know why they did that to him.' The suits at Billabong pray for a Parkinson victory to save a whole lot of egg being smeared over a whole lot of faces. Their prayers are left unanswered. The Billabong reject humbles the Billabong poster boy. For the first time in living memory, the personification of mild-mannered humility has claimed a wave. You claim a wave to let the judges know you think it's been especially points-worthy; the drop has been more steep than they realised; the power hack was more brutal than it may have appeared from the judges' ivory tower; you're losing and need help. You can claim a wave in the traditional manner of throwing your hand in the air like every other man and his dog. Or you can grab your balls and flip the bird like Damien and CJ Hobgood. Or you can stand on your board and shoot everyone on the beach with your imaginary machine-gun-like Andy Irons. We *hope* it's imaginary. Little has overcome big. Broke has overcome the big bucks. 'Yeah, that was the first wave I've ever claimed,' he says, making sure his white board is in full view of the cameras. 'I just wanted to show everyone I could surf.'

Slater's quarter-final is against the red-headed Mick Campbell. You cannot remember the last time you saw a redhead. Where'd they all go? Campbell is no shrinking violet. He's thrown punches at Irons after a heat in France. That's the spirit. Beat them in a heat then do your level best to punch their fucking lights out. Slater advances.

Fanning faces Australian rookie Josh Kerr. The future of the sport has taken off, grabbed his rail and landed. Kerr has talked himself up over the summer, but no-one has really known what to expect. He can find a punt on any wave and launch himself into the stratosphere, but it's fraught with danger. If it works, 10 isn't a high enough score. But stuff up an aerial before a perfect peak feathers down the point without you on it, and you're going to look like an A-grade tit. Nobody wants to look like an A-grade tit. Not in front of 15 000 knowledgeable people. 'I want to make a statement to myself and everyone else,' Kerr says. 'I've watched Mick surf out here, and I've watched Mick surf this event. This is going to be awesome.' Fanning is unmoved. 'It doesn't matter who you're up against,' he says. 'You just have to go out there and do your thing.' People old enough to know better start wading through the windswept shallows to get a closer look. Feast your eyes on this little sucker.

How To Make A Ball-tearing Start, by Josh Kerr: He latches onto his first wave straight after the siren has finished its wailing. Rocket-launches himself into a heaving pit. Stays in for five seconds, a lifetime, and shoots free. Grabs his rail for a roundhouse verging on a circumnavigation of the globe. Disappears into a foam ball for the briefest of moments. Glides along the open face and does a reo. Does another reo. Go on, do another one. And another. He slaps the lip like he hates it, loves it, one of the two. There's never much difference. He lands his floater and cocks an ear to shore to hear his opening score: 9.17.

How To Brazenly Capitalise On A Ball-tearing Start, by Josh Kerr: The jet ski whips him back into the teeth of the cyclone. Kerr jams into one of the ocean's deepest, darkest caverns, bigger than the one he's just passed through on the way to 9.17-point heaven, comes out, looks back to make sure what he just saw, what he just *did*, was real. It was. He awaits his next score and surely he cannot have rattled up another 9-pointer, surely he can't be treating Fanning with this much contempt, surely he can't be even better than anyone suspected a week ago. The scores are calculated. The beach is silent. Liz needs oxygen. Judge number one gives Kerr 9.93. Judge number two gives him a 10. Judge number three gives him a 9.8. Judge number four gives him a 9.5. Judge number five decides on another 10.

Kerr gets a 9.97.

You have got to be fucking kidding.

Kerr has 19.1 points and Fanning hasn't even started. No surfer in pro tour history has won a heat from this position. His eyes narrow to slits.

How To Launch The Mother Of All Comebacks, by Mick Fanning: He vanishes behind the curtain, comes out, gets his bearings, launches an extravagant snap; infinitely more barbaric than anything seen all day. Fanning clubs the foam. Rack off. Fanning spreads his arms like the wings of a condor for a succession of cutbacks, carves and roundhouses. He knocks the top off another lip, and another, completes his journey down the point, hears the cacophony he's created—you've never heard a noise like it—and puts one arm in the air. He's not celebrating or claiming. He wants

the jet ski. He wants it NOW. Game on: 9.73. Game *right* on.
Fanning's army are on their feet. Liz claps. How good is this. That's
not a question, but a statement of fact. How. Good. Is. This. The
wind fades. Kerr has priority but Fanning slides smoothly into a
barrel so clear that from shore, his red shirt travelling through the
funnel makes him look like blood flowing through a vein. It's not
an angry tube. It's a controlled, serene tube; a moment of sanity
in an otherwise nonsensical 30 minutes. This time, Fanning punches
the air because, you know what? This is extraordinary. These two
waves, these four waves, have been extraordinary. His arm isn't in
the air to get the jet ski, not this time. Three more razor-sharp
hooks, slashing the face so severely there should be a wound. The
announcer doesn't say Fanning's score, he bellows it: 9.8. Your name
is Mick Fanning and you've hit the lead. And then the heat enters
its eighth minute.

Fanning is manic, pick-pocketing waves at a furious rate, an
addict needing one more fix, but nothing can or will better his
opening salvos. Kerr keeps searching, too, but he can't improve
his score, either. With just seconds left, a moderate wave hovers
above Kerr. He needs a 9.6. All he can hope to do is go absolutely
fucking ballistic.

How To Go Absolutely Fucking Ballistic, by Josh Kerr: Three
carves. Each carve is bigger than the one before, 85 per cent
velocity, 90 per cent, never losing control even on the last carve
when he's approaching terminal velocity and his body faces the
right but his board is going left and there must be some kind of
G-force at work here, his white hair a vapour trail. He does another
carve, so many carves, 95 per cent, 96, running along the face
almost at full throttle now, 97 per cent, 98, his right arm behind
him like a rudder trying to control a speed boat on the very outer
limits of its capabilities. Kerr builds momentum, precious
momentum, sliding into another bottom turn, faster, faster, standing
high then swinging low before springing back up, more speed, more

speed, his eyes fixing on an impossibility. One hundred per cent. Go. Go, you mad bastard. Go hard. Kerr rams his board up the face with his head still below. He's upside down. He sends his board under the closing lip and then puts *himself* under the lip as well, hooking his board through the roof of the close-out as he keeps hanging the wrong way up in what appears to be a complete contradiction of the laws of gravity. The roof of the wave folds and Kerr goes with it. He cannot survive this—but he needs a 9-plus. He has no right to make this without straps—but he needs a 9-plus. He's vertical, back to front and upside down and wrong. There's no escape to the left. There's no escape to the right. The only escape is *up*. The whitewater swallows him. Bravo, he's had a lash. Respect. He's gone, completely out of view, never to be seen again. One second, two seconds, three seconds, he's still gone. You look away. Imagine if he'd made it . . . And then he makes it! Kerr re-emerges like a mountaineer coming out of a blizzard three days after he'd been given up for dead. He adjusts his shorts because that appears to be his greatest inconvenience. He casually finishes his 28-second ride. Liz gently places her binoculars in her lap. 'That could be the best manoeuvre I've ever seen on tour,' Slater says.

How To Get Away With Cold-blooded Murder, by Mick Fanning: Judges have the befuddled expressions of university students trying to answer an exam question they do not understand. Fanning hears the roars and sees the arms in the air. His heart stops. What was that? What the fuck was that? This is what it was: not enough to get Josh Kerr into the semi-finals. He's given an 8.3 and no-one knows whether it's right or wrong. Might have been a 2. Might have been a 20. How do you put a value on a move no-one has ever done before? A move no-one will ever do again because, well, you just can't? Kerr comes in and he's the epitome of not knowing whether to laugh or cry; wallow in disappointment at a lost opportunity, or revel in the glory of making a name for himself. He receives a rousing reception from the illustrious group he's just joined: the men's world tour. Fanning runs through the crowd like he's stolen something. Which he has. He puts his board in the rack of the surfers' VIP area with trembling hands. Liz has not moved a muscle. She appears to be frozen solid. 'How do you like them apples?' Fanning beams. 'I got two smokers.' He shakes his head. Slater sticks his hand out and Fanning slaps it.

'A heat like that is what you live for,' Fanning says. 'I didn't know Josh had two 9's—I only thought he had one. I knew good waves were going to keep coming.'

Kerr doesn't know what to think. 'I got off to such a good start. I knew Mick was going to fight back. Hats off to Mick—he's a competitor. I'm happy, we put on a good heat, it was a great experience. That last wave, I just had to give it my all. I didn't even think I was getting near the score. I just wanted to do something to show off.'

Mission accomplished.

Fanning and Burrow will square-off in one semi; Slater and Bede Durbidge in the other. Theories on why Burrow is yet to reach No.1 range from laziness to sex addiction. A lazy sex addict. There's a contradiction. Burrow is blessed with such an abundance of natural talent that people think there *must* be some sort of logical explanation for his filling every position in the top ten—except first. His heats have been efficient but little else. Contests are the only times you will see Fanning and Burrow together. They are by no means enemies—absolutely nothing of the sort—but they're not best mates either. 'It's all pretty cool, you know,' Fanning says of tour life. 'It's like an extended family. You have your mates you hang with during the day and then more mates you party with after the contest and some guys you probably don't seem to see too much. It's all pretty cool. Everyone is pretty friendly to each other. There's not too much garbage going on, not too much aggro. If you give any aggro, you're going to hear about it and get shit about it for the next twelve months. You don't want that. People can start talking it up in the water, but I just try to block all that out. It's probably sounding like all I ever do is try to block things out. But it's true in a way. I just shut everything off. I don't talk to anyone in the water. I don't look at anyone in the water. I just want to surf my heat. I just want to concentrate on myself out there. I just want to do my business.'

'I think Mick is going to bring it,' Slater says before the Fanning–Burrow showdown. 'He's here to put his stamp on this place and this tour. He may prove to be the most fierce competitor we have right now.'

Burrow has watched Fanning and Kerr's extravaganza. 'It was a good one,' he says, 'but I've erased it. I don't want to talk about it. I just hope Mick has peaked.'

Mick hasn't peaked. Cameras zoom on Burrow's impending doom. Fanning storms through a close-out like he's kicking down a door. The beach is heaving and swarming and rumbling like distant thunder. The beauty of sport: the atmosphere, the emotion. The look on a mother's face. Fanning mutilates it for 18.13. Burrow can only scrounge together 7.33. It's a bloodbath. Burrow will lay down infinitely more serious challenges for Fanning as the year unfolds, but for now, he says, 'I'm really pissed off. It's a good result, third, but I just felt like I couldn't do anything right. He was just getting those little drainers. I'm bummed. Whatever, I'll take a third. Mick just has that local knowledge.'

Yes, Mick Fanning has local knowledge.

Drive down Boundary Street often enough and you'll see a ribbon wrapped around a large Norfolk Island pine tree—the site of the collision on 14 August 1998, that took Sean's life. Yes, Mick Fanning has local knowledge. Mick Fanning has a whole lot of local knowledge. Occasionally, Mick Fanning has more local knowledge than he cares to remember.

Slater faces Durbidge for a place in the final. Tropical Cyclone Odette—Odette? What kind of piss-weak name is that for a force of nature?—is pushing through lump-and-bump six-footers. She's hanging in there, the old girl, huffing and puffing. What a contrast. A humble guy from North Stradbroke Island trying to make ends meet facing a superhero with more cash and kudos than he knows what to do with. The stakes are huge; the pressures extreme. Crack The Big Five and you're a millionaire. Fall out of the top 28 and you're back to your crapola day job. Durbidge is a cruisy individual, but don't be fooled. None of these blokes surfs a heat to make a new friend. They surf a heat to blow the other guy's brains out. It really is an odd sight in pro surfing, a white board. 'I'd like to see Bede on my team,' Slater says. 'But he's not going to be on my team in the next half-hour.' They enter the lion's den and you've never been in the middle of such a one-sided crowd. Everyone is baying for Slater's blood except his Hollywood connection. It's no surprise. When video highlights of Durbidge's win over Slater at Trestles were shown at the ASP awards night, the ovation was deafening. When Slater's victories at Snapper and Bells were shown, not to mention his coronation as world champion, you could hear a pin drop. Why are all these people death-riding him? Don't they get who he *is*?

Durbidge shoots into a six-second barrel, fitting into the tall walls like a hand going into a glove, and follows it with the kind of tail-spin last seen in the dirt car park at 3 a.m. after the ASP tour launch. He's ahead. When Slater attempts the same slide but the nose of his board digs into the H_2O and he falls, Durbidge is even further ahead. Slater goes bodysurfing after his tumble, travelling a good 15 metres on his stomach until his board thumps against the top of his head. And then his board comes to rest along his back, riding *him*. Neither Slater nor his board are getting enough points. Durbidge hands Slater a couple of gift waves and turns blue an otherwise grey sky. But one more late love shack gets him home and it's an all-local final with Fanning. Durbidge has followed his 18-plus against the mercurial Parkinson—who has just ordered a hamburger at the Rainbow Bay, happy as a fucking clam—with a 19.4 to beat Slater. It's impossible to overstate the surprise on Slater's face. He's been beaten when he's been *on*. His 18.73 would have brained virtually every other heat of the contest, including the other semi against Fanning, but it hasn't been good enough to beat a man on a white board with no stickers. Durbidge's girlfriend is practically hyperventilating, blinking away persistent tears. Slater makes his way to the shower. In his more maniacal days, he kept a log of every heat. Losses were explained with terms such as 'Impatience' or 'Catching Too Many Waves'. Here and now, he just shrugs. They're rejoicing in his demise, but offering commiserations. He taps his board with his spare hand in acknowledgement of the ovation he's getting. 'What do you do?' Slater says. 'You can't be bummed losing a heat like that. He was just in better sync than me. He surfed better than me.' *He surfed better than me.* Bede Durbidge has locked horns with eight-time world champion Kelly Slater in the semi-finals of the Quiksilver Pro and surfed better than him. Rip Curl? Quiksilver? Anyone?

Slater has made a threatening, if not dominant, start to the year. There are ten events on tour—the best eight will count for each surfer's ranking, with two throwaways. 'You have to have semi-final finishes and better to get the title,' he says. 'The guys I'm expecting to be there are Taj and Mick. I'll match Taj with this result but Mick will get more points from the final. I'd like to lose to the winner, so I hope Bede wins it.' He appears to have given Parkinson the old heave-ho as a threat, and wouldn't mention Irons if there was a nuclear attack and they were the only survivors. Burrow sits on a red lounge. Slater climbs into a green T-shirt and laughs with Hudson. *Well, hello.* She's lovely. You sincerely hope that dick McConaughey isn't trying to get his greasy mitts on her. Fanning and Durbidge embrace momentarily in the surfers' VIP tent, slapping each other's backs hard. Fanning pecks Karissa on the cheek. Poor old mums, eh? They always miss out. The rain is bucketing down and umbrellas are being blown inside out. Just before the final starts, with the water cleared for Fanning and Durbidge, a lone dolphin appears from nowhere, riding a set wave around the point with unmistakable joy, shooting out of the water right where everyone can see. And then it vanishes again. Go figure.

The storm still rages. Durbidge starts the final by seeking shelter inside another Superbank cave. *Somebody sponsor me?* He sticks his head out after a short while to see if the weather has improved, or if anyone is waving a contract in the air, but there's no luck on either front so he pulls down the shutters and goes back inside. He shoots up and down the line, up-down, assaulting the last section like quiet people sometimes do when they snap. Fanning's mask remains as immovable as a plaster cast. It could rain for the next three weeks and you doubt his game face would slip. You're starting to think it's the only face he has: buzz cut, thick white hair, those piercing eyes, the no-bullshit aura. He's fighter-jet fast and strong as an ox and every turn is a tornado. Every barrel is longer. Just. But just is all you need. This isn't the most riveting heat apart from the substantial prize on offer: immediate possession of the world No.1 ranking. Durbidge has thrown so much into beating Parkinson and Slater that he's running on fumes. His final score is a 12. Fanning wins with a 16.17, punches the air and is carried up the beach as camera flashes ignite the Coolangatta sky. Woody, the bearded security guard, offers him a can of Fosters, and Fanning does what any self-respecting Australian does with a can of Fosters. He takes one swig then pours the rest out. Cat's piss. Fanning's left bicep bulges. It's bedlam on the beach, along the boardwalk and in the Rainbow Bay. It's New Year's Eve and the clock has struck midnight. People are on their feet and hugging and clapping and jumping up and down and throwing their arms in the air as if they were the ones under pressure and the pressure has become too much.

'I'm so pumped,' Fanning says. 'To win at home—awesome. I live up the road, all my mates are here, my family. It's the perfect way to start off the year, surfing perfect Snapper with a mate. To have everyone see this, I'm ecstatic. There have been times in the past when I've said I want to be world champion but when the pressure has really come, it's been a different story and I haven't really believed it. But I feel comfortable now. Even when I was in bad situations today, I just felt like the waves were going to come. I can take the world title. I really believe that now.'

In the background, kids frantically paddle behind the old lava rock to try to surf like Mick Fanning, Kelly Slater, Taj Burrow and the guy with the white board and no stickers. These are early days, and you don't know the full Mick Fanning story yet, not really, but you remember being stopped in your tracks at the following sight: Fanning sitting on the sand before the final, all alone despite 20 000 spectators getting in his face, all of them gawking at him, all of them crowding him, but him being this oasis of calm. The hordes backed away and gave him his space. There was a silver ring on the third finger of his right hand. It's a traditional Irish ring called the Cladough. Liz bought them in Ireland and all the Fanning siblings wear them. Beneath his red—the most dominant of colours—singlet was a gold necklace with a pendant: the Celtic Irish cross. Fanning's legs were crossed and his eyes were shut. He looked relaxed, but intense. He looked calm, but pumped to the eyeballs. He clasped his hands together, the tips of his thumbs gently touching, as though he was in prayer. A black watch on his left wrist told him it was time to go. A tattoo underneath his left bicep told him: 'Sean'.

2

Memorial

Pre-dawn. Jet-black. Cold. Quiet. Nine years since Sean died. The place where Mick goes. Birds on a wooden railing. The light improving. A garden plot, 13 metres long. A block of concrete for Sean Fanning. To the right, a block of concrete for Joel Green. Fresh flowers. On each block, a small metal surfboard with inscriptions. SEAN JAMES FANNING. FOREVER YOUNG. JOEL GREEN. FREE AS AN EAGLE. Next to each plaque, a small wooden cross. The simplicity of the crosses—just bare wooden crosses with the name of the deceased, their birth date, their day of passing. In the end, maybe that's all we are: names, numbers and a small wooden cross.

A gentle breeze. Surfers Paradise to the north. Snapper Rocks to the south. Kirra directly below. One tree. A half-moon. A dog barks. The sun's glow makes a path from Snapper to the memorial. An old man walks down the road.

From dawn to dusk, the following sights and sounds: people having barbecues, people riding skateboards, click-clack on the pavement cracks, people having birthday parties, people wearing bikinis, people wearing board shorts, people wearing jackets, people saying hello, people keeping to themselves, people being rude, people being considerate, people walking briskly, people walking slowly, people sitting on benches, people sitting on blankets, people laying on towels, old people hunched over on benches with their hands on their knees, people with red hair, people with blonde hair, people with black hair, people with no hair, people with hats, people drinking coffee, people drinking beer, people drinking wine, people holding surfboards, people holding bodyboards, people showering, people wiping sand off their feet, people not caring about the sand on their feet, people stopping and reading the plaques dotted along the Oceanway walk between Kirra and Snapper dedicated to the long lost souls. WILLIAM GILL 1935–2004. People holding hands, people yelling, people laughing, people arguing, people leaving their footprints in the sand; the people and the footprints only temporary; people walking across rocks, people crossing the road, people climbing the hill, people driving cars, people riding motorbikes, people boarding buses, people in taxis, people walking dogs, people taking photos, people making videos, people wearing shoes, people wearing sandals, people throwing frisbees, people being busy, people doing nothing, people smoking cigarettes, people drinking water, people getting drunk, people getting sober, people with eye patches, people with dogs, deaf people, blind people, dumb people; people ignoring their children, people losing patience with their children, people doting on their children, people dressed to the nines, people going out, people getting home. People on the sand, people on the grass, people doing cartwheels, people playing cricket, people kicking a football, people worrying, people not caring less, people being awkward, people being free, people swimming, couples walking close, couples drifting apart, couples nuzzling, people chewing gum, people sweating, people crying, babies sucking on their fingers, babies sucking on their mother's breast. People parking cars, people being good, people being bad, people taking care of themselves, people giving up, people looking after their parents, the circle of life: the eleven-year-old having the birthday party becoming the 40-year-old mother becoming the 75-year-old grandmother becoming a wooden cross. People thinking how good the day has been, people wondering where it all went wrong, people exhausted, people re-energised, people with regrets, people feeling blessed, people feeling robbed, people feeling lucky, people feeling up, people feeling down, the old man having another walk, the sun disappearing, the half-moon again, jet-black again, cold again, quiet.

Same things, different faces.

Forever.

3

Mecca

RIP CURL PRO
BELLS BEACH, TORQUAY, AUSTRALIA

Mick Fanning visits the small wooden cross before he travels *anywhere*. 'Just in case I don't make it back.' There are no photographs of Mick standing alone at the place where Sean's ashes are buried. Nor should there be. Ever.

He's made the pilgrimage to Bells every Easter for ten years. His first major triumph was at this sacred surfing site as a scrawny seventeen-year-old wildcard who doubted he deserved to have his name on the trophy because he was still just a rat-bag kid. He dedicated his breakthrough win to Sean. He was so weak he couldn't lift the bell above his head. Simon Anderson handed over the trophy and declared: 'Look out world, here comes Mick Fanning.' It was his arrival in the big time. The christening of White Lightning. But in reality, the transformation from greenhorn to potential great had come a year earlier on the south coast of New South Wales in a frenzied money-grabbing exercise otherwise known as the Konica Skins. An unknown Fanning slayed Occhilupo, Luke Egan and various other goliaths at Sandon Point on an unbeaten seven-heat rampage that proved, in one fell swoop, he could blitz anyone on the planet. Fanning's prize money ticked over like the fare on a taxi meter with every merciless heat win. It was his first serious contest after Sean's death and he didn't give a stuff. Young men become dangerous when they throw off the shackles of giving a stuff. He had no idea how much he had won. He jumped on stage to grab the loot and they gave him $21 000. On the day that Sean would have turned 21.

Fanning remembers thinking: 'Shit—that's a bit weird.'

At 2 a.m., a text message: 'Swell coming. Bells will be huge.' You have one, and only one, recurring thought: Bells will be huge. You're booked on a 6 a.m. flight from Sydney to Avalon, the airport south of Melbourne and therefore closest to The Great Ocean Road and therefore closest to Bells Beach and therefore closest to the promised land. You have never been to Bells and you imagine a wild place with ice-cold water and wind. You imagine the end of the Earth. You can feel the aura. Laying in bed, thoughts running through your head, already you can feel the aura. You dream of dirt roads and beautiful wide open spaces and the chilled fresh air filling your lungs and you imagine sheer cliffs and the invigoration of it all and this is mecca. You wonder if there's swell.

Bells is hard-core. It's a festival. It's mountainous waves marching across the Pacific Ocean with faces like glaciers, whitewater crumbling like an avalanche. Bells is vast and rapid alcohol consumption. It's pre-dawn surf-checks. Bells is a thousand ways to hurt yourself, maybe a thousand ways for a man to find himself. Bells is walking home with no shoes and a ripped shirt at 5 a.m. on Good Friday, nailed. It's Michael Petersen's hat trick; Mark Richards' hat trick plus one; Anderson's triumph in 15 feet of clean, mean southern ocean grunt the year Fanning was born (a historic win because Big Saturday produced the biggest contest waves ever seen in Australia and was the moment Anderson unveiled the revolutionary three-finned design which dominates the global market to this day, the Thruster). Bells is Cheyne Horan winning on a winged fin the year Ben Lexcen's winged keel gave *Australia II* the America's Cup. It's Occhilupo versus Tom Curren in '86, the all-time heat. It's the kid you used to see at Merewether, Nicky Wood, winning as a sixteen-year-old then disappearing without a trace. (Where'd he go? Fair dinkum, where'd Nicky Wood go?) It's Occhilupo winning in 1998 to trigger one of the most inspiring comebacks in world sport. Bells is Occhilupo's speech: 'This is such a special moment for me and it's such a special event. It's been such a long time. It means a lot to me to be a professional surfer and to be allowed to come here where the land isn't built on. I'd like to dedicate this win to my father, Luciano Occhilupo, who passed away in 1990. I've been waiting a very long time to say that. Thanks very much—and thanks.' That's an immortal quote and Occhilupo in a nutshell: 'Thanks very much—and thanks.'

So let us see the bell. Let us touch the bell like Catholics touch the feet of Saint Peter in the Vatican City. Let us see Fanning, Burrow or Slater ringing the bell. Let us see it all today. Is there any swell? Give us swell. Give us a whopping great low-pressure system smack-bang in the middle of the bowl and a thumping swell charging across the ocean like cavalry. Problem. Hertz have no rental cars. Neither do Budget, nor Europcar. Avalon airport is shit creek. Avis don't have a paddle. Organised travellers are driving away in their cars and you're thinking: lucky fuckers. The last counter is for Thrifty. They have one car. You pay $55. Bells Beach is 50 minutes away. Swell? The beginnings of an adventure, the anticipation. Swell? Two seconds from the airport, and it feels like the never-never. Swell? Dry fields and sheep, horse shit, no buildings. No anything except grazing sheep and brown grass and that constant smell of horse shit. The news is on the radio. Swell? They read the general news. Swell? They read the finance news. Swell? They read the sports news and you do not give a crap about anything other than the swell or lack thereof. Your day is about to become an anti-climax of unfathomable proportions—or an endless possibility.

Swell?

They don't say.

The super-quick family history is that Fanning was born in Penrith in the western suburbs of Sydney on 13 June 1981. Any further from the beach and they would have been cutting his umbilical cord on Uluru. He skateboarded, kicked a football, threw stones at bottles. Mick, now 26, was the youngest of five children behind Rachel (38), Peter (35), Edward (32) and Sean (who would have been 29). John Fanning and Elizabeth Osborne emigrated to Australia from Ireland with one-year-old Rachel shortly after Liz had completed her nurse's training. She was nineteen. John and Liz separated when Mick was two. The details are nobody's business.

'The kids went to live with their dad for a while in 1986, in Coffs Harbour,' Liz says. 'That's where they started surfing. Mick was four and Sean was six. It was the worst time of my life. I missed them so much, but I thought it was right for the boys. It just didn't work out. Rachel was at university and Peter was starting college when Edward, Sean, Mick and I moved to Ballina. Sean and Mick started catching waves under the Ballina bridge. That's where they really taught each other to surf—but Mick wasn't all that interested. He had started soccer. He was an amazing little midfielder and played in the State Under Twelves. He was a very happy child, Mick. His brothers and sister loved him. He idolised Sean, and Sean always looked out for him. We didn't have much money. I had great jobs but the rent was expensive and I always wanted to give them good food. They didn't have many clothes. I used to buy their clothes from K-Mart and sew labels on them. But the money didn't really matter. They could all walk to the beach and that's all they needed. I'm so glad they liked the beach. It got them into a great sport and kept them away from too much mischief. They spent all their time in the ocean or in Mick's case for a long time, playing soccer.

'We were all very happy. It was so peaceful. In 1993, Sean and Mick wanted to move to the Gold Coast so Sean could get more exposure for his surfing. They were both sponsored by Quiksilver the first week we got there, so Mick forgot about soccer and started surfing a lot more. That's how it all started. Both Sean's and Mick's careers took off from there. They were in the Australian team and won the most titles in their age groups. They were very active members of the Kirra Surfriders Club with Peter and Edward. Mick and Sean were both doing really well but then Sean died and it was the worst day of all our lives.'

John Fanning lives near Wollongong on the south coast of New South Wales and works as an earth mover. Mick is getting to know him because he wants no regrets. 'The relationship between John and all the children has steadily improved over the last few years,' Liz says. 'Mick and his dad are in touch regularly. It's been great to see that happen. John is very proud of Mick. He doesn't know that much about surfing, but he's getting better. Mick and the other children used to see John occasionally but they'd never had a dad who had been with them. He always showed them a lot of affection when he did see them, and they rang him whenever they wanted, but I was very disappointed for them that he didn't spend much time with them. They missed out, but one of the most touching moments for me was when we were all together after Sean died. John came to us. Mick was so deeply, deeply grief-stricken but John and I were both there for him, holding him. He had both his parents together, putting our differences aside for our children. That was very special to me.'

Fanning went to Ireland two years ago to delve into his family history. He lost a morning heat in France and flew to Ireland that afternoon with Joel Parkinson and Nathan Hedge. He met his godparents, saw the house his father was raised in. He's proud of the Irish blood coursing through his veins. By his front door is a framed scroll detailing the history of the Fannings who originate from County Limerick. *Dominick Fanning, mayor of Limerick, greatly distinguished himself at the siege of the city in 1651, hanged as a result of his patriotic and uncompromising stand.* On the opposite wall to the scroll is the family crest. There's a chevron—or the rafters of a roof—which stands for protection and 'generosity and elevation of mind'. Mick has a picture of Sean in every room. He has kept all of Sean's old boards. He occasionally—very occasionally—rides the board Sean was using the most before he died. Goes alright, too.

For the first time, John Fanning is at Bells to watch his son compete.

Fanning is travelling with Liz and Karissa. He no longer hunts with the pack.

'I've done the whole travelling with everyone deal,' he says. 'I guess it just didn't work for me. I'd have some good results here and there—but I just had to start doing my own thing. They're my mates, and they'll always be my mates, and I'll always love hanging out with them. But if you want to do the best you can, sometimes you have to be a little bit selfish. I have a hard enough time looking after myself without worrying about anyone else.'

Fanning used to suffer from loneliness on tour. You can arrive at a hotel on some magical island with 30 other people—but everyone still checks in by themselves. Fanning no longer OD's on solitude. Rip Curl have hired Matt Griggs as the pit boss for all the company's tour surfers—and Fanning's world-title charge is his priority. 'I'm their mother and brother and coach and trainer and mate and whatever they want me to be,' Griggs says. Phil McNamara hovers as another coach. Gary Dunne, the man who recognised Fanning's potential a decade ago and lured him to Rip Curl from Quiksilver in the greatest sponsorship coup of the modern era— with more money than a sixteen-year-old Fanning could comprehend—treats Fanning like a son and is always there or thereabouts.

'There was just something we saw in him right from the start,' Dunne says. 'We saw him surf at the Australian junior titles. He didn't win, but we thought, "We should talk to this boy". He was with Quiksilver at the time, but we spoke to Mick and his mum about coming across to Rip Curl. Quiksilver weren't in the position to support him quite as well as we were.' Fanning is surrounding himself with friends and family, the two groups of people he believes define a man. If there's one certainty in the months to come, it's that he will never be alone unless he wants to be. Fanning has people by his side who genuinely want the best for him and they're good people, this lot, every single one of them. Fanning is extricating himself from the temptations that arise when he's staying with his mates and even though there will be uneasy moments when he worries if Parkinson and the rest are taking it the wrong way, he will stick to his guns and turn his back when he thinks he should. When contests go on hold for days on end while everyone prays for swell, he'll be less tempted to go and drink a dozen schooners.

Boards are strapped to the roofs of cars like a scene from 1973. The open road. Freedom. Isolation is supreme. Just you and your thoughts. David Rastovich is a soul surfer. You suspect soul surfers can't handle pressure—needing a 9.5 with three minutes left isn't always fun. Rastovich went through a phase of not talking on Tuesdays. He says he never felt more at peace. You like that. No talking on Tuesdays.

Torquay is the gateway to Bells. So. Close. Now. You hurtle past the Bells Beach Hotel. A massive Rip Curl store next to a massive Billabong store next to a massive Quiksilver store. A billboard of Mick Fanning. You slow on the top of a hill. Is that swell? You swerve past a tree. Three more dips and rises on a tar road, one quick glimpse of water. Bells. A steady procession of rusty cars and Kombi vans with the tails of single-fin boards protruding from windows and boots. Miles of bushland, a golf course to the left, a fast food joint, and is there any swell? A turn-off to the left and onto Bells Boulevarde—an unobtrusive two-lane road with a 40km/h speed limit—and more expanses of wide-open spaces and cattle and is there any swell?

There is swell.

You can see it.

There is swell.

Slater hasn't won an event since Bells last year. He's level with Tom Curren for the most career wins and it's starting to bug him. Victory number 34 is elusive. 'I think I've been suffering a mental block about passing Tom's record,' he says. 'It's been playing on my mind. Maybe if I'd put that to bed it would have freed me up for a couple more wins last year. It'd be meaningful to win my thirty-fourth here because Tom is so synonymous with Rip Curl and Bells Beach. I was hoping to put the record to bed at Trestles last year because Tom and I both won our first pro events there and I thought that would have been pretty ironic. But it'd be special in Torquay. I turned thirty-five last month and it's the thirty-fifth anniversary of the contest so Bells and I are sort of in alignment right now.' Slater's two wins have come in 1992 and 2006. 'It hasn't always been one of my better events on tour. But with Tom and some of the other greats being here for the anniversary, if for some reason I could pull off a win, it'd be pretty special for me. I'm ready for another win. Not that I didn't try last year but I didn't *have* to get that win to get the world title. I probably didn't focus very well in the final in Spain. I drank a couple of beers before it and Bobby Martinez got me. I was sort of celebrating before the final event finished. I have to get out here and perform. It's not easy to win a contest these days.'

It costs two dollars for parking. Your money is taken by a large bearded man. His neck is the size of a tree trunk. He says two words: 'Finals today.' You want to hug him, but he does not appear to be the kind of man who would appreciate being hugged. Out of the car and onto a dusty field. It's the Bells Beach Surfing Recreation Reserve. Another car pulls up and the occupants pile out. Over the PA system: 'Kelly Slater beats Travis Logie.' A soft-faced boy with freckles says, 'We missed him.' He's devastated. His father tells him that Slater will surf again. The soft-faced boy with freckles is no longer so devastated.

You walk to the ticket booth. Tickets are eleven dollars each. Problem being, you don't have any cash and there are no ATMs in the wilderness. The girl behind the counter says, 'Don't worry about it. Have a freebie.' If only all the stressed-out dickheads in the city thought like that. You walk to the edge of the cliff. Winki Pop is a rip-roaring 250-metre right-hander over a flat-bottomed reef. There's not a cloud in the sky, it's cool and crisp like a snowfield on a clear day. You buy the biggest goddamn coffee you can get your hands on. The steam from a hot pie rises like midnight mist from a lake. People wear hooded jackets and stuff their hands in their pockets. They shuffle along the cliff like a clan of monks. Cold sand stabs your feet like shards of glass.

Finals today.

Fanning's thousand-yard stare.

'Mick is just such a focused guy,' Slater says.

Fanning has made a movie called *Mick, Myself and Eugene*. He's asked the meaning of life. 'The meaning of life?' he says. 'I don't know. Don't you find that out when you die?' He laughs. It's a haunting laugh you will not forget. He's asked for his message to the youth of the world. 'Fuck,' he says. 'I *am* the youth of the world.'

Fanning has been in Bali, shooting footage for Bobby Martinez' movie. His campaign will revolve around peaks and troughs, starving himself of waves before gorging himself around the time of contests. He used to focus on the tour all year, but now his brow will only furrow in carefully planned bursts because to be world champion, Mick Fanning doesn't need to be the best surfer every day of the year. He needs to be the best on about 40 of them. And on those 40 days, he only needs to be the best in specific 30-minute explosions of energy and desire and no-holds-barred commitment.

'I'm trying to put the tour into different compartments,' he says. 'We've got the Australian leg. Chile and J-Bay are pretty close and then there's a break. Trestles and Europe are all in one group. There's a couple of weeks off before Brazil, and then it's Hawaii. I want to extend myself at the right times and take it easier when the time comes for that. I'll still think about the whole thing. Even when you try to turn off, you're still thinking about it because there's a bit at stake. But I'll try to go and do things which are just totally not surfing. Just go to places where there's no surf so I'm not tempted to think about it too much. I find that gets me really hungry. After a week off, I'm so fired up to go surfing again. I'm just frothing for it.'

Fanning runs down the steps and nearly trips over. He's built like a greyhound. Strong and light and tight as a coiled spring. Slater eats an apple on the viewing deck. He turns it over in his right hand, pondering it as though even eating an apple requires deep analysis. For fuck's sake, just eat it. Slater has been late for his first-round win over Mick Campbell and Owen Wright. And early finishing it. 'I was here on time,' he says. 'But I sort of mistimed it. The fins I wanted on one board were on another board and I was just switching fins. Then I did a full-length paddle from the beach up to the point about six times in twenty-five minutes. I was dying. I had to come in and take my wetsuit off.' Imagine being Campbell, who reaches a stoush with Fanning in the fourth round anyway, and Wright. Imagine being treated with such contempt.

Fanning leans into his turns like he's navigating a corner on a motorbike. The white blur gets a 9.7. At that speed, he should get a nose bleed. Damien Hobgood shakes his head and says something about smoke. Fanning is into another quarter-final. Kids swarm. With his board is tucked under his right arm, he signs *Tracks*. He's on the cover. Fanning posed naked in *Black and White* magazine— you'll believe that when you see it. Cameras start rolling. A white Rip Curl hat is placed on his head because heaven forbid Mick Fanning has his photo taken without a Rip Curl hat on his head. Dragon sunglasses protect his eyes. Video cameras are everywhere. Mick Fanning is lucky if he can take a crap without Rip Curl putting out a DVD. 'Just rolling along,' he says. In the front row of the autograph-hunters, getting squashed from behind, is the soft-faced boy with freckles. He looks up at Fanning with the wonder of a child seeing fireworks for the first time. One of the beauties of sport is the look on that kid's face. Fanning ruffles his hair.

The crowd builds. Cool weather becomes unseasonably warm. Layers of clothing are shed. Woo-hoo. You wonder how anyone can beat Fanning. You watch Parkinson beat Bruce Irons and now you're wondering how anyone can beat *him*. Slater watches Parkinson intently, puts on his wetsuit, looking distant. He's making phone calls to the Gold Coast, checking the waves in Fiji.

Slater faces Tom Whitaker. Whitaker has been to Las Vegas— on the way to snowboarding in Colorado—with Fanning and Karissa in January. 'There was nothing on that trip to suggest any great surfing from Mick this year,' Whitaker laughs. 'We had a mad time.' Whitaker climbs a slab for a 9.5. Slater tumbles over twice. He's not here. Wherever he is, it's not here. He said at Snapper: 'You have to be on for every wave. You might come fifth instead of first from missing just one little manoeuvre and just that one little incremental difference can make all the difference at the end of the year. If you win that one close heat, you invariably get through another few rounds or win the contest and get another six hundred points and that can be a world title. You can't have any slides during the year. You need that intense focus for every wave.' Fanning is riding every wave as though it's his last. Slater, for now, is not.

'I haven't surfed in a couple of days,' he explains later. 'I've been kinda sick.' He needs a 7.67 with seven minutes to go.

Irons paddles out for his quarter-final against Damien Hobgood. He circles Slater and Whitaker. 'What are you doing?!' he yells at Whitaker. 'SIT ON HIM.'

Whitaker says, 'I was like, "He's got priority. *You* sit on him".'

Six minutes, five, four, three, two, one minute, ten seconds, Slater milks his last wave for every last drop, but it's too small. He turns around and claps Whitaker. 'Good job, Tommy,' he says. Wrap your head around this. The world's greatest surfer has just been knocked out of one of the world's most prestigious events. His peers have been unashamedly vocal in their support of his opponent. He will fall further behind in the rankings if Fanning or Burrow get through a few more rounds. His pride is dented. He's far from home. He's cold. Yet he's happily standing on the sand, having a chat, posing for photos, doing the autographs-with-the-tips-of-your-fingers trick so the paper doesn't get wet. He's giving everyone his time. Nothing is an inconvenience, no question too dumb. He doesn't talk to the other pros. Just the fans—his people. Slater says he knows that one autograph can make a child's day. You tell him about the soft-faced boy with freckles. He wants him pointed out, but you can't see him. Then you can: he's following Fanning.

'I need to sit down and think about where my head is at,' Slater says. 'Usually I don't get rattled in heats, but in that heat I felt a little bit physically weak. I'm trying to get healthy again but I felt a little jittery. I've had a bit of a flu, some kind of bug. I tried to sweat it out yesterday and drank lots of fluids, but I didn't get much sleep. That's no excuse. I was out there and had the same conditions as Tom. I fell on three or four waves. There was one, especially, where I fell on my third turn. If I'd made that, it could have been a different story, but he had one really good wave, a 9.5, so what do you do?' His face hardens. 'It's already a different situation to last year,' he says. 'I started with two firsts and that took the pressure off for the rest of the year. Now the pressure is back on. I'm going to have to step up to that. I'm playing catch-up already.'

The eternal question: Will Slater quit? 'We'll see,' he says. Eyes roll. 'I don't know. I surfed very uninspiredly today, I know that much, and I have to work out why. I generally get to Tahiti and start feeling it. That's the moving contest for me every year. It's the event which makes me get up and get going. It's an event where, if you really play your cards right, it's . . . not easy to win, but if you get that one good wave and control of the heat early, you can get through. If I get my head right, I can start playing catch-up from there.'

Mick Fanning will face Joel Parkinson in his quarter-final. They have been extremely close friends since the age of thirteen. They've surfed Snapper and Duranbah since they met at Palm Beach/Currumbin High School. With Dean Morrison, they became known as the Coolangatta Kids because the three of them dominated junior surfing in Australia for the next half-dozen years. They were inseparable. Come their early twenties, they distanced themselves to forge their own identities. But they are still tight. There's still a deep bond. 'Joel and Dean used to cane me when we were kids,' Fanning says. 'They're the guys I've got to thank for becoming a decent surfer. If I didn't have them as sparring partners when we were younger, I would never have tried so hard. I only ever wanted to do the extra yards because those guys were so talented. I was only ever trying to keep up.'

Morrison was unbeatable at thirteen and fourteen. Parkinson started catching him at sixteen. Fanning was always one step behind. He's been on tour for five years and has not registered one win over Parkinson. Not one. 'He *was* my best mate,' Parkinson jokes. They run past Slater. Symbolic?

Consider the records of The Big Three—plus Parkinson and Irons—against each other:

Slater v. Irons: 29%   Irons v. Slater: 71%   Fanning v. Slater: 33%
v. Fanning: 67%   v. Fanning: 70%   v. Irons: 30%
v. Burrow: 71%   v. Burrow: 63%   v. Burrow: 57%
v. Parkinson: 0%   v. Parkinson: 43%   v. Parkinson: 0%

Burrow v. Slater: 29%   Parkinson v. Slater: 100%
v. Irons: 38%   v. Irons: 57%
v. Fanning: 43%   v. Fanning 100%
v. Parkinson: 0%   v. Burrow 100%

Parkinson has never lost to Slater, Fanning or Burrow. NEVER. He beats Irons more often than not. Slater has eight world titles, Irons has three and Parkinson has none. Why does Joel Parkinson have none? It makes no sense that Joel Parkinson has none. He's broken all his boards while getting footage for the biggest surf movie of the year—*Trilogy*, to be launched in California in October—and he's needed an emergency batch for Bells. It appears to make no difference. He could ride a door and get an 8. His daughter, Evie, giggles.

'It's so hard surfing against your mates,' Fanning says. 'Joel has beaten me every single time and it's hard because I know exactly how well he can surf. I know exactly what he's going to do, and he knows exactly what I'm going to do. I've just got to get the right waves and forget that he's my mate. You're still mates, even out in the water, because you don't hassle each other or anything like that. But you have to block everything out. He's been my mate since we were thirteen, so I want him to have a good contest. But I just don't want to be the one to lose to him. I want to win, but I don't want to be a prick about it. There's no mouthing off when we come in. The competition stays out in the water. We respect each other. Joel is one of my best friends and he always will be. Even if we weren't surfing, he'd be one of my mates. He'd always be someone I'd want to hang out with. He's a great surfer. He's a great father and he's a great husband. He's a quality bloke but when we get a singlet on, I want to beat him every bit as much as he wants to beat me.'

Parkinson's domination of Fanning cannot last forever.

Or another half-hour.

'Finally got him,' Fanning says. He's squeezed past by a third of a point. A curse is broken. A cameraman fumbles with his equipment. 'Come on,' Fanning says impatiently. 'Let's get this over with. I want to get out of here.' The ASP instructs every surfer to be interviewed for the live webcast after every heat. Win or lose, they're supposed to speak. It's incredible they have agreed to such an inconvenience. Fanning will spend an entire year saying he's taking it heat by heat, his boards feel great, it was a tough heat and he was lucky to get through, there were a few fun ones out there. It's not in his nature to talk himself up. His 6'1" spear will say enough. Microphones and cameras are shoved in Fanning's face. His eyes are darting around like those of a caged animal. His board clips an ESPN Brazil microphone. 'Sorry mate, sorry,' Fanning says. Then, for the cameras, he says in one short, sharp burst, 'I'd surfed Joel seven times and never beaten him, but I've finally got him. I want another final. I want another bell.'

Irons reaches the semi-finals by smothering Damien Hobgood. Ice-cream cones for everyone. 'Here we go, brother, here we go,' he says to someone who isn't his brother. He watches Fanning and Parkinson. He sits on the steep wooden steps to pour bottled water and Red Bull down his throat. The cliffs are swarming with spectators by now.

'Mick looks like the guy today,' Slater says. 'He could get a big lead on us all. He's gotten the Parko monkey off his back.'

Burrow beats Whitaker in the first semi. Who knew? Again, he's been sneaking through without the hype generated by Fanning and Slater. Nothing spectacular. 'There were a few fun waves coming through,' Whitaker says. 'I was having fun out there and got a few fun ones, and if I say fun one more time I'm going to shoot myself.'

Burrow is riding a new brand of board. The Firewire threatens to be the most significant movement in design since Anderson's Thruster. It's lighter and stronger than regular boards. It has a balsa parabolic stringer around the rails instead of the traditional stringer from the nose to the tail. The idea is to increase the whip in and out of turns. Like a snowboard on water.

Irons gives a thumbs-up before battling Fanning. All's good in the hood. Fanning's face has shades of white and brown. Irons, seeping with machismo, struts through the crowd. 'Here we go, now we're going,' he keeps saying. He runs to the water as though it's dawn and he hasn't surfed for three months. Fanning is in his shoreline trance.

'Mick is one of my favourite guys on the tour,' Irons has said. 'If I'm not winning, I want to see a friend of mine winning. But once the heat starts, it's on.' Irons has 16.9. Fanning has 16.17— and falls. There's an unusual silence across the beach. Nothing but the hush of waves crawling up the sand. Irons' eyes are bloodshot and spinning. His shoulder-length brown hair is matted. Fanning hasn't come in yet. He's punched the water at the final siren. Then punched it again. Then sat out there for a good 20 minutes. He's still out there when they start the Expression Session—the free-surfing exhibition held before the final of every contest to give the winner of the second semi-final enough time to catch his breath. Slater contests the Expression Session with gusto and you give up. He surfs without passion in a heat with consequences, then goes nuts in a heat which doesn't mean jack?

'How long is this going to take?' Irons says of the Expression Session. He has little interest in watching Slater show off.

Fanning's chin is dotted with white stubble. He's direct and honest. There is no bullshit in Mick Fanning. You look into his eyes and see a hard edge. But you also see compassion. *Sorry mate, sorry*. Maybe that's what you get when your brother dies on you: compassion with a hard edge. Fanning is forever looking at the waves. No matter what he's doing, or who he's talking to, he cannot go five seconds without looking at the waves.

'All over,' he says.

Not really.

Fanning climbs the 60-odd steps. He has a board tucked under each arm. His head is down and he looks defeated; suddenly, his legs look tired, his shoulders are slumped, the excitement has drained from his face. He peels off his singlet and grabs a towel. Karissa walks over. She's tall and tanned and young and lovely. They hug. They're smiling, talking softly. She rests her forehead against his. Liz swears Mick is firing like a semi-automatic because he's in love. Get a bucket. But maybe she's right. It's easier to gamble when you're in love. You can't lose *everything*.

The beach is full to overflowing. The car park is clogged with cars, utes, trucks and motorbikes. A dog is tied to a bench with a steel chain. Thousands of spectators now. Nude toddlers thrash around. Burrow and Irons make their way to the water. Burrow yawns. Sand is scooped into water bottles for people to take home. The bowl is a blessed little corner of God's green Earth, a natural amphitheatre. Then you see the trophy—the bell. It's as high as your belly-button. A rectangular wooden box with a silver bell hanging from the top. You thought the oldest trophy in pro surfing would be tattered and worn, but it's not. Wautharong Aborigine dancers gather for the presentation. They have white paint on their bodies, faces and hair. Two of them carry didgeridoos. They watch the 30-minute final and make the occasional *brrrgh* in the quiet time between waves.

Burrow has been watching Fanning, Slater, Irons and Parkinson score 9's while he's barely managed a 7 and confidence, confidence, confidence (the never-ending search for Taj Burrow's confidence) has eluded him. But now three of The Big Five are watching HIM and his faith has been found in the rubble. His Firewire isn't a dud. Don't throw it on the bonfire and sell your shares just yet. But it's felt too light. By a mere 100 grams.

One hundred grams. No more, and no less.

'I wasn't coming to Bells but I flew down to do some secret work,' says Firewire designer Nev Hyman. 'I've spent a couple of days with Taj, doing some videoing and some weight changes to the board to increase its momentum. I only added a hundred grams but I'm telling you, a hundred grams can make or break a pro surfer. We did it, he surfed, we videoed him again and he was raving about it. He said he couldn't believe how much better it was going. Nobody knew we'd put on those hundred grams. Nobody knew how it was done.'

One hundred grams.

A doctor conducted experiments on six terminally ill patients in the United States in 1907 to determine the weight of the human soul. He weighed their bodies immediately before and after the confirmation of death in an attempt to prove the soul was a tangible thing. His first patient lost 21.3 grams so 21 became his magic number. It's a flawed theory but let's go with it. Nev Hyman has added the weight of the souls of The Big Five to Taj Burrow's board and there has been a resurrection.

A wave rattles his rib cage. He leaps stiff-backed over the foam and dives onto his board. Zinc cream protects a burnt face. His blond hair is as messy as when he got out of bed. Burrow looked this way when he was a child. He'll look this way when he's 60 and getting all fins-out on his 9-foot mal. The tide rises. So does Burrow's temper. 'I was struggling at the start,' he'll say later. 'I was getting two turns then slipping behind every wave. I got completely shut down on one. My board hit me on the shins so hard, I was just ... *argh*.' There's a 7-pointer when he almost decapitates a cameraman. Additional points are not available for the decapitation of a cameraman. Thirty-three minutes of the 35-minute final are in the can. Irons has surfed with precision. He reminds you of Parkinson. Funny, that: three-time world champion Andy Irons reminds you of no-time world champion Joel Parkinson. Irons leads but on a board which suddenly feels like a magic wand because of the addition of nothing more than 100 grams, Taj Burrow requires 6.19 points with a minute-and-a-bit on the clock and with confidence, confidence, confidence (the never-ending search for Taj Burrow's confidence) seeping from every pore, he does not doubt for one second he will get it.

And here comes a set. And here comes the chance for Burrow to win his first contest in three years. And here comes his chance to join Fanning as the world No.1. And here comes the $64 million question: Does he have *it*? Does Taj Burrow have the balls to stare down an opportunity? If he's serious about this race, if he really is going to man up and try to stare down the biggest dogs in the kennel, he must be able to grab opportunities like this and wring their bloody necks. Another $64 million question: Does he take the first wave of the set, the devil he knows, the wave making all the promises in the world, or does he roll the dice on the next? It might be bigger and better. It might not be. The hordes on the cliff are pointing out to sea, screaming for Burrow to take the second wave. He rolls the dice. Taj Burrow paddles across the water's icy skin. His eyes grow wider than they've ever been.

Freeze-frame. Burrow is getting to his feet. Underneath, Irons is about to duck-dive. He tilts his head upwards and to the left. He's not watching Burrow. He's looking down the line to make an instant calculation. Is there a 6.19 in this? Burrow peers down the same line. He will make the same calculation. Pros can tell the scoring potential of a ripple. It's an 8. A 10. A 4. They just know Burrow's feet find the wax. His toes curl, getting grip. His left foot is splayed, his right foot jammed hard against the rubber tail pad. His back knee is flexed low, his front knee inverted. Irons goes under and Burrow takes off and they've come to the same conclusion. There's more than a 6.19 in this. Unless Burrow gags. 'I looked at the wave and thought, "Unless he falls, he's got the score",' Irons will say. 'Bad luck for me, good luck for him.'

Every move of every heat. They all count. Back at Snapper, in round three, Burrow was a hand-clap from disaster. He trailed Trent Munro when the hooter sounded, but he was up and riding. He needed a 7.5 and got a 7.67. World titles are made of such things. Burrow sling-shots right. A cacophony becomes a din. The previously bored Aboriginal dancer leaps to his feet and his didgeridoo rolls down the slope, clunking. Irons doesn't want to see spray off the back of the wave. He doesn't want to see Burrow's fins. He wants to hear the beach groan. If it's going to happen, it had better happen soon. The dice stop. There are no moans, no groans. Burrow is halfway to shore. His score rapidly accumulates. *Six-point-one, six-point-two.* Burrow tells himself he's done it. Nailed it. It's better to travel than to arrive. Except now. Now Taj Burrow just wants to arrive. 'Me and Andy were surfing our arses off,' Burrow says. 'But then that last set came through. The second wave is always good at Bells. That one, what a dream. It was the best wave we had for the whole final. All I had to do was ride it. All I had to do was not mess it up. I was so nervous. I knew that was it. Unless I fell, I'd win. They were all screeching and yelling on the cliff. It was insane. I could feel all these eyes on me. I just had to compose myself.'

He's been given a 9. A bit generous, but it's a moot point. 'I tried not to think too much,' Burrow says. 'I just wanted to finish that wave and not worry about how many people were watching or how many points I needed or how many seconds were left or how much pressure was on me or any of the outside circumstances. It was pretty heavy and a picture-perfect ending. I could hear the crowd. The most nerve-racking thing was all that noise when the wave was coming. My heart was pounding. I just had to put everything out of my head.'

Burrow's crimson face is painted white by the Wautharong. He lifts the trophy high and for a moment this all looks so ridiculous— the Aboriginal face paint beneath the Billabong cap, all the Rip Curl slogans strategically placed behind him, all the microphones and cameras—but then you see it's just the way surfing is. A bit of nature, a bit of tradition, a bit of opportunism; a multimillion-dollar business where every last skerrick of exposure counts. If Taj Burrow has to squeeze in some Aboriginal symbolism between his Rip Curl contest singlet and Billabong hat while he's clutching his can of Fosters and holding a Firewire surfboard, so be it. As American basketballer Shaquille Neal said: 'I'm tired of hearing about money, money, money, money, money. I just want to play the game, drink Pepsi, wear Reebok.'

The beach is alive. Burrow is surprised by the reaction. 'Maybe I thought everything was going to come easier when I was younger,' he says. 'I don't know. But it feels like I've got a lot more support out here than I originally thought. So many people have said, "Come on, you can do it—you should be winning these events". I never used to think there were that many people on my side. It's made me feel good. It makes me excited to try to do better.' He heaves the trophy above his head once more. He staggers like a weightlifter with more kilograms than he can handle. His knees weaken, his neck and arms tremble. He stumbles back and forth, forth and back, and damn near drops the trophy. Imagine. Imagine the bell breaking on the concrete near the pile of didgeridoos, rolling lifelessly across the stage. Burrow hangs on. He's told to hold it out in front and shake the be-jesus out of it. 'Good job, buddy,' Slater says. Burrow says thanks. Thanks heaps.

'Mick has been the form surfer by a mile,' Burrow says. 'I feel like I've slipped under the radar a bit, but I'll take it. This is pretty sweet.' And there he sits, contest singlet, big Billabong logo-covered cap, a can of beer on the desk, a bigger set of headphones than they use at NASA, the face paint smeared across his cheeks and forehead. And he's talking earnestly about one of the biggest moments in his career. Why do you laugh? Why is this so bloody funny? Four of the last six winners of Bells have gone on to win the world championship. 'I'm liking that stat,' he says. He watches a replay of his last ride. 'Alright,' he says. 'Unreal.'

Slater climbs the stage. He receives a cheque for $1000 for winning the Expression Session. The irony. Parkinson gets a grand for the wave of the day. The irony. Fanning collects a thousand for the wave of the event. The irony. Irons is given a miniature bell which makes as much noise as the triangle he may—or may not—have played at primary school. Bing. 'Congratulations to Taj,' Irons says. 'He's a good guy and great surfer and I've been battling him my whole life.' You've been *battling him your whole life*? Like Superman and Lex Luther? That kind of thing?

And there they are, The Big Five, all up on stage at the one time. Burrow has beer poured on him. 'If I could pick any contest I'd like to win, this is it,' he says. 'It's in Australia and there's so much history. To get to ring this thing—awesome. I get my name on the best trophy there is. I can't remember the last time I was on top of the rankings. There's a lot of hungry guys out there. It's going to be epic this year and I've made a great start. It feels like there might be a little changing of the guard and I want to be part of it. Andy had me. It wasn't happening for me, but I just knew there would be another set. I'm riding that last wave thinking, "I'm going to fucking win it. Just finish this". Good times tonight. It's unbelievable. The best feeling I've ever had. Me and Andy have had such an intense rivalry all our lives.' *All your lives?* Like Superman and Lex Luther? That kind of thing? 'He's had my number and I just wanted to win today more than anything I've wanted in my whole career. There's so much prestige to this. The best surfers in the world are on that trophy and it's the longest-running event in surfing history and you add all that up and you want it more than anything. It's surfing. It's what I do all day, every day. I'm stoked.'

Taj Burrow's stoked count: 53. With a bullet.

Burrow used to be a bit of a porker, you know. He's always been fit, because you can't surf all day every day for a quarter-century without being in decent nick. But he hasn't been super-fit. Three weeks after Slater won his eighth world title at Mundaka, Burrow made a telephone call that confirmed his resolve. He hired a full-time physical trainer/physiotherapist/dietician called Luke Pickett to travel with him all year. If Griggs is Rip Curl's pit boss, Pickett is Burrow's. 'I've started doing the right thing,' Burrow says. 'Nutrition, fitness—I've never felt better. I normally just go through a year doing whatever, but I see guys like Mick and Andy training and doing everything they can to get an edge, I'm going to do the same. I'm going to step up and do that for myself. Everyone is surfing so good, you've got to do anything you can. I used to be kind of lazy and didn't put in as much effort as I could. Not anymore. It's the best start to a year I've ever had, and it's cool to see the Aussies leading the way. It sets me up perfectly. It's been three years since

I've won a contest. I've been runner-up so many times. I've had lots of bridesmaids.'

Come again?

'I've had lots of bridesmaids.'

Let's not revisit the time Burrow's lack of a world title was blamed on sex addiction. OK, let's. Our first thought is that there could be worse things to be addicted to. He's told *Tracks*: 'There have been some stupid things written about me and chicks. For the first few years I was on tour it seemed like I was one of the only single guys so I had a lot of focus on me relating to chicks, but it definitely didn't distract me from competition. The articles about my supposed "sex addiction" were mostly coming out when I finished runner-up for the world title to Occy in 1999, so I think that's proof the girls didn't have an effect.' But in another interview on the topic of the ladies, with Surfer magazine, he's said: 'They just do my head in. There've been a few times when I've spotted really cute girls down the beach, so I'll walk down their way on the way to my heat, just to check them out. The next thing I know I'm paddling out in the impact zone just getting hammered, just getting out of rhythm. It's not good.'

Although you don't know this for a fact, you're guessing Busselton High in remote Western Australia was no Playboy mansion. If Burrow has gone out into the big wide world and not only discovered the fairer sex, but discovered they're pretty keen on him, good on him for making the most of any available opportunities. Back in his single days, you doubt Burrow ever felt the need to lie down on a psychiatrist's couch and say: 'It's horrible, Doc. All these beautiful women want to have sex with me. How do I make them stop?' 'The ladies haven't affected me,' Burrow says. 'I'm just a normal dude with a normal libido.' Hang on. He IS a sex addict. The days of playing the field are over, though. He's had the same girlfriend for two years. Her name is Cheyenne Tozzi. She will be making her presence felt soon enough.

You look at Burrow's board. On the underside are the words: Nev, for Taj.

'It was on my mind the whole time, that it would be pretty significant to have a win here on new technology,' Burrow says. 'So much history has been made at Bells with Simon Anderson's thruster. This is new equipment I'm riding and I'm the only one riding it on the tour. I'm proving it works.'

Fanning's training is a program called Corrective Holistic Exercise Kinesiology. CHEK revolves around posture and core strength. He started it in his rehabilitation from his renegade hamstring and used it to correct his scoliosis. Griggs admits the only downside with Fanning dedicating every last ounce of determination to his world title assault is that his career will be cut short. 'It's a bit of a secret what Mick does but then again, even if people knew, not many of them would be committed enough to do it,' Griggs says. 'I doubt Mick will get the longevity in his career because of how hard he's going right now. I can't see him still on tour at Kelly's age. It's pretty full-on.'

Fanning does gym work. Eats right. Surfs. Doesn't guzzle beers and shovel in junk food like he used to. 'It depends what the waves are like,' he says. 'If the waves are pumping, I just surf. But when the waves are flat, I try to get to the gym. The nutrition is the big thing. It's amazing what it does for your energy. I used to get really tired all the time. I'd have one surf and I'd want to go to sleep. Now I can surf all day, every day. Taj has all the talent in the world but he's never wanted to train before. He's never wanted to do anything extra. But he's gone out and gotten a physio to travel with him. He'll get his diet right, start training—good on him. It's amazing what having a healthy body can do to your mind. You start to feel invincible.'

Fanning is the first to leave Bells. Slater and Parkinson remain on stage. They're giggling like schoolgirls. Perhaps it's no good for Parkinson to be as happy as a fucking clam. Maybe it makes him less ruthless. Maybe he'd get better results if he had the shits. Maybe Joel Parkinson's life is so good he doesn't *have* to fight. And maybe he doesn't even realise. Whether he comes first or last, he'll have his big house and lovely family and his childhood sweetheart Monica as his wife and that's terrific, but maybe being as happy as a fucking clam isn't the ideal state of mind for Joel Parkinson when it comes to competition surfing. He laughs more than a circus clown. He's still laughing while Burrow and Irons perform their official duties; i.e, never-ending interviews where they're asked identical questions by different people. How does it feel, Taj? *I'm stoked*. Yeah, but how does it *really* feel?

'I know they're hungry,' Irons says of Fanning and Burrow. 'They're going to have a really big push this year. They've always been up there. It's just a matter of them putting a whole year together. But there have only been two events. Let's wait and see how they're going when we get to the tenth event.' Yes, Andy, let's.

Fanning gives his cheque to Liz. 'If he loses, I don't go near him for a while,' she says. 'I just let him have his space. I usually go and do my own thing until he's had enough time to have a think. I think we're all the same, aren't we? I never intrude on Mick. I'll never say to him, "Will you take me here?" I'm usually very lucky—he'll come and knock on my door at the hotel and we'll go out to dinner together. But it can be a bit stressful. I don't always enjoy watching him. I'm just like this . . .' An unsteady right hand. 'I'm always shaking. My daughter says, "Well, you shouldn't watch it". And I say, "Well, I have to watch it". She says to me, "I don't understand why you get so stressed". She sat down to watch it on the internet one day and was so stressed, she said it was the pits and she was never going to watch it again.'

Karissa carries one of Fanning's boards. 'A first and a third is pretty good,' he says. 'I'll take that.'

The beers are free at The Rose in Torquay. They're consumed at a frightening rate. About 11 p.m., four hours after kick-off, a man in his mid-30s arrives in a wheelchair. He parks himself near the revelry. Everyone is trolleyed. Parkinson turns up late, happy as a fucking clam. Burrow is blowing his dough at Crown Casino in Melbourne. No sign of Fanning. This is no place for Liz and Karissa. The man in the wheelchair goes unnoticed until Mick Campbell catches his eye. Campbell is wearing bright white sneakers with the laces undone, black socks, loud red board shorts plunging below his knees, a white T-shirt and a white cap tilted to the side like Snoop Dogg. He looks like a fourteen-year-old trapped in a 32-year-old man's tattoo-covered body. And he's going off—hugging his mates as though he'll never see them again, buying drinks for people he doesn't know, telling everyone he loves them. You keep an eye on him. He sees the guy in the wheelchair and does a classic double-take. He walks away from his head-banging gang to visit the man in the wheelchair. He gets down on his knees. They talk animatedly. Campbell buys them drinks and puts an arm around him. 'It cuts me up, seeing someone like that,' he says. He could weep. He spends a large portion of a long evening looking after the guy in the wheelchair and all the while you think: more power to Mick Campbell.

Fanning is having a quiet night. He's hatched a plan, and it starts tomorrow. He is going to confront his fears. Yes, more power to Mick Campbell. And more power to Mick Fanning for what he is about to do. The next stop on this jaunt is no place for the faint of heart. It's a killing field. It's a place where the pretenders are separated from the contenders, where the weak are separated from the strong and where, if you're unlucky, hesitant, petrified or just fated to be stuck in the wrong place at the wrong time, your head will be separated from the rest of your body. It's a place that scares the living daylights out of Mick Fanning. It's a dead zone. It's the most terrifying wave on the planet. It's Teahupo'o.

Liz will never go to Teahupo'o. It's too dangerous and nerve-racking. She returns to her house on the Kirra hill. She walks the

65 steps to her front door. Sea eagles nest in her backyard. They're teaching their chicks to fly.

'This is a very special place,' she says of her home. It's high on the Kirra hill, overlooking the Tweed Valley, Fingal Beach and Mount Warning. Parkinson and Morrison live on the other side of the same mound. Mick bought a vacant block of land and built on it because this was where he always wanted to spend the rest of his days. Parkinson's uncle is in the house between Mick and Liz. Liz's home is called 'Seanian Oig'. It's Gaelic for 'Young Sean's Rock'. She could only ever afford rental accommodation before moving onto the hill but she was able to buy with the money she received from being the beneficiary of Sean's life insurance. 'This house is his gift,' she says. Sean died on a Friday. On the Monday, he had signed up for life insurance for the first time. It was his first day in a new job at a window factory. He was getting money together because he was ready to go on tour.

4

Fate

Mick was offered a ride in the car that killed Sean. He declined in favour of walking. He had imagined the future. He had not imagined this.

'They were so close,' Liz says.

Her eyes drift. 'We called them "the little ones". They did everything together.'

Liz Osborne is a warm and lovely woman. She has an open face and curly hair. She is the type of person who will treat a stranger as though she's known them all her life. 'I hope the universe shines on him,' she says of Mick. 'He's a decent young man. He deserves it so much.'

This is without doubt the most difficult interview you will ever conduct. What right do you have to ask a mother about her dead son? There can be nothing as harrowing as out-living your child. You have three daughters. If they go before their time, you will be tempted to go with them.

'It just happened,' Liz says.

'It just ... happened. It was the worst day of our lives. It's so sad but Sean lived his life to the full and he loved every moment of it. He was a leader. He was so loved by everyone. He was very inclusive and cared for everyone. Our house was always full of boys who wanted to be near Sean. He was a larrikin, but he was very straight and did not take drugs. He always went to school. He got his Higher School Certificate and wouldn't let Mick wag at all. Sean harassed their headmaster until he gave in and they started a sports excellence program for surfing. The headmaster, Mr Bonfield, is so proud of them now. They had the best surfers in the world in that program.

'Sean had so much respect for me and made sure all his mates were polite and caring towards me. When someone came into the house, he always introduced them to me and told them to say please and thank you even if they just wanted a drink. He was very funny. I guess it was just his time. We're the ones who are sad because we have to miss him. He's probably really happy. He's definitely around us, he's definitely watching. We all feel that.'

That night.

'Mick was at the same party,' Liz says. 'People think he was overseas but he wasn't. He was there. Sean and Joel got in the car with their girlfriends and the two boys lay in the back of the station wagon. They didn't have seat belts on. The two girls were in the front seats. The car hit one of those big pine trees on Boundary Street, just down the road from where we live. Mick didn't know. He was walking home right behind them, right along the same road. Some older guys that we know went and found Mick and took him away because the accident scene was going to be right there in front of him. He would have walked right into it. They brought Mick home. He came in and woke me up and told me Sean had died. That's what he said: "Mum, Sean has died". He wanted to go down and see it but we didn't let him. We didn't want him to see it until they cleared the wreck. We kind of locked him in the house for the rest of the night.

'There's no reason for it. I think the girl put her foot on the accelerator instead of the brake, but none of that matters now. Like I said—it just happened. It's a very dangerous spot. They're always trying to change it. You know where the roundabout is? She hit the kerb and went straight into the tree. They were OK, the two girls, but the back door came open and I think Sean was lying ... I'm sorry ...'

A pause.

'I don't like to think about ... the accident scene ...'

A long pause.

'It's alright,' she says. 'It's good to talk about him. It's good to remember him. Sean's girlfriend's father was an ambulance driver and he was called to the scene. But when they found out who it was, they had to take him away. It was a terrible thing for the whole community. It's still going, but we try to see it in a positive way. It inspires us to live with an appreciation of the gift of life. Mick knows his surfing is important, and he's trying so hard, but he also knows it's not the be all and end all. It's just a shame they never got the chance to do the tour together. Mick would have loved that, and I really do think it would have happened. It was devastating for all of us, but Mick in particular. He's being loyal to Sean's memory. He's being good to his word. I respect him for that.

'We all had to grieve how we thought best. Mick was expected to help people and that's what really pissed me off about the whole thing. He was only seventeen and he was expected to be the comforter for the whole community—but he was the one who needed comforting the most. He'll never get over it. None of us will. I think you just learn how to live with it. We try to remember Sean in good ways and that's the most important thing for us. People get embarrassed when we talk about him and tell stories about him. It can make them feel uneasy, but it makes us feel better. I guess they're just not sure how to be around us. Joel's parents were very different. I had the house open after Sean died and kids from everywhere would come over and sit with us, but Joel's mum had to close herself off. That was her choice. I can understand that. There's no right way or wrong way.

Tears.

'You know, Sean had Mick running around like a little servant. "Mick do this, Mick I need you to get this for me", and Mick was like, "Oh yeah, sure, Sean, I'll do it for you".

More tears.

5

Broken skull

BILLABONG PRO
TEAHUPO'O, TAHITI, FRENCH POLYNESIA

'You've got to tuck your balls in and just go,' Mick Fanning says. 'You've got to go mad. It's an epic event. Everything about it is crazy, radical, wild. I love it. You've got this amazing backdrop of the mountains, the water is so blue, you can see the coral underneath, everyone is screaming from the channel, the atmosphere is enormous. It's pretty overwhelming. I want to go and get a result there to prove to myself I really can do it. I haven't done much there before. The wave is scary. If it's big, it's *really* scary. I don't think anyone who paddles out there isn't scared. If they say they're not scared, they're lying.'

Teahupo'o can give you the ride of a lifetime, or kill you. She's a little difficult to predict. If there's one place which can end Fanning's campaign—if not end *him*—it's this little dot on the map. This little fishing village. This little beauty. This little beast. The translation of Teahupo'o depends on who you ask. One man with arms the size of a Norfolk pine will tell you it stands for *The End of the Road*. It's the most logical explanation because Teahupo'o is the furthest you can drive south from the Tahitian capital of Papeete before you come across a river. The hidden meaning is that it's *The End of the Road* for this particular lifetime if you're crushed onto the razor-sharp reef in an explosion of coral, flesh and bone. They're not tubes, these things, they're death chambers. But another man will shake his head and say no, no, no. He'll say Teahupo'o really translates to *Broken Skull*. Given the carnage you've witnessed in this freak of nature over the years, the winner's trophy of a spear is an appropriately deadly memento. King Teahupo'o's son avenged the death of his father by feasting on the murderer's brain.

Ka-boom.

It's not a wave. It's a mutation of a wave, a distortion of a wave, a *thing*. It's a hissing, spitting, howling *thing*.

Ka-boom.

Sunny Garcia has won the Triple Crown in Hawaii six times. Sunset Beach, Waimea Bay and Pipeline make up the Triple Crown on the North Shore and they are formidable arenas—but Garcia can treat them with the disdain of Kiddies Corner. He is scared of nothing in the world. He's spent most of the year in jail and barely flinched. But even he admits Teahupo'o gives him the creeps. He's scared when it's big because the reef becomes a slaughterhouse. He's scared when it's small because sooner or later it will get big again. 'I'm just sitting there, waiting for it to come and get me,' he says.

Surfing has a lot to do with self-respect and there's no greater crime against yourself than backing off a wave. You're a coward. You're pathetic. It's the ultimate humiliation. It goes against the whole ideal. Surfing is for free spirits and to hell with the consequences. You're supposed to throw yourself into the great unknown. Who cares if you fall? Who cares if you get hurt? Squibs are not welcome. Back off and you wallow in self-loathing. There's nowhere to hide. You get dirty looks. You're mocked and ridiculed and so you should be. There's more honour in taking off on a dead-end—because you just might make it. 'Eddie Would Go' is a famous mantra. Hawaiian Eddie Aikau went, and drowned—legend. There's idiocy in that, of course, but the need for bravado is real and everyone understands it. You have no credibility until you have conquered waves of serious consequence. Every reef, sandbank and point break you will ever visit has the same rule: Go. Teahupo'o, though, is the exception to the rule.

One of the larger sets of balls on the planet are residing inside the board shorts of Mark Occhilupo, but even he freely admits he's shied away from the thing. It was the Billabong Pro, in a heat against Patea 'Poto' David. 'I've been in some hairy situations out there,' he says. 'I remember when I lost to Poto. I had a really sore back at the time. I had some good medium-size barrels and he didn't have much and then right at the end a really big wave came through. I had priority and he asked me if I was going. I said, "Ahh...nah". I couldn't do it. It could have been my worst wipe-out ever because I just didn't have the right mental space. I thought that was a good decision. I lost the heat because of it, but I saved my life.'

Ka-boom.

Fanning gets scared. He just feels lost out there. He's never quite sure where to sit. He's never quite sure which waves are makeable and which ones are going to scrape him along the reef like cheese through a grater. He needs help—and is not too proud to admit it. This is one of the most crucial stages of the year. He flies to Papeete the day after Bells when Burrow, Slater and the rest haven't even thought about packing their bags yet. Previously, he's arrived with everyone else a week before the contest and been forced to fight for waves like a seagull over hot chips. He's always been eaten alive. Close to a hundred of the world's best surfers—the tour guys, the trialists, the kamikaze locals wanting to make a name for themselves with one hypnotic ride—cram onto the small take-off zone. It can be virtually impossible to get a wave but Slater and Irons have cracked the code. They can paddle out and dominate. They'll arrive with an air of authority and swing straight into a pit next to a hundred guys who have been crapping themselves for hours. Fanning holds no such sway, feels no such self-assurance. He's never placed better than a ninth. Ninths are no good. At the start of the year, when he started plotting his course, he decided he has to get to know Teahupo'o a little better. He needs to go and see her on his own. He arrives in Papeete for a secret ten-day mission, his face an atlas.

Ka-boom.

Fanning stays at the back of the waterfront home of Alain Riou. His bungalow has a thatched roof and white salt-encrusted walls. Three wooden steps lead into water more clear than diamonds. Fanning jumps on a jet ski and arrives on the reef within two minutes. Mick Fanning will surf Teahupo'o for ten days by himself and every second counts. There's only one way to get to know a place. Surf it until you can surf it no more. Even the moments that don't feel as if they count—they count. It's just Fanning and the *thing*. No distractions. He will introduce himself, stick his head into every nook and cranny. He will study her in microscopic detail. She will consider him. He will attempt to understand her. She will contemplate his worth.

Ka-boom.

'I'm not disciplined enough to go and do that,' Kelly Slater says later. 'I'm not even disciplined enough to intentionally practise a certain move, or whatever, time and time again, like the other guys might do. I've been competing for twenty-seven years. That's most of my life, ever since I was a little kid. When I get into competitive situations, I become aware of a lot of things that I'm not aware of normally. I notice where the waves are breaking, the way the tide is, the way my board is getting through the water, the way my fins are reacting to how I'm turning. I get on auto-pilot in competition. If I'm not in competition, I don't notice those things.'

Ka-boom.

Taj Burrow is front row at the Australian Fashion Show in Sydney. His girlfriend Cheyenne Tozzi is on the cat walk. Burrow is flying high. He's followed his win at Bells by taking out the Boost air contest on the Gold Coast, where not even Slater and Josh Kerr have been unable to halt his freight train of momentum. 'I couldn't have asked for a better time of it,' Burrow says. Split the screen: Burrow is living it up. Fanning is busting a gut out on the reef. It's not that Burrow isn't hungry. He is. It's just that Fanning is becoming ravenous.

'There's a lot of motivation there to take Kelly down,' says Tom Carroll, Australia's world champion from 1983 and '84. 'The big thing for those two guys is going to be who can stick it out for the whole year. It's a huge ask for anyone. They have to find a way to keep their focus and keep improving their performances but they've also got to find a way to stay in the moment. The more they think about the end of the year, the more they'll get distracted. Talent-wise, Mick has the leap on most guys. He's got a lot of world titles in him—if he wants it. He's gotten a few runs on the board this year but he has to keep that going. He can be an easily distracted guy and he's got to keep himself in check. He's the biggest hope for Australia, in my view. Taj has shown some form but he's yet to show he can hold out for a whole year. Anyone can have a good event. You need nine or ten of them. You just need that unwavering drive or you're going to screw up. It's so easy to get caught up in all the shit that goes on. You have to be really humble and really open to adjusting to all the changes that come and go over the course of a year. You have to keep yourself on the job, and I think that can be especially hard for Australians because we have such a good life at home. It's so alluring and easy to fall back into the comfort zone. It's all there, just waiting for us, the easy life. You have to know when to bring yourself out of that and get back to the task at hand. Kelly and Andy have the hunger, all the time, but it's not a part of our culture to be so hungry. We like to have a good time. We like to take the piss out of each other. That's just a part of who we are in Australia. There's the beer-drinking culture and a lot of guys don't know how to get out of that. It's something I found very difficult to pull myself out of, to be honest. I ended up with that sense of purpose and I was lucky to find that. If you're out there training for the world tour and you've got your mates saying, "Ah, come on mate, let's go for a beer, don't be soft", that whole thing can be a huge distraction and something very hard to escape. Some guys might not want to pull away and that's fine. But if they don't, they're not going to win a world title. It's that simple. You know what I mean about Australians? We like to have a good time. 'The passion gets lit in Mick. I can see that.'

Carroll knows about passion. He refused to compete in South Africa in 1985, robbing himself of another world title but making his stance against Apartheid. He's overcome injuries: infected fin gashes, ruptured stomach muscles, a knee reconstruction, torn ankle ligaments, countless cuts and open wounds requiring stitches, back strains, concussion and a fin fair up the bum. And he's overcome sorrow. His first win at Pipeline came from an almost suicidal attack on giant waves highlighted by his legendary 'snap heard around the world', a maniacal re-entry under the lip of a giant wave that could have killed him. Just before the final, Carroll had been told his sister had died in a car accident.

'There's been incredible brilliance from all these Australian guys at times, but I really, really enjoy Mick's surfing. Mick, to me, can hold himself above the rest if he gets his head right and it looks like he's doing that. I think there's more focus in him this year. He's getting close to where Kelly and Andy are. He needs to keep it up. If he doesn't, they'll be all over him. Just one opening is all they are going to need. Kelly can bring focus at any time and that's a rare skill. If Mick can bring that same focus to the table, look out. But he's got to do it at every single event. He's got to get on that roll where he starts winning heats without getting his hair wet. That's how I used to think of being in that state where you keep winning heats with a minimal amount of stress. You get that aura where the other guys sit back and let it happen for you. Kelly has that. The other guys are half-expecting to lose to him. You get a big reputation because you get big scores and then, to a degree, you keep getting big scores because of your reputation. Mick has the potential to get himself into that position.'

Ka-boom.

Fanning arrives on the reef. Alone.

Ka-boom.

Spend ten days with someone, some *thing*, and you're going to get comfortable. Fanning catches a wave, gets barrelled, paddles back out, does it again. Repeat. Catches a wave, gets barrelled, paddles back out, does it again. He wants it to become automatic. You've seen him be painfully shy around people he doesn't know— then outlandishly extroverted around his mates. There's a bit of that in everyone. He wants it to be the same with the *thing*.

Ka-boom.

Teahupo'o is pronounced Chow-poo. Chopes for short. Local surfer Thierry Vernaudon claims to have first ridden the *thing* in 1985. But it was small, so doesn't really count. Anything under 6 feet doesn't count. Mike Stewart and Ben Severson—riding body-boards, otherwise known as Esky lids, otherwise known as shark biscuits, otherwise known as complete and utter abominations—

embarked on their historic white-knuckled rides in genuine size in 1986. But it took until the mid-90s for bona fide professionals to tippy-toe up to Chopes for photo shoots like children creeping up to knock on the door of the local haunted house. Run up, knock, run like hell. The real legend was born in 1998 at the first professional contest. It was just a world qualifying series event but the *thing* bared her teeth at the intrusion after her thousands of years of supreme isolation. She lashed out. Treated the pros with disdain. How dare they come here! It was 10 feet and scary as shit. Renowned hell-men cowered. Wannabe hell-men decided they didn't want to be hell-men anymore. Months later, the photos hit the magazines. The focus was not on the surfers. It was on the *thing*. The general reaction: WHAT THE FUCK IS THAT?

Ka-boom.

Laird Hamilton's death-defying 18-foot wave on 17 August 2000, is a part of surfing folklore. It left him crying in the channel. He swore he had come closer to God.

Ka-boom.

They're alone, Fanning and the *thing*.

Ka-boom.

'I guess anything I've ever done, I've wanted to try to do it properly,' he says. 'What a nerd. But if eating better is going to make me feel better, I'll do that. If putting in extra effort at the gym will make me stronger, I'll do that, too. I knew my weaknesses coming into this year and Teahupo'o has always been one of them. If I'm serious about this, I have to get this right.'

Fanning gets 3-to-4 feet Teahupo'o. He gets 5-to-6 feet Teahupo'o. He gets 7-to-8 feet Teahupo'o, punishing Teahupo'o. He doesn't get 15 feet Teahupo'o, king-hit Teahupo'o, but he gets very frigging solid Teahupo'o, challenging Teahupo'o, competition Teahupo'o. The *thing* plays with him for a while. Shacks him. Smothers him. The perfect host. But then the devil inside hurls three monsters at him, breaks his board and knocks the wind clean out of him.

Grabs the back of his head and smashes his nose against the fibreglass.

Mick Fanning keeps coming back.

Ka-boom.

No matter what the *thing* does, Mick Fanning keeps coming back.

Ka-boom.

It's the dark room you were too afraid to enter as a child.

Ka-boom.

Teahupo'o is vivid on a clear day. The water becomes beyond blue, a deep and rich blue as though all God's blues have been thrown into a bucket and splashed across the reef. The mountains are so, so green. They're so, so lush and vibrant. This is nature. This is the way to live. No shirt, no shoes, fruit and vegetables, peace and quiet. Island time. You walk more slowly, talk more slowly. At night, the stars are so close you can touch them. Is that right? Are the stars closer here? There are more of them and they're bigger, you're sure of it. Or maybe when you're at home, you don't look for the stars so much. But when the storms hit, Teahupo'o is dark and full of shadows and frightening and Armageddon.

Fanning is nearly a kilometre from shore. Nobody sees and nobody hears. 'I've been able to surf it in a bit of peace,' he says. 'In a way it feels like the first time I've ever really surfed it. I don't know if I've ever backed myself here before.'

Ka-boom.

The weekend before the Billabong Pro, the ASP stages a 30-year reunion for the most pivotal contest in tour history: the 1977 Stubbies Classic at Burleigh Heads. Thirty of the 32 original combatants perform an exact re-enactment of the draw. Back in '77, with 20 000 people lining the point, one immortal beat another in the final: Michael Peterson downing Mark Richards. Peterson no longer surfs. He cannot accurately be described as wafer-thin. He has agreed to watch the reunion without taking part. Wayne 'Rabbit' Bartholomew, ASP chairman and 1978 world champion, asks Peterson to nominate his replacement in the draw. It can be anyone. It can be Slater. It can be one of his friends. It can be one of his peers from the good old days. He chooses Mick Fanning, who flies back from Papeete for the one-day reunion before turning around and going back to his bungalow with the thatched roof and salt-encrusted walls. He will re-enact Peterson's semi-final against Bartholomew. And then he will take to the water with an immortal.

Mark Richards was Superman. Seriously, he was. He would paddle out at Merewether Beach in Newcastle when the waves were too big and ugly for anyone else to jump off the rocks and when word spread that Superman was out on the third reef, no-man's land, hundreds of people would run down the hill to watch him. Television cameramen shot footage from helicopters as Superman carved out his long, swooping lines because back then he provoked awe. You know he did, because you were there. You were barely ten years old and your father was barely 40 and he really did provoke awe in you both.

Superman won four straight world titles from 1979 to 1982. Superman tamed some of the most gargantuan swells to have hammered Waimea Bay and Sunset. Superman's logo on his 'MR' boards bore a striking resemblance to the symbol used by the other Superman, the poor imitation you saw in the comics. Superman would return home to Merewether from his heroics in Hawaii and paddle out in his silver wetsuit and you were convinced he would never grow old. He turned 50 in 2007. Time waits for no Superman.

He says if anyone can break the domination of Slater and Irons, it's the square-jawed and intense young man with whom he's about to share the water at Burleigh. But he fears that in Slater, Fanning is confronting the equal of any top sportsman in any discipline from any era. 'To me, Kelly is one of the greatest athletes in history,'

Superman says. 'Take any sport at any time, I don't care. He's in the Muhammad Ali, Tiger Woods, Michael Jordan, Michael Schumacher echelon.'

Superman still lives across the road from Merewether Beach. He owns a surf shop in Newcastle. He leads a quiet life, still surfing at Merewether, mostly at a spot called Ladies. He's a gentle soul, calmer than the Dalai Lama. Little punk kids who should show some damn respect occasionally drop in on Superman at Ladies, but he never complains. Those kids should be taken out the back of the surf club and shot by Matt Hoy or one of the other gung-ho locals because no-one should be allowed to drop in on Superman, not ever. He isn't the type to bask in past glories or hang around the tour so people can fawn all over him. As much as they'd like to. Unless you call him at his shop, or get him at home, you're unlikely to get him at all. He doesn't have a mobile phone because he fears it will give him cancer. He steers clear of computers for the same reason. Funny old world, eh? Superman was brave enough to conquer the North Shore of Hawaii but he's too scared these days to put a little telephone to his ear.

'Burleigh was the beginning of the Dream Tour,' Superman says. 'Man-on-man heats instead of four- and six-man heats. Just two guys in the water in absolutely perfect conditions. It felt like this was the way it should be. It felt like the future and it was. We finally had a format that worked and promoted good high-performance surfing. It was amazing. There was a massive crowd, probably fifteen thousand or twenty thousand people. It was where it all began.'

On why Australia hasn't produced a world champion since Occhilupo, Superman says: 'They've encountered the two most competitive surfers in the history of competitiveness. Kelly and Andy—those two guys want to win and keep winning. They want to leave bloody carcasses in their wake. They're like gladiators. They could be bleeding to death on the sand but still go out for their heats. Someone else will lose an event and go home and think, "Oh well, that's the way it goes". Kelly and Andy will go home and punch walls. It doesn't matter whether it's marbles or recreational tennis or a muck-around game of poker, those two guys want to win like no-one else has ever wanted to win before. That's the problem for Mick and everyone else on the tour right now—the two most competitive guys in history have taken over the sport. They're basically butting heads, trying to bash each other up. It's like they're the two biggest bulls in the paddock and everyone else is too scared to go up to them. It's like everyone is going, "How do we stop them?" They're phenomenal.'

Get Fanning to nominate his ten greatest moments and high on the list is the first time he met Superman. It was at Coolangatta. Superman had designed a board for Fanning. They talked for hours. 'I do follow the tour—from a distance,' Superman says. 'They've named it very aptly: the Dream Tour. It's where we all hoped it would be by now. It was always the vision—having the very best surfers in the world competing in a format where the best surfer should come through in great conditions. It's hard to see how the tour could be in any better shape. Guys are making money, the surfing is phenomenal, the events are held in amplifying waves in out-of-the-way places and you've got some really passionate ex-surfers running the show, people like Rabbit, and a crew who really believe in it. They're not doing a job they don't give a shit about. They passionately believe in the sport and where it's going.'

Fanning beats Bartholomew—because that's what Peterson did. Liz accepts the trophy—because that's what Peterson's mum did. It's 2-foot and onshore. Crap, really, but crap is in the eye of the beholder. You'll go out in anything if you're in the mood. Sections and peaks look better than they really are. You'll see them because you *want* to see them. And you'll find fault in perfection if you want to. It's a bit flat, a bit onshore, a bit nothing. Peterson gives Fanning his original Stubbies medal. Fanning is speechless. He stands next to Superman for photographs before the final. Fanning has the single fin and Superman has the thruster. Fanning opens his mouth but no words come out. The Burleigh reunion was shaping as one of the highlights of his career. Surrounded by Australia's former world champions, all of them telling him how much it would mean for the crown to be brought back home, and how genuinely capable he is of doing it, it's become a highlight of his life.

You wish you could tell Superman how much you worshipped him when you were a boy. You wish you could tell him that one of the greatest days of your life was sitting in the water with him at Ladies in your early twenties. You wish you could tell him that your first surfboard was a classic little red 'MR' you found under the Christmas tree. You wish you could tell Superman it's one of the few possessions in your life you will never throw away. You wish you could tell him how you plan to give it to your own kids when they start surfing, and how you'll tell them all about the man who designed it. You wish you could have been on the headland at Burleigh 30 years ago for the last day of the Stubbies, or at Waimea when it was 10 metres and he slaughtered it. You especially wish you could tell Superman he will always be the hero of all those kids from the Merewether hill who have long since grown into adults. You wish you were brave enough to say all that.

The *thing* rises, rearing like a mountain, blacking out the sky. It mutates and haemorrhages—the lip spewing forward. You tell yourself this is impossible but it's too late. The ocean unloads. Detonates. You attempt to stand, but your feet don't even touch the board. You free-fall, horrified. You shouldn't be out here. You have made a serious mistake. You didn't know it was this big. You imagine cracking your chin on the bricks, jamming your top teeth through your gums, your mouth filling with blood like an overflowing bath.

You're a kilometre from shore. Cut to ribbons. The skin of your back has been shredded. Your board is snapped in two. Salt water burns your red flesh. A Teahupo'o tattoo requires no ink.

Burrow is staying at the home of local charger Hira Terinatoofa. Nev Hyman gives a long and detailed explanation of the Firewire phenomenon but you're not really listening because all you're really thinking is that he's going to make a deadset fortune out of all this. And so you say to him, Nev, old boy, you're going to make a deadset fortune out of all this. 'Hope so,' he says. 'We've put enough bloody time and effort into it. It's been a pretty good start. Having Taj as the face of it all is priceless.'

Ka-boom.

Taj's face won't be so priceless if it hits the reef.

Ka-boom.

Thank the Lord for having created such a wondrous place.

Ka-boom.

The first question: How big is it?

The real question: How big will it get?

Teahupo'o can get too big, see. It can get so big that one day the ASP and Billabong will be up for manslaughter when they send out two surfers and only one comes back. 'I hope it's going to be bombing,' Irons says. Sometimes, you should be careful what you wish for. You won't be surfing this cussing, howling, demonic *thing* again unless Andy Irons puts a loaded gun to your head and even then you might not paddle out because taking a bullet from Andy Irons might be the quickest way to get the same trip to heaven or hell, whichever you're destined for. Tahitian Briece Taerea is the constant reminder, his white board protruding from the water like a tombstone as he stayed under too long. His skull was mangled beyond repair and he spent two days in a coma before he was pronounced dead and all the divine mountains did was look on.

Some Day

Ka-boom.
What is this?
Ka-boom?
No swell.

Fanning doesn't know if he's won his first heat against Anthony Walsh and Raoni Monteiro. He can't hear the judges. Back in his boat, he has to wait until he gets an SMS from Liz. 'I'm six thousand miles away and I'm waiting for a text from Mum to either say, "Well done", or "You idiot". Luckily it was, "Well done". I didn't get a single barrel the whole time—it definitely wasn't the Teahupo'o I saw last week.'

Liz is glued to the internet. But she isn't enamoured by the commentary when they start talking about Fanning's propensity to try too hard. 'That's what people like to say,' Liz says. 'They were talking about it when I was listening and I wasn't very happy. They were trying to say he was too focused. Look, the training, yes, I think he was too much into that for a while. He had to tone it down, so he did. But I don't think he's *too* focused, no.'

The Big Five reach the third round. *Ka-Boom?* The beast is snoring. Next day, no *ka-boom*. The day after that, no *ka-boom*. Mick takes Karissa to the island of Moorea. They'll stay there until word filters through of swell. They're there for an eternity. Fanning is keeping a low profile, knocking back the vast majority of media requests—or making sure he doesn't even receive them. 'I've turned my phone off,' he says. 'I'm hiding.' Fame is a curious creature. You can work all your life to be recognised for your achievements then when people start taking notice, all you want to do is vanish.

Then there's a bump on the reef. Burrow racks up 17.66 in round four against Cory Lopez—but loses. He's not stoked. He's so un-stoked he can barely speak. 'I'm not sure how I lost that,' he says.

Fanning murders Chris Ward and he's going places he's never been: the quarters. Burrow's demise means the No.1 ranking is his again. The last eight are Fanning, Parkinson, Irons, Jeremy Flores, Lopez, Luke Stedman, Damien Hobgood and outstanding Australian rookie Kai Otton. Scan that list. A big name is missing. The biggest name of all.

'Bonus,' Fanning says after Slater loses to Flores.

The king has coughed up a ninth. 'I just didn't have the sync with the waves,' he says. 'You've just got to pay your dues. The last two years have come my way. This year is looking to be more of a struggle.'

There's such a distinct lack of *ka-boom* that Bartholomew has no option other than to extend the event for two days and pray for swell for 48 straight hours because it will be an embarrassment of nuclear proportions if the ASP can't finish an event at Teahupo'o because the waves are too small. They will become a laughing stock. There will be misguided but inevitable suggestions that Teahupo'o isn't *that* breathtaking after all. 'Mother Nature doesn't care about a contest,' Fanning says. Bartholomew extends the waiting period until May 16.

Parkinson beats Irons in the first quarter-final in 1.5-metre waves. 'Andy was having some issues with his equipment and having a bit of a meltdown,' Parkinson says.

In his quarter-final, Fanning faces Luke Stedman. 'He'll probably make life harder for me than I will for him,' Stedman says, and he's right.

It's still not real Teahupo'o, not the death-defying Teahupo'o that turns the medical tent into an emergency ward and rips shoulders from sockets and leaves the unlucky with pools of blood forming at their feet. The ambulance driver is asleep behind the wheel and he can stay that way. Fanning's semi-final is against Kai Otton and the surf is bordering on the sublime with overhead barrels, and something happens here that you are unable to explain.

Otton leads. Fanning paddles straight to the spot he wants. No more uncertainty. No more paddling around in circles. He's up and surfing. His board is pointing at five o'clock. It goes to three o'clock. His back knee touches the wax. His left hand drags behind him— the brake. He falls deep. But he's gone too deep and the *thing* envelopes him. Even Mick Fanning can't understand what happens next.

There's whitewater everywhere. He's blinded and he's a good 15 metres too far inside. There is no way out. You can't even see his singlet. There are photos of this wave and they are of nothing but a wave. You can usually see a man's silhouette inside a barrel but there is no sign of life when Mick Fanning goes into the darkness. There's a burst of spray as the *thing* explodes and at the moment when surfers usually appear from the cavern, Mick Fanning does not come out with it.

But then he does.

He kicks off his board and does the most extravagant claim of his life: knees bent, forearms flexed, fists closed tightly. Watch footage of that wave if you get the chance. Watch it all day and night and try explaining it. Fanning gets the only 10 of the contest. He gets his first 10 at Teahupo'o. 'That was a pretty special wave,' he says. 'I—um—I don't really know what I was doing in there. I was double-pumping, trying to do what I'd been doing the week I was here but it didn't really seem to be working. I couldn't see. I thought I'd blown it—but then I got out.' You'll spend an entire year watching replays of that barrel without once being able to make sense of it. Miracle is derived from the Latin *miraculum*, and refers to the divine intervention of a supernatural being. Just in case you were wondering.

Fanning loses the final to Damien Hobgood. Doesn't matter. He's come to his worst event on the tour and taken a second. Burrow: ninth. Slater: ninth. Fanning has turned a glaring weakness into a strength. Which pretty much means there are no weaknesses left. He has the satisfied look of a man who has completed a mission he wasn't entirely sure he was up for. And he's done it courtesy of a Teahupo'o barrel—the one *thing* he had never mastered before, the one *thing* he spent ten straight days trying to perfect while everyone else was putting their feet up, the one *thing* he wanted to get right in case an important heat came down to his ability to go left and hang on for dear life and make it out. You are unsure about the merits of karma in this life but it's the only explanation you can find for Fanning's 10 and you suggest it to him and he says: 'Maybe. I've seen the replays and I'm not real sure myself about what happened there. Maybe you're right. Maybe that's the way it all works. You put in the hard work and you get your rewards.'

The *thing* has a sense of humour. The day after the finals she offers double-overhead barrels, boards being crushed, Slater being dragged through the lagoon for 30 minutes, photographers falling out of their boats in the rush to get close-up pictures of the real Teahupo'o. Irons and Slater sit on the inside and stage a private war, taking turns getting waves, pushing themselves to outdo the other. What you'd give to see them in another real-life heat. The two best sessions of the Billabong Pro have been immediately before, and immediately after, the event. The *thing* has a *cracking* sense of humour.

You can pay the price for having high expectations. Maybe it's better to expect nothing and then whatever you get is good. You have no expectations whatsoever about your next destination. You log on to the ASP website and the venue for the Rip Curl Pro Search is officially listed as Somewhere in Chile. There's *no* destination and you like the sound of that. You like it very much.

Teahupo'o will forever remind you of Morgan Beck. He was a surf writer for Australian Associated Press, and an outstanding man. He lathered himself in sunscreen every day so he wouldn't die from skin cancer. He surfed a lot so he stayed fit. He ate healthy food so he would live long and prosper. He was in his early 30s when he died. He was throwing a frisbee with his girlfriend, Anna, on the beach at Collaroy on Sydney's northern beaches. They went home early because Morgan felt ill. They had an early night because he still felt ill. He went to the bathroom and Anna heard a thump. Morgan had collapsed onto the bathroom floor. The thump was Morgan dying of a heart attack. Why? A good man who looked after himself drops dead at 30. How can that be? Halfwits who ply themselves with drugs and alcohol and treat people with no respect will live till they're a hundred. You surfed with Morgan once and he looked out to sea and said: 'What does it all mean?' Maybe now he knows. Maybe he can shed some light. You were in Teahupo'o in 2002 when you heard Morgan had passed. You'd been talking to him about doing a book together. It was going to be a book on the Dream Tour in the hope it would coincide with an Australian winning the world title. The day he died, you caught a wave for Morgan Beck. It was only small.

6

Snap

A mistimed floater snapping his board; the splits ripping his hamstring off his pelvis. Put your fingers in the corners of your mouth and stretch your lips until they snap and you're on the way to understanding the kind of blinding pain Fanning experienced when he horribly misjudged an innocuous little 2-foot wave at Bawa in Indonesia in 2004.

'The pain was ridiculous,' he says. 'I bawled. I was kind of under the water thinking it couldn't be too bad and I could stay out and that it was cramp that would go away. But I couldn't even get in the boat. It felt like my leg was going to fall off. We had to get out of there but it was a nightmare. We ended up having to sail for ten hours and get three flights before we got home. I had to bribe a seat on a plane to get to Singapore. I didn't know what I'd done. I'm thinking. "What's wrong here? Something is really wrong here". It took me forty-eight hours to get home. I thought I'd be out for six weeks. I was shattered because I was going to miss J-Bay. I'd been having a bad year and I needed to turn it around. I was pissed off because it was going to be a *really* bad year. We found out how severe it was, but it was still another couple of weeks of trying to work out what we could do for it—if anything.

'My chiropractor knew a really good surgeon in Sydney, Merv Cross. Merv rang me and said, "You have to get down here straightaway and get that thing fixed". I went down and I didn't see Merv, I saw Dr Peter Wood. Between the two of them, they had done the most amount of surgery on that injury in the world. But even that was only, like, thirty-five times. They didn't know what was going to happen. They were like, "Well, we suppose you could surf again some day". But they didn't know if I could. They didn't know if I'd ever get back to the level I was at. I was gutted. It was so daunting. The thought of not being able to surf again was killing me.'

The operation in layman's terms: 'They basically peeled back my arse and put this grappling hook in there and I had to wait for the scar tissue to grow back over it, they screwed the hook into my hip then sewed the muscle onto the hook. It was so strong they could lift me clean off the table just with the grappling hook. They had me hanging over the table like some kind Silence-of-the-Lambs freak. They told me it was a one hundred per cent success and I was going to be fine and I'd be able to surf again.

'I had about six weeks after the surgery at home, just watching movies and being a sloth. I wasn't allowed to move because the muscle could tear away again. I didn't go near the ocean for three months. It's insane to think about that now. I was completely immobile for most of the time. I couldn't drive and I wasn't even allowed to sit properly. I had to sit on this weird angle all the time. Then they had me on crutches.

'It was such a blessing in disguise. I'd started taking everything way too seriously. I started surfing because it was fun, but it wasn't feeling like as much fun anymore. It was feeling too much like a job. Half the time I didn't even want to get in the water. I was exhausted. Everything had happened so fast that I'd never had much time to really think about surfing and just my whole life. They told me I could surf again and I had to work out what I wanted to do with it.'

Fanning's previously hectic lifestyle had ground to a halt. 'His house had just been completed and he spent a lot of hours sitting alone in there with the doors closed, just thinking,' Liz says. 'I think it gave him the chance to work out what he really wanted to do. I think he found a lot of courage in that house.'

In 2005, *Surfer* magazine asked Fanning about the changes he would make when he returned to the tour. He told them: 'One big thing is being ruthless. I got told by [his board shaper] Darren Handley years ago that when I go in to negotiate contracts with him, it would be like, we'd look at each other and as we walked in, we were friends. But as soon as we got inside the door, it was business. And there are no friends in business. And now, as soon as I put on that wet shirt, it's like, "Fuck all you guys. You can get fucked". I think that's where Andy's got an edge, and Kelly. I notice Parko did it a lot this year. Just watching around the contests, watching the magazines and interviews, he's really changed his whole perspective. I still try not to be a big head, but deep down you know what you can do. As far as I'm concerned, those guys haven't got an edge at all.'

Mick Fanning has begun to practise what he preached. If you hear him say *heat-by-heat* one more time, you'll slash your wrists. But he's right. It's not rocket science. The one and only thing Mick Fanning can do is win his next heat, whenever and wherever that may be. There's no point worrying about the future. It will come around soon enough.

7

Somewhere in Chile

RIP CURL SEARCH
EL GRINGO, ARICA, CHILE

The shimmering lights of the dead-flat city of Santiago disappear into the background as Fanning's flight from the Chilean capital takes him along the roof of the Andes, the snow-capped peaks bursting through thick clouds, endless proof of the magnificence of nature and the timeless and immoveable beauty of a mountain. He arrives at Arica in the dead of night. Gun-barrel waves push down the ice-cold and barren coastline. When he wakes the next morning, Fanning believes he is on another planet. Arica is the world's third driest city with an average of less than one millimetre of rain per year. 'It's like being on the moon,' he says. 'I've never seen a place like it.' The ancient town is 2000 kilometres north of Santiago and surrounded by thousands of miles of dust, dirt and sand amid the imposing backdrop of the Andes. The mountains are quiet. They're so quiet.

Fanning takes two steps outside the foyer of Hotel Arica, peers skyward and sees El Morro, a large hill overlooking the town and all its people. El Morro does not have one blade of grass. Not a tree. It's the same lonely landscape all the way from Arica to the lifeless and waterless wasteland of the Atacama Desert. On top of El Morro, visible from every house and every street, every nook and cranny in this far-flung place, is a giant statue of Jesus Christ. His arms are spread in front of him. His palms are open as he savours all before him, rejoicing in the peace forged between Chile and the neighbouring nation of Peru. Wherever you are in Arica, no matter the time of day or night, no matter what you are doing or thinking, you can see Jesus.

And Jesus can see you.

'Everyone has been going, "Where's Arica? What is it? What's it like?"' Fanning says with bleary eyes. 'We kept getting told it was Chile Pipe—and it is. We got here really late so we couldn't tell what was around us. We had no idea. It could have been anything. It was pretty wild to look outside this morning. You go, whoa, where are the trees? Where is *everything*? I've had a few surfs. Got a few beatings.

'First time, I'd had too many coffees and I got really, really excited and just started trying to catch all these waves, paddling around like mad and getting smashed. I was thinking, "When am I going to make one of these things?" But then I got a couple and it was fun. My first wave was only small, about three feet. I went over and broke my board and started swimming in. There was no problem at all, it wasn't like I was about to drown, but as I was swimming in through the keyhole—it sucks you out then sucks you back in again, you've just got to sort of beach yourself the best way you can—I looked up and two lifeguards are right there with me. They've got the rescue buoys, the whole bit. They were being so full on. I'm telling them, "Nah, thanks, I'm alright, I can just swim in". Just as I said no, this wave came through and bowled them over and rolled them across the rocks. It was hilarious—the poor blokes.' Avoiding an international incident over an Australian surfer taking the piss out of the local lifeguards, he hastily adds: 'It was good they tried to help out.'

Fanning sits at a small circular table on the second floor of Hotel Arica. Outside, half a kilometre from shore on a reef called El Buey, a solo figure rides gargantuan crests. Fanning doesn't know it's Kelly Slater; the king has strolled into town typically late before venturing straight out into a restless and domineering swell. He's either taking it easy or taking the piss by arriving at the eleventh hour. The contest will be run at a wave called *El Gringo*. Slater's first wave at El Gringo will be in his first heat. 'I got a couple of good surfs in,' Fanning says. 'But we're all in the same boat. No-one has surfed here before. We've only seen bits of footage. It's a tricky wave and it's hard, but guys like Kelly surf so good it'll just take him one surf to be where the rest of us are.' Bruce Irons is cracking jokes in the foyer, but Slater isn't laughing. He puts his head down and walks slowly along the corridor back to his room. He's alone and has a hang-dog expression. So often, he's alone.

'Somebody asked me, "Are you really showing up and just expecting to surf this wave?"' Slater says later. 'I guess when you've surfed so many waves all over the world . . . I just guess this is the kind of wave I'll like. I think it suits me really well. It's like a beach break, but on a reef. It's a short punchy little wave and it's really hollow. That's the kind of wave I love. I've watched a lot of video of the spot. I'll put in a little time out there in the next few days and see where the reef is shallow and see where I can safely get caught inside and where I'll get in trouble. Just a couple of things like that, more for safety than anything else. When a wave comes in that's going to barrel, you can line it up and know where you need to be, so that's not the biggest problem. The biggest problem is, where is the reef really shallow? Where am I going to get hurt? That's the concern for all of us.'

ARE YOU GOING TO RETIRE OR NOT? FOR THE LOVE OF GOD—YES OR NO?

'I'm in the position now of trying to make that decision,' he says. 'It's whether I have the passion. Basically, I'm here and ready. I've realised that if I don't get a result here, if I were to drop in the ratings, it would have me steering the rest of my year towards other work and personal things. I haven't really surfed an inspired year so far. The only good thing is that I have a good throwaway from Teahupo'o. That was the worst result I've had since, I don't know when, a couple of years. It's still not bad—a ninth isn't horrible—but I just haven't found that inspiration yet this year and I'm sort of re-evaluating where I'm at with a lot of things in my life. Realistically, I'm going to put a hundred per cent into the goal.' And what's that, then?

'Ten world titles,' he says. 'But there are other things popping up in my life that I love and want to do. Most of them are based around surfing and promoting the sport, but I'm probably speaking a little early on things right now because I need to sort them out for myself.' Slater has a small speaking role in an animated Hollywood movie called *Surf's Up*. He might make surfing films, but he might concentrate on music. He might do another two years on tour, but he might quit tomorrow. There's always a but with Slater. He might do this, but he might do that. 'It's a long year,' he says. 'I've been back on tour for five or six years now and I'm just trying to decide if I want to try to go for another world title—really put myself there in my mind, put all my energy into it. I can't be indecisive about that.' The irony, of course, is that Kelly Slater is chronically indecisive about whether or not he's indecisive. 'It's not something you can be indecisive about and still do.' That's really what he said. You have a moment where you can understand Irons' frustrations. And then Slater repeats his speech from Bells about not planning to come here until he heard the forecast. You've heard all this before, at countless other contests in numerous other countries and you're thinking: is this guy for fucking real?

'I'm basically motivated here by the quality of the swell and the wave that we get to surf,' he says. 'My brother came to Chile for two weeks and stayed for six. He loved the country, and I've been wanting to come ever since.' There's also his sense of duty. 'It's the first time we've ever had an event in Chile so I thought because of that, it was important to be here and see what it's all about and meet the people.'

He's just being honest. He can't tell people what he's doing—because he doesn't even know. People ask whether he's going to retire, and he tells the truth. He just does not know. He's asked what he would do in retirement. 'For one, just go surfing.' So why retire?! You *are* surfing! 'Just having the freedom to go and surf anywhere, any time, in the best swells. Going to places I've never been. I had a taste of being off the tour for three years and I just loved the freedom I had. But I love the competition, too.' But, but, but . . . 'I love playing music, I love working on surf films, and films outside of surfing that I'm working on now. Just trying to find time for family, getting home.' He wants to compete, but he doesn't want to compete. He wants to dedicate himself to the tour, but he wants to get off the tour. At the absolute most, if Slater was to surf every round of every contest, he'd surf 70 heats a year. That's an absolute maximum of 35 hours a year when he has to work. There's all the travelling and crap airline food and sterile hotel rooms and lay days when you're stuck somewhere against your own free will with nothing to do. Media and sponsors are always knocking at your door. But still. For people slaving away in a claustrophobic office for 60 hours a *week*, Slater is already blessed with what sounds suspiciously like freedom. Don't get the wrong idea. He's not complaining. He just doesn't know which of his two idyllic lifestyles he wants.

Later, a member of Irons' Billabong posse is sitting on the rocks at Ex-Isla Alacran, the bomb site of an area facing El Gringo. He's talking to a woman. She's asking him about someone she's become infatuated with—Slater. The Billabong man is annoyed to a staggering degree. He starts telling her about Slater's constant maybe-I-will-quit-but-maybe-I-won't speeches. He's enraged. He tells her: 'You know what, Kelly? Shut the fuck up. He doesn't hang with anyone, he blows everyone off. He only says he might quit so he can hear people saying, "No, Kelly, please stay, Kelly, we need you, Kelly". If you want to do the tour, just get on with doing it. If you don't want to do it, don't do it. Just spare us the bullshit talk. Come up with all the excuses you want because you're getting your arse kicked right now. If you want to go, just fucking go.' The Billabong man stops abruptly as though he's stunned at the ferocity of his own outburst. He's raised his voice. Everyone is listening. He walks away.

Fanning is again being bombarded with media requests. It's not in his nature to be as expansive as Slater. Opening up to a room-full of strangers doesn't always appeal. The irony being that deep-down he has more to say than most. 'All you can do is go with it,' he says. 'Sometimes it gets a bit much, you know. You just want to kick back and relax and do your own thing, prepare for an event or whatever, but people are saying, "Give me this, give me that, it won't take a sec". It'll always take more than a sec. That's cool. I know it's part of the deal. I don't really mind it. You just have to know when to say yes and when to say no.' Not that Fanning has been previously invisible. He came fifth in the race as a rookie in 2002 and has since been fourth, seventh (despite his injury), third and third. He's had a high profile since he won the Konica Skins but he was, and still is, a shy person. He's summed up his confusion about being a recognisable figure in demand from sponsors by saying: 'I just don't know what they want from me.'

The less he thinks and talks about the tour, the better. 'One thing I found really hard in my first few years was being able to pace myself and forget about it all when I needed to,' he says. 'I thought about it so much, all year, it would just wear me out. It's ridiculous to try to keep really focused on one thing for twelve months but I always tried to. It's exhausting. A couple of years ago I tried to stay up for the whole year, from the first event on the Gold Coast to the end of Hawaii, and we got to France in October and I had nothing left. I could barely move. We went to Brazil and I was still buggered. I didn't realise until I was home before Hawaii how much it takes out of you when you try to think about it every day. You have to turn off. You have to force yourself to. You get home and if there's only one week between trips, you probably keep your level of focus up there, but when there's a longer break you have to let it go. We've just had a month off and for two of those weeks, I was on a boat trip with my mates. That was cool. That was getting away from it. Then I had two weeks of getting fit before I came here, and I feel really refreshed again.'

The boat trip was with Joel Parkinson and Dean Morrison to the Mentawis. Some days they surfed. Some days they put their feet up and had a beer for breakfast. Burrow passed by on a different boat. The world No.1 and No.2 did not exchange a single word.

The Atacama Desert is a 966-kilometre plateau wedged between the Andes and the Pacific Ocean. The river beds have been bone-dry for more than 120 000 years. There is no sign of life. Not a single fly because there is nothing for the flies to eat. Deep into the desert, this is a land without people, birds, animals, trees, vegetation, no life. There is nothing here, nothing, just a road.

Homes are derelict. A string of houses halfway up El Morro are painted pink, yellow and green as if the colours will camouflage the reality. The front walls are as thin and flimsy as cardboard cut-outs. They look fake, painted on, as though these are not real houses but those from a movie set where there's nothing behind the front wall but an empty stage. The centre of town has a park with fountains, and a stretch of designer shops. It's nice. People wear suits and floral dresses. But this isn't the real Arica. Come towards the desert, and the more quiet it becomes with every passing mile. Stray dogs go hungry, wither and die. Dirty faces. The people time forgot. A man could lose his mind out here.

You stand beneath El Morro at dusk. There's a rotting doll's house at your feet. In amongst all this emptiness, there's a child's play house. Bizarre. You crouch and peer inside. You can still see Jesus, just his grey eyes. Inside the broken-down doll's house are candles. They've long since burned out. Wax has poured across the floor and dried. Flowers are decomposing. No-one looks after this anymore. A plaque for Judith Alejandra Vergara Godoy reads: *'Jesus respondio: Yo Soy la resurraccion la vida. El que cree en mi, aunque muera, vivira. Juan 11:25.'* The translation: 'Jesus responded: I Am the resurrection and the life. The one that he believes in me, although dies, will live.' And you think: is that right? Maybe if you believe it's right, then it's right. Maybe the belief is enough. Maybe the belief makes it true. One black car flies past. You walk home and the wind has faded. The waves are only gentle now, the calm before the storm.

A tourist was the first to ride the suck-hole of Ex-Isla Alacran but no-one thought to ask his name so the wave became known as El Gringo. *The Foreigner.* El Gringo can pack a punch. It's not a beach—do not come here on holidays—there isn't a speck of sand. It's mostly cold. Most of the surfers will never return. You can't paddle in. You're just washed onto the jagged and unforgiving rocks, hoping for the best, praying for minimal damage. Your board will be dinged. It's an inevitability. *You* will be dinged. The rocks are covered in mussels and barnacles. They're sharp and unavoidable. *El Gringo* is not a pleasant wave. The best that can be said for it is your sense of accomplishment when you get back in without requiring the kind of medical treatment that leaves Adriano de Souza requiring fifteen stitches to his forehead.

Vultures circle Fanning as he prepares to tackle Dean Morrison. They're as frightening as a scream. Fanning sits awkwardly on an uneven rock. 'I sit there and I visualise,' he says. 'I started doing it last year. I see myself surfing the waves and the *way* I'm going to surf them. I started winning heats straightaway, so I kept doing it. I'd been getting all flustered and over-excited at the start of my heats. I don't surf well when I'm flustered. I go a bit mad. So this one heat, I just sat down and breathed a couple of times to settle myself down. I wasn't trying to do anything in particular, just breathe. But I started picturing catching these waves. I won the heat and I've been doing it ever since. A lot of athletes do it. They've done tests on these sprinters where they put sensors on their muscles and get them to visualise running their races while they're sitting still. The visualisation actually turned on the same muscles they would use in the race itself. I'm no scientist, but I can believe that. The mind is a powerful thing. It works for me and it works for a lot of people.'

Fanning paddles like fury for 50 metres. He wears booties even though he hates them. There's an A-frame peak. You can go left or right. The barrel is more likely to present itself to those going left. A big steep wall is more likely to be made available to those going right. Fanning and Morrison paddle for the same wave. Fanning goes right, Morrison goes left. Fanning's arc is like the opening of a hand-held Chinese fan. Morrison tucks inside a deep barrel and lives to tell the tale. The thousand-odd spectators in front of the lighthouse go el berserko. The commentator screams: '*Gracias gringos!*' Fanning has been good, but Morrison has been better.

The vultures fly straight at Fanning and Morrison again. It's grey and overcast and a scene from Hitchcock. Morrison ducks. With twelve seconds to go, Fanning is heading for uncharted territory. *Alrededor dos.* Round two. You don't want to be in round two. It's where bad things can happen to good people. He needs a 6. He goes right and pinches an 8. Stick that in your pipe and smoke it. Fanning wins with a millisecond to spare. It's uncanny how often the big guns win in the final seconds. Slater used to say he felt so in tune with the ocean he could *will* waves his way. Maybe it's that. Maybe it's just luck. Whatever the whimsical reasons, the B-List guys need a 6-pointer with five minutes to go and the ocean turns its back on them. The A-Listers need a miracle with one minute left and their prayers are answered from high on El Morro.

Fanning comes in and takes off his leg rope as though there's never been any doubt he'd get through. 'I cut my fingers getting rolled along the reef,' he says. 'It's dangerous out there. It's a pretty serious wave. I knew I could get the 6 or 7 if I could just find the wave. I was looking at those rights all day. I was lucky I snuck into one. I haven't beaten Deano in so long and I'm stoked to get him back. You don't want to be in that second round here when you've got guys at their local break. There's no pressure on them and all they want to do is take you down.' Fanning puts on a fur-lined hooded jacket and goes into the commentary booth like he's on his way to the electric chair. He'd rather have a tooth pulled. But this is a Rip Curl event and when you *are* Rip Curl, you do as you're told.

Policemen in khaki uniforms and knee-high boots roam the streets. They carry batons and loaded guns. Where did all the guns come from? When Jesus stands on El Morro and surveys all this, does he think: where did all the guns come from? His monument is illuminated at night. It gives the impression he stands beneath a halo. At the airport in Santiago: guns. On the border of Peru: guns. In front of Ex-Isla Alacran: guns. Outside the department store where people shuffle out with bread and bottles of water and not much else: guns. When you finally completed your journey from the other side of the world and set foot in Arica's airport: guns. Where did all the guns come from? Jesus, where did all the guns come from? Don't just stand there. Do something.

De Souza looks as though he's been belted across the face with a plank of wood. The broken board count starts moving into the 30s. Andy Irons bails out. There aren't many places in the world where Andy Irons bails out. Slater jostles Chris Ward for a wave. Not keen? Crap. 'If you're going to go out to do your job, do your job,' Slater says. 'I do what I have to do to get a win. It was a little bit of a dog fight. I think I got here about ten minutes before my heat. I wasn't the most prepared. I've only surfed twice in the last three weeks. I've been in California and the waves have been small and I haven't been surfing too much. I'm getting excited for the swell that's coming.' Fans yell. KELLEEEEE! KELLEEEE! 'I'll be warmed up in a couple of days,' he says. No hurry, then.

Irons and Burrow are frog-marched into round two. Burrow has arrived without booties. Fanning is commentating when Burrow is beaten by Hawaii's Kekoa Bacalso and Australia's Ben Dunn. The trouble for the usual suspects at a mysterious place like this is that they can come up against some freewheeling barrel merchant who just happens to run hot. 'There's no pressure on guys like me,' Bacalso says. 'I just go out and surf and have fun and enjoy myself.' Burrow is out of sorts. He doesn't like *El Gringo*. 'Taj is a bad-arse surfer but I couldn't worry about him,' Bacalso says. 'Luckily I got a couple of good waves and didn't get washed into the parking lot. It's going to be, like, a hundred-foot in the next couple of days so I'm just going to go out there and give it my all, hopefully not get too pounded. I'm sure I will get pounded but everyone is in the same boat.'

'Taj will get through the next round just fine,' Fanning says before Burrow beats Christian Merello. But he's out of whack, looks awkward.

Liz is here. Slater pecks her on the cheek. 'Good to see you,' he says. Slater is walking round telling a lot of people how good it is to see them. The general consensus is that results—and not swell charts—will determine how long he's on the tour. Andy Irons is livid at the mere suggestion of Slater pulling the pin early. He tells him so, in no uncertain terms, at the hotel bar. The next two stops of Trestles and Jeffreys Bay are among Slater's favourites. If he doesn't make a move there, it'll be *adios*. 'I guess it'd be easier to be in full preparation mode if I were a bit higher on the rankings,' he admits.

The Pacific Ocean covers one-third of the Earth's surface—165 million square metres. The Chilean coast stretches for 4630 kilometres. With three seconds to go, Irons needs a wave to arrive within a foot of him. And it does. He beats mortified Chilean Manuel Selman with a 9.7. 'I was ready to go home,' Irons says. 'I was seriously about to pack my bags and go and have a two-week break. It's just the way my year has been going. It was a really low and sketchy heat. The local kid knew where to surf and got a couple of 6's. I only had a 3 and needed an 8.5. I thought that was it because there weren't too many 8.5's coming through. I was in trouble.' Selman is beyond devastated. He was *this* close to becoming an instant cult hero. But Irons has been covered by pit and snuck through. If there's one man who can get on a red-hot streak, win three straight contests and blow the title race wide open, it's Andy Irons. He's exceedingly dangerous. You think of a snake. You think of a snake that cannot be killed. You can chop off its head but it will not die. Perhaps comparing Andy Irons with snakes is a bit harsh—on snakes.

Burrow is eliminated by Brazil's Bruno Santos by 13 points to 6 and this is what Carroll was talking about and herein lies the frustration of people who are besotted by Burrow's level of surfing and desperately want to see him bridge the miniscule but vast gap that currently separates his abilities and accomplishments. 'It's a difficult one,' Burrow says. 'I think it's a pretty bad wave to have a contest on. It's a hard place to get a score—I hate it. There were a couple of sick ones but I don't know if it's a fair playing ground. It was horrible.' Burrow's only saving graces are the throwaways. He can have two shockers without them counting to his final ranking. Problem is, he's already had them. On top of his third at Snapper and first at Bells, he needs four more high finishes. And there are only six events left. If Teahupo'o or Arica end up being among his best eight events, he will not be world champion. The only semblance of success for Burrow is at a game of No Limit Texas Hold 'Em Poker against Irons to decide who gets the final scene in the *Trilogy* movie. Burrow wins with a pair of tens—hollow, meaningless. His 33rd at Arica and a losing score of 6.17 against Santos—disappointing, problematic. You honestly cannot believe he's lost to Bruno Santos.

Irons belts Victor Ribas and comes in five minutes early. 'I got smashed on my first wave, got a good barrel on my second, a pretty good one on my third and broke my board on my fourth,' he says. 'Wrapped it up.' Simple. He's a funny bastard, Andy Irons.

El Gringo is a black-and-white photograph, that harsh. There are endless ghost towns: Chacabuco, Humberstone, Puelma, Pedro de Valdiva. But in an oasis right in the heart of the wasteland, about 2000 metres above sea level, lies the village of San Pedro de Atacama. There's a 400-year-old church and people, quiet people, slow-moving people. You think there might be a God, but you are not a religious man. Is that possible? Can you believe in God and not feel religious? Perhaps religions are more trouble than they're worth. You pray every night for an eye to be kept on the people you love. But out here, you're not entirely sure it does anyone any good. The Atacama Desert is no place to live.

Fanning is about to face Chris Ward in the fourth round. Liz watches him walk awkwardly across the rocks. She has a pained expression on her face. He's putting his heart and soul into this. 'He's always been like that. He's always put everything he has into everything he does. What you see is what you get. He was doing very well at school and a lot of people said to me, "Why are you letting your kids go surfing?" I said, "This is their life. I want them to do whatever makes them happy". I'm glad for having done that. Surfing is a very mystical and spiritual thing, I think. You're dealing with nature and what can be more beautiful than that? Mick's always said he wishes he finished school, but I think he's doing pretty well for himself.'

Liz has been to Tahiti on the way to Chile, staying in the white bungalow at the back of Alain Riou's house with its thatched roof and white salt-encrusted walls. She's going to the Amazon on her way home. 'Mick says I can have two trips a year,' Liz says. 'I go to Hawaii every year, and that's all business in a way because it's the end of the year and the sponsors are all there and it's better if I deal with all that. And this year I've come here. It's amazing to be able to come to places like this. I'm very grateful to Mick. He's very good to me. He said to me, "Look, Mum, I want you to have a really good holiday this year. You've looked after me for twenty-six years and I'm going to pay you back". We've got some friends in Tahiti so I went there. And after this, I'm going down the Amazon. What about that!' You picture Liz quietly packing her bags to come to the other side of the world to support her son. There's something heartbreakingly beautiful about that.

'He's doing everything he can,' Liz says. 'I guess it's just up to the gods. He'll do it some day.' As the statue of Jesus on El Morro is your witness, that's exactly what she said: He'll do it *some day*.

Fanning beats Ward to reach another quarter-final. Parkinson literally pushes Cory Lopez in the chest to make the last eight but Irons knocks him out. Morrison beats Slater. DEAN MORRISON BEATS KELLY SLATER. 'To surf against him and have a good heat against him, it means a lot to me,' Morrison says. 'I'm really proud of that.'

Slater gives credit where it's due—but there's an edge to his voice. He does not enjoy playing second fiddle but at the moment, he's about fourth or fifth. 'You surf a good heat and you lose,' he says. 'Good on the other guy. What do you do when a guy takes off on a wave, it looks like a close-out but he gets a 10?' You pack up and leave. Slater goes.

Every day at 2 p.m., the wind comes.

Irons beats Parkinson in the quarters. The saving grace is that Parkinson can get home in time for the birth of his second daughter. But he ain't happy, either. Fanning's quarter-final is against Bobby Martinez. Martinez has a thick goatee, muscular frame and a work of art printed on his back: a tattoo of a Mexican gunslinger. Martinez was raised in gang-land on the outskirts of Santa Barbara in California. Pro surfing has allowed him to avoid jail and/or a bullet to the head. Martinez starts with a 10. Trouble. He only needs a 2-pointer—but does not get it. What the ocean wants, the ocean will get. Martinez punches his board, punches it hard. Fanning will go toe-to-toe with Irons in the semi-finals.

'Mick is pretty unstoppable right now,' Irons says. He does not sound as though he means it. Damien and CJ Hobgood are in the other semi. They're twin brothers. They're so alike CJ doesn't know which one he is. They're Christians. Jesus keeps watching. Fanning has tan zinc spread across his frozen cheeks. He's on the rocks.

Irons slaps his hand. Fanning's board is resting across his lap and points straight towards El Morro.

Fanning is on a bright white board with sharp blue spray. He creates the designs himself. He wears a slick sky-blue wetsuit under a bright yellow singlet. He's off to a flyer. Irons is slithering around on the inside. He's worked out this place with sheer rat-cunning. Fanning has priority and therefore the next choice of wave but he's too far out and Irons steals the winning right-hand barrel from under numero uno's nose. He comes out and gestures to the judges: *How good was that?!* Go on, tell him. Tell Andy Irons how good that was. Give him a number between 1 and 10. Nine. Both his scoring waves have come under Fanning's priority. Irons has beaten him for the second time this year and his joy is as plain as the nose on Joel Parkinson's face. Fanning has let the heat-winner go.

'I looked at it—the left didn't look that great and the right didn't, either, so I pulled back,' Fanning says. 'Andy was in the right spot at the right time, swung left and got the score. Another third, another keeper for the end of the year. I've just got to keep pushing along. I've made a great start but there's a long way to go. You've got to keep attacking and that's what I'm going to do. I'm going to keep attacking and I'm not going to stop until the end.'

Damien beats CJ. You think. Who knows? They're the most identical set of identical twins you've ever laid eyes on. Their best mates don't say hello; they say, 'Damo? CJ?'

Irons straps on his leg rope before the final, tucks it under his black wetsuit, does three squats with his hands on his knees, picks up his board, does one large leap into the air and bolts towards the rocks. He looks totally and utterly convinced he will win. He starts stronger than Hobgood and he's such an enigma. He finishes stronger than Hobgood and he's such an enigma. He's more solid during the middle stages of a tragically lopsided final and he's such an enigma. He chooses better waves than Hobgood and rides those waves better than Hobgood and everything he does is better than

Hobgood. He does four double fist-pumps. A single fist-pump. Three more singles. A killer smile. Another single pump. A kiss on the internet camera. A kiss for his fiancée, Lindy. 'I didn't go anywhere,' he says. 'I've always been right there in the race.' He stands on the stage yelling, '*Muchos, muchos—PERFECTO!*' Then he yells, '*Viva ce Chile!*'

The hardcore crowd yells back: '*Viva ce Chile!*'

Later, quietly, his eyes shifting left and right like a crocodile preparing for the kill, he considers the ramifications of the result and his rise to No.3 in the world behind Fanning and Hobgood. Coldly, he declares, 'Game on.'

You walk up the hill to the statue of Jesus. You're on the top of El Morro, looking over Arica and all its people. The concrete Jesus is a hundred times your size. You read what he's saying: '*Amos Los Unos A Los Ostros Como Yo Os He Amado.*' The only reliable translation you receive for any part of that text refers to the phrase, *I have loved you*. In the past tense? He used to love you? What about now? You want to know if Jesus is real. That's a serious question: is he real? You fly back to Santiago and the eternally majestic Andes keep you company and a single road weaves through the interminable Atacama Desert. Surreal, so real. You sing. It's a beautiful thing that can make a man sing. The road never ends. It never ends.

8

Eugene

Mick Fanning has an alter ego. His name is Eugene, and he's a certified lunatic. Eugene makes a brief appearance the night of Fanning's loss to Irons in Chile. He bumps into people, pretends he's going to steal all the handbags lined up next to the dance floor of the Soho Bar, laughs, slumps into a chair, pulls the hood of his jacket over his face and quietly goes to sleep. No harm done.

Eugene appears when Mick has indulged in too many beers. Or vodka and Red Bulls. Or tequilas. Or too much of any form of alcohol. Mick goes home and Eugene kicks on. He will stay out pretty much until he passes out. Eugene will have a drink in one hand and his pants in the other. Eugene will hug people like the world is going to end. Eugene will talk about himself in the third person. Eugene runs wild and it's a fascinating transformation. Someone so driven and dedicated turns into the polar opposite. It's as though Mick needs to release his own pressure valve. He becomes the anti-Mick and you get the impression every now and again that he gets sick and tired of trying so hard. Mick is asked for a complete character assessment of Eugene. He turns red and looks at his feet.

'Eugene is—I don't know what Eugene is,' he says.

Mick Fanning cares about doing the right thing. But Eugene does not. It's all fun and games because Eugene is a happy drunk. It's just that he's *so* drunk. It's as though Mick wants to be someone else—just for one night. What's that song about wanting to change your clothes, your hair, your face? There's only one person on tour more universally popular than Mick: Eugene. He's taken on legendary status. Mick will win a contest, sip a beer during the presentation and the crowd will chant, 'Eugene, Eugene, EUGENE!' The pros will join in. Griggs will look at Mick becoming Eugene and he's glad he's letting his hair down. He's glad Mick's giving himself a break. But sightings of Eugene this year are virtually non-existent. He's been locked in the basement with instructions to stay there because if anyone can stuff the whole thing up for Mick, it's Eugene.

'The first few years on tour, it's almost too exciting,' Mick says. 'You come off the WQS and there's a party at every contest and you're like, "Let's do it. Let's have some fun". But there's a time when you have to get serious and get away from all that. You have to make the right decisions for yourself and your career. It's still fun partying with your mates. That will never change. But you just have to get your work done before you go and play.'

Eugene's coup de gras came at the US Surfer Poll Awards while Slater was making a serious speech about the clean-living habits and respectfulness of the younger generation. Two thousand of surfing's heaviest corporate hitters were in the Sun Theatre in Anaheim. It was a grand occasion which even Fanning called the Oscars of surfing. Eugene started yelling from the crowd. 'Jimmy Slade! Jimmy Slade!' If there's one thing Slater hates, it's being called Jimmy Slade—the name of his cheeseball *Baywatch* character. 'Jimmy! Jimmy Slade!' Eugene decided to join Slater at the podium. Slater hugged Eugene and asked what would happen if he acted this way at such an important and formal occasion in Australia. Eugene grabbed the microphone and yelled: 'You'd get laid!' And then he proceeded to polish off the rest of the free drinks. He tackled Irons to the ground as his mate tried to make his way to the stage to receive an award. Eugene was told to leave the premises. Mick later nominated himself for dickhead of the year.

'I used to party a fair bit at the wrong times,' he says. 'I thought the surf would be flat and the contest would be on hold the next day so I'd go off and party, and then there would be waves and I'd get beaten. I just woke up one day and said, "You idiot. That's enough". I'd lose my heats and just feel like a total fool. Now there's no partying until the end of an event. That's the rule and I'm not even tempted to break it. They might be the best parties in the world but it's not worth it. You wake up with all these regrets and you've ruined what you're trying to do. It's just stupid. I'm engaged and Mum comes to a couple of events now. I suppose things are a lot more settled. I'm just more settled in myself. Don't get me wrong. I still like to party. But it's got to be at the right times now.'

When a gang of pros hits Casino Arica, Fanning wasn't one of them. When others were hitting Soho, The Chill Out Bar or The Sunset Bar during the event, Fanning was nowhere to be seen. When stragglers were doing a line of speed off a 5000-peso note at 3 a.m. in the back streets of Arica, both Mick and Eugene were sleeping like logs. Mick says it's reasonably safe to assume all hell will break loose around Coolangatta if he takes the crown but until then, Eugene had better stay out of this. Mick is asked again for a character assessment. He shakes his head. 'I honestly don't know what he is,' he says. 'I have a couple of beers and just start going wild and there's Eugene. It's just one of those things. Some people change when they have a few beers and I guess I'm one of them. I turn into this other person and everyone starts calling me Eugene— it's my middle name. Eugene goes a bit mad. Eugene is ... I'm trying to think of the right words. Nothing matters to Eugene. That's what Eugene is: it's when nothing matters.'

9

J-Bay

BILLABONG PRO
SUPERTUBES, JEFFREYS BAY, SOUTH AFRICA

Mick Fanning's feet are bound. His heart is thumping against the wall of his chest. He's petrified. The black man jams the knot of the rope tight. Whites and blacks do not always get along in South Africa. The knot has frayed edges. Fanning cannot move his feet one inch. The black man pushes the white man to the edge of the highest bridge in South Africa, the Bloukrans. Below is a straight drop of 216 metres. Fanning is 40 kilometres east of Plettenberg. He does not dare look down. He stares ahead. A few wisps of cloud out there in the never-never. This cannot be happening. Sharp breaths. One more step, *just one more step*, and he will disappear into the gorge. The black man laughs and inches Fanning forward. Fanning takes one deep breath. And then throws himself off.

He screams.

Fanning is plummeting into the gorge and he can picture himself being blown apart on impact. He wonders if his safety harness is still on and doubts it is because he can no longer feel the straps.

The frayed rope holds firm. If there's a better way than doing the world's highest bungee jump to unnecessarily put yourself in a position to suffer a horrific injury halfway through potentially the most important and gratifying year of your life, you'd like to hear about it. But he wanted to do it, so he did it. Mick Fanning, like all of us, will die in the years to come. But he will not die wondering.

'I think if Mick is going to win, it's going to be this year,' Slater says. 'If he doesn't, it will probably make it harder for him to win in the future because he's had such a good start and it would really be a let-down for him to not capitalise.' Are these mind games? The truth? Both? Maybe Kelly Slater only ever speaks the truth but it's perceived to be psychological warfare because that's what the truth is: just one big mind-fuck. 'I have all the respect in the world for Mick and his surfing and just him as a person,' Slater says. 'He's one of those guys who is fearsome in the water—but he leaves it in the water. He doesn't make things personal. Mick is a true professional. If he wins it this year, if he becomes world champion, I'll be proud of him and stoked for him.'

And that's the first and last time you will hear Kelly Slater use the word stoked.

J-Bay was first ridden in 1964 when a group of Capetown surfers wandered in on their way to a contest at Port Elizabeth. It was Easter. They stopped at Coetzee's Fish Shop and decided to go looking for a quick wave. There was one hotel, a couple of shops and a sparse collection of holiday houses. The pioneers spread the word for the word was good. J-Bay became a haven for South African hippies, vagabonds and various other layabouts. It was a feral place, but there's not always a lot wrong with feral.

Some Day

Care for an opinion? J-Bay is the greatest wave on the planet. If you had ten minutes to live and the choice of one last wave, you would come here. You want to pack up your family and move to Jeffreys Bay tomorrow. Imagine doing that, just picking out your favourite spot in the world and moving there. Imagine having that much courage.

There are two ways to get amongst it at J-Bay. You can paddle out from the beach near Magnatubes, or throw yourself into the fray off the point between Boneyards and Supertubes. Elsewhere on this wondrous planet, different breaks have different names because they're so far apart. Most of them are prime examples of stating the bleeding obvious. There's a place in the eastern suburbs of Sydney called Ours because the Bra Boys, in all their infinite wisdom, think it's theirs. There's a spot at Newport on the northern beaches called The Peak because it's where there's an A-frame peak. Further south, there's The Reef because it's, well, a reef. Off-The-Pool at Palm Beach is located just off the pool. The best way to highlight the length of ride at J-Bay is to say that the *one* wave passes through *six* different locations. On a single four-minute voyage, accompanied on various occasions by dolphins, whales and occasionally a great white shark that wants to skin you alive, you rattle through Magnatubes, Boneyards, Supertubes, Impossibles, Tubes and Albatross.

You cannot believe your eyes.

This cannot be real. It's *so* good.

You jump off the rocks and cut your foot. Blood spurts and you're shark bait. You're nervous, so you piss in your wetsuit. Blood and piss? May as well slit your own throat and be done with it. A one-minute paddle leads you to pole position. Your feet are numb with cold, but you don't care. The tips of your fingers hurt with what feels like the beginnings of frost bite, the kind of cold you'd get if you pressed your fingers firmly against a block of ice and kept them there for an hour, but you do not care. You do not care because this is J-Bay. If you enjoy surfing, you must surf this place. Just once. It'll cost thousands of dollars to get here. It'll take forever and a day by the time you fly to Johannesburg, catch another flight to Port Elizabeth then drive for an hour on the N2 West. But it'll be worth every cent. Just one wave will be worth every cent.

The wave peels close to the rocks.

Anyone can get out at J-Bay. Anyone can catch a wave. It's not a dangerous break, so beginners and pros can surf their heads off. The take-off is easy. The shape is so curvaceous that only the greatest kook will fall off. If you can't surf J-Bay, you don't belong here. If you can't surf J-Bay, you can't surf *anywhere*. The pros can go nuts, but it's a challenge. It's the most technically demanding wave on the tour in that it's so fast and pure. You can't rely on one atomic bomb of a move to get a score. You can't grab your rail and tuck into a barrel and just hang on and hope that's going to be enough. That requires courage. This requires skill. Any technical deficiencies will be exposed. There's no air to be had, not really. You have to *surf*. Look at the list of winners since 2002: Fanning, Slater, Irons, Slater and Fanning. Parkinson's breakthrough win was at J-Bay when he was a happy-as-a-fucking-nineteen-year-old-rookie-clam in 1999. It was an almost identical elevation to the upper echelon as Fanning's first triumph at Bells. J-Bay is for the traditionalist. The surfer who travels at blistering speeds. The wave rifles down the point so fast that there's no time to waste. Every move must be executed with absolute precision because if there's one split second of delay or hesitation, if you're too high on the face or too low or just too *slow*, one of J-Bay's scorching rights will shoot away without you. Miss one turn by a millisecond and you're gone by a mile, stranded as your train disappears into the morning light. Goofy-footers struggle so badly to travel at the required rate of knots that not one of them will make the quarters. Which just goes to show why the man Fanning is trying so hard to emulate as an Australian world champion, Occhilupo, is such a freak. He won here in 1984. Copy that? Mark Occhilupo won J-Bay in *nineteen-eighty-four* and he's still on tour. That's outrageous. Fanning was four back then.

A wave jettisons from Magnatubes as whales make their imperiously slow journeys along the point like nomads moving towards another pasture. Dolphins play. Boneyards is a quick and hollow section, slipping and sliding. You jump to your feet, the cut now a cavernous ulcer and still you do not care. Faster, faster, into Supertubes, a rollicking pipe and the ride of a lifetime within the ride of a lifetime. Supertubes is offering everything a wave can possibly offer—lightning-quick walls stretch farther than you know, caves where you can escape the Devil Wind, places to thread, places to shred . . . Faster, faster, flying to the end of Impossibles . . . Faster, faster, blinded by the sun but at least it's out, faster, faster, a million miles an hour, the view a blur of aloe gardens, sand, an untouched coastline. The weather is bad and it feels like the end of the world. Or the bottom of the Earth. Or both. Everything is exaggerated and extreme. There's no place so invigorating. Thunderstorms shake the walls. The hot days are blistering. The cold nights are ice. Faster, faster, down to Tubes, so close to the rocks, the bricks. It's so shallow that your brain, the smartest part of you, is screaming at you to stop because the weakest part of you, your legs, are jelly.

There's only one place in the world where you have literally surfed for nine straight hours in a day and that place is Jeffreys Bay. It's a non-descript country town where time doesn't really exist. There's just day-time and night-time. The time when you're either getting ready for a surf, having a surf or coming in from a surf. If it's night-time you're warming your bones with whiskey and crawling into bed from the blissful deep-seated exhaustion of it all. Nothing feels so good as being surf-wrecked. You will come here again.

Flashback—22 July 2003: Taj Burrow versus Damien Hobgood in the semi-finals. The winner will take on a rampaging Kelly Slater in the final. Burrow stops mid-paddle. He knows what he's seen. He just doesn't *want* to know. He catches a wave and does not make a turn. He's coming in long before he's supposed to. No moves, no nothing, he just wants to get in as soon as fucking possible. Burrow keeps looking behind him. He scrambles onto the rocks. Mike Prickett is a water photographer who knows a shark when he sees one and he scrambles in, too. Burrow runs up the beach. Great white sharks feast on human flesh. The biggest great white shark of all time is likely to be feasting on the flesh of Damien Hobgood unless somebody tells him what's going on. Nobody does. Because nobody believes what Burrow is saying. Whatever the reason, they just don't believe him. You can tell when someone is lying, or exaggerating, or trying to convince themselves more than they're trying to convince anyone else. Taj Burrow is not lying.

Shark.

Burrow is told it's a whale. He vehemently protests. 'No, no, no—it was a shark. I swear it. It's *this* big.' He points to his board. It's as big as your board? No, he says. The *fin* is as big as his board. You can hear the theme music to *Jaws*. 'It was a thick perfect triangle and it scared the shit out of me and I know what I'm talking about,' he says. 'There's no way it was a whale, no way it was a dolphin, no way. It was the biggest shark I've ever seen in my life. Whales don't have fins. There was a fin, I'm telling you there was a fin. I've never seen anything like it.'

Burrow is told by officials—who would want to have been pretty sure about this—that he's seen a whale because a whale has just been sighted further up the point. Burrow is told to get back out and finish his heat and surfer in red, you require a 6.7. Eyes swing to the water. Damien Hobgood is still sitting out there. Prickett has spent most of his life in the water. 'It was a shark,' he says.

'Believe me. They're out there.' Burrow returns to the water with less energy than he displayed while getting out. Down on the rocks, he takes one last look back up at the officials. *Out there? You want me to go OUT THERE?* He falls off his next four waves and loses.

Slater spanks Hobgood in the final. Later that night, Burrow grabs you by your shirt collar and says: 'I fucking swear on my fucking life it was a fucking shark!' He's laughing. Now. Just a few weeks later, a surfer is mauled by a great white while warming up for a Pro Junior contest. Its fin was as big as Taj Burrow's surfboard.

Faster, faster, you're into the last leg, Albatross and . . . shark? You arrive at a shallow section which takes you *really* close to the rocks and . . . shark? You're hurtling along and your brain is still screaming at you to pull out because your fins are inches from being ripped from your board by the bricks but your hands are clamping your head because this is so fucking good . . . Faster, faster, and you're picturing yourself in *Tubular Swells*, that classic movie with footage of the 22-day mega-swell in 1977 that will never be matched and . . . shark? You're still going and . . . shark? How has nature come up with this? Where did the boards come from? The waves? The riders? Albatross is where the wave begins to slow and it's almost a relief because you cannot go at breakneck speed for one second longer or your head will blow clean off your shoulders. Albatross is a humble little section across a weedy reef, and you're done. You try to remember the intricate details of the greatest wave of your life but you can't remember a damn thing.

So you have to do it again.

It's like a barrel: your memory card is wiped clean as soon as you get out. As if the real beauty is beyond the capabilities of human understanding. The paddle back up to Boneyards is wide in the deep water and . . . shark? It's dark now and every other surfer is a shadow, a faceless shadow. You feel cold and silent and no-one is talking and no-one has any expression on their faces and there's another grim reaper and there's another one and they're all taking off and disappearing down the line and you will never see any of them again and all the grim reapers have gone and you're out here by yourself but there's a dozen more grim reapers and your mind is playing tricks and it's night, it really is night-time now, you've stayed out too long and you're petrified. What's that bump? What's that ... shit ... you can see sharks, you swear you can, the men in grey suits, their lifeless eyes on you. You want to scream. You're horrified by the thought of a shark tearing you apart, beheading you, skinning you. Why? You're happy enough to skewer a fish through the neck with a cheap steel hook. You're more than willing to deceive it with the promise of food, only to kill it and tear apart *its* flesh. You'll decapitate it, gut it. And you'll do it without so much as a fleeting second of remorse. But now you're pleading for a fish to leave you alone. Pathetic. Perhaps you would think differently if you could hear a fish scream.

You paddle in.

MARK OCCHILUPO: His first round is against ... who cares. You are determined to savour every moment because Occhilupo, the *original* Raging Bull, won't be around for much longer. Retirement is imminent. He won't re-qualify for 2008. Anyone finishing below 28th on the rankings loses their ticket for the following year and Occhilupo is in the 40s. Occhilupo has retired before, two years ago, in comical circumstances. It lasted a millisecond. Billabong organised a major press conference on the Gold Coast. Every major TV station, radio station, newspaper and surfing magazine in the country was in attendance. Occhilupo said all the right things— that he appreciated the chance to travel the world and surf, that he would never forget winning the world title in 1999, that he was very much looking forward to the next stage of his life. He thanked everybody for their attendance and gave assurances that he knew in his heart he was doing the right thing. He went outside and told a mate: 'I don't know if I'm doing the right thing.' He was back for the first day of the next event, keen as a kid.

American writer Rita Mae Brown once wrote: 'Sport strips away personality and lets the white bone of character shine through.' That's Marco Jay Luciano Occhilupo. He's been everything, nothing and everything again. He's made people shake their heads at the wonder of such a God-given talent and kick the dirt during the lost years when he couldn't shake the demons in his head. He's been angelically good, devilishly bad, deliriously happy and desperately sad. He's reached mind-blowing highs and plummeted to unimaginable lows. This has been a full life and truly remarkable career, and even though it can't be over—it just can't be—it nearly is. Time marches on.

The facts: Occhilupo is 41 and this is his farewell year, having been ranked No.2 in the world at seventeen. He won J-Bay in 1984 and the world title was thought to be a given—but it didn't come until he was 33. The lost years were spent locked up in his Gold Coast unit, losing his mind, fitness, willpower, pride. He was too ashamed to venture outside in case the kids who worshipped him saw what he had become: a sad reminder of what the Bull used to be. A pathetic ghostly example of what could have been.

What could have been—words to put a lump in the throat. Occhilupo kept hearing them, and the loudest voice was his own. Just when all hope seemed lost, he had a dream that told him to go surfing again. He went to Western Australia and started training, running, doing a thousand sit-ups a day, getting himself back into chiselled shape, rediscovering the magic, the love of riding waves.

He just had this gnawing feeling in his gut that he could still match it with the young punks back on the world tour, and so at the age of 30 he swallowed his pride and slogged his way through the wholly unglamorous World Qualifying Series in an attempt to return to the big time.

He made it, becoming the oldest world champion in history in one of the greatest imaginable examples of how you're never so far down that you're completely out.

Occhilupo still has the wild spray of blond hair that screams hardcore surfer, the square jaw you want in a hero and the wholehearted respect of every other member of the tour. He's a rock, but bawls like a baby. He cried when he became world champion because his father, Luciano, HIS hero, was no longer around to see it. He is genuinely loved by his peers on a tour which will have gushing tears running down its collective cheek when he returns to the shore after his final heat. He's made more friends than he knows. He's made a lot of people smile. That's not a bad thing to take with you—the knowledge that you made a lot of people smile. Occhilupo is so magnificent he'll surf three-metre Teahupo'o like it's a fun park. But he'll stub his toe walking across the rocks at Jeffreys Bay and scream like a little girl.

He is so awe-inspiring he can terrify an opponent with nothing more than a look in their direction. He looks like a colossus but has the high-pitched voice and giggle of a grommet. His mother, Pam, used to think the winner of a surfing heat was the first to make it back to shore. She thinks he never really grew out of his childhood and applauds such an accomplishment. He has two sons, Jay and Jona, and you will never see a more doting father. His wife, Mae, says he's a beautiful man. There's no arguing. He's eccentric, radical, normal, shy, extroverted, introverted. He's hopeless, great, perfect, imperfect. He's told you he lives for the feeling of the first wash of water over his face at the start of the day; of going into his first duck-dive with sleep in his eyes but coming up with an almost superhuman strength. He honestly believes anyone who doesn't surf is doing themselves an injustice and he wishes he could show everyone the light. He met Mae at a ten-pin bowling alley. They still go there. He's a man of the world; he's a homebody.

'I'll be right,' he says of retirement. 'It's no big deal.'

But it is.

For all the unforgettable heats, victories, comeback from oblivion and world title, one little moment sums up the man: that speech at Bells after his victory in the 1998 final, having been through hell and back to win his first event in twelve years. Thousands of people in front of the presentation dais fell into a reverential silence when he said, 'Thanks very much—and thanks.' Someone should take the last sentence of that speech, print it in big bold type, frame it and give it to Occhilupo when all this ends. For all the entertainment he's provided, friendships he's made, inspiration he's delivered to three generations of surfers and just for everything he has contributed to surfing, someone needs to walk up to Occy, shake his hand, look him in the eye and say: 'Thanks very much—and thanks.'

'He's pretty much a legend of our sport,' Fanning says. 'He's such a character and such a cool guy. I remember that day, when he won the title. I went surfing really early then later on I was listening to the radio and they started talking about how Occy was the world champion. I was so pumped. I was still pretty young when Occy won and I suppose in some ways I was still a kid. Kids think about what they want to end up doing and I wanted to do what Occy was doing. It can seem like a long way away but you've just got to tell yourself it's possible. You might not end up doing what you want. But you might.'

You remember being there when Occhilupo christened his son at J-Bay, right near Supertubes on a clear, windy morning with a hundred people wearing shell necklaces and no shoes. You remember it being nice. Nothing extravagant or pretentious. Just nice. Now he walks quietly through the aloe gardens and down the steps towards Supertubes. The neat haircut doesn't suit him because it doesn't match the memories. Raging bulls don't have short-back-and-sides hairdos, do they? There should be a long mane of wild and unkempt blond hair, muscles bulging through his chest and shoulders, the vicious head-snap of the zealot accompanying every turn. Where are the loud red shirts and board shorts? He loses his opening heat to . . . who cares. He has Mick Campbell in the second round. He's lost seven of his eight heats this year. Campbell is as tough as nails but he's quivering because Occhilupo at J-Bay is the stuff of legend. His backhand attacks are immeasurably above and beyond anything a goofy-footer will ever do here again because it's verging on a physical impossibility. Campbell, another goofy-footer, is paraletic with nerves. Occhilupo appears to have brushed his hair. You hope not.

Occhilupo leads Campbell, and as much as you like Campbell, you hope for a miracle. You hope Occhilupo is allowed one more win before he leaves. Give him this event. It wouldn't kill you, Huey. Campbell takes off late as though his elevator has snapped a cable. He makes the drop, launches himself upside down and makes that drop, too. He gets the wobbles, steadies, sets the radar on a spot over his right shoulder to hit and annihilate. He throws himself into the close-out. And makes it. Occhilupo paddles for one last wave, but misses. His shoulders slump. Another 33rd. Another step closer to the end.

There are lay days, half days, clear days, cold days, unseasonably warm days, raining-cats-and-dogs days, good days, inconsistent days, flat days and on all the days, The Big Five start being whittled down to The Big Three. The big guns are wheeling themselves out.

MICHAEL FANNING: Mick and Liz were staying in a house overlooking Supertubes in 2004 when they became friends of the maid, Primrose.

She's a beautiful young black African woman. Fanning befriended her over cups of tea. They made each other laugh. It's all you need. Blacks can be treated like door mats in South Africa—still. You've stayed with friends at a house in Port Elizabeth where, after three weeks of the maid—whose name was Nantando, which means happiness—making everyone cups of coffee, an offer was made to return the favour. Nantando was embarrassed by the offer and refused. She kept shaking her head as if the mere suggestion was preposterous. Heaven forbid a white person makes a cup of coffee for a black person. She got down on her knees and started scrubbing the kitchen floor. You have seen few more dispiriting sights in all your days.

Primrose was six months pregnant when she first met Mick and Liz. She spoke excitedly about being a mother. Her face was the type to come alive. Primrose was dirt poor and struggled to pay for so much as a box of nappies, so Liz went out and bought a few. No big deal, and most certainly no large amount of cash, but for Primrose, it was the equivalent of three months' wages. The contest ended and Mick and Liz stayed in touch with Primrose. Three months later, good news: her child was born. Six months later, bad news: her child had died of AIDS.

Primrose had contracted HIV along the way. It had developed into AIDS and she passed it on to her baby. AIDS had already killed two of her brothers. Primrose's health started deteriorating badly. The Fannings sent money for her medication. They do not admit to this—but they were helping to keep her alive. By the Billabong Pro of 2005, Primrose looked weak and fragile. A film was growing over her eyes and she was going blind. Without an operation, she would lose all sight within twelve months. The bills were taken care of by the Fannings. Primrose wept when she was told. The operation was a success and her sight was saved. She did a computer course and started a salon with her sister, Timberland, with another round of financial help from the Fannings. Primrose is a confident and upstanding young woman who gives no clue as to the hardships she has endured. There are some remarkable people in this world who no-one ever hears about. An invitation—and air ticket—was extended to Primrose for Mick and Karissa's wedding. Go to the list of World Vision sponsor parents and you'll see Mick Fanning's name as providing support for two children. Not that he'll ever talk about it.

He has another military-style buzz cut and his head resembles a block of granite. He looks unbreakable. He thumps Jeremy Flores and Sean Payne in round one. 'Just wanted to get a good one off the bat,' he says. His first wave is an 8.17: big hook, barrel, message of intent. *Still here, boys.* Told he's popular at J-Bay because of the hell-raising nature of his victory parties, the defending champion replies: 'We won't worry 'bout that till the end.' There's a rumbling storm on the horizon. Bolts of white lightning. 'It's time to start building towards the end of the year,' he says. 'You've got to put the bricks in the right places to build the house. We've only had four events and I've only got four bricks.' What shrink has put that in his head? Fuck the bricks, Mick. Just get out there and surf.

South Africa's 1977 world champion Shaun Thomson has seen Fanning recently and, according to Thomson, conversation turned to the title race. When Thomson told Fanning he expected it to go down to the wire with a winner-takes-all finale at Pipeline, where Irons and maybe even Slater would take a whole world of stopping, Fanning replied: 'Mate, it'll be over before Pipe.' There are 48 egos on the tour and Fanning admits to being one of them. He has to be.

Shark?

'I thought I saw something,' he says after wiping the ocean floor with Payne again in round three. 'There was a bit of a splash. There was only a minute to go, so I thought I'd just man-up and not say anything.'

Some Day

Fanning meets Pancho Sullivan in the last sixteen. They're staying at the same place with uninterrupted views of Supertubes. They're competing under the same Rip Curl banner alongside Taylor Knox, who's been signed up in Chile. Fanning and Knox get on like a house on fire. Back when Fanning was returning from his injury, he hung out with Sullivan in Hawaii because Sullivan's traditional arcs and deep incisions were a source of inspiration for someone who had not been able to complete a single turn for a stupefying six months. Sullivan helped Mick Fanning. Out in the water, he'll be getting no favours in return. 'It sucks, but when your mates are the best surfers in the world, you can't avoid them,' Fanning says. Karissa is with him again. Burrow is within a stone's throw with no idea of the drama about to knock him sideways.

'He's just so supremely confident,' Thomson says as Fanning takes off like an intercontinental ballistic missile. He has 15.66 points after sod-all minutes and Sullivan doesn't have one. Not a point. Nil, nada, zip. He ends up with 4.84 and a red backside from the kicking he's just received.

Fanning scurries back to the house. 'I'm keeping to myself,' he says. 'Keeping it low-key.' He's into the quarter-finals against Danny Wills.

No-one has feasted on J-Bay more than Wills. Anyone scanning the point at any time of the day sees the rocks, dolphins, low-hanging clouds, whales, maybe flamingoes . . . and Danny Wills. There's ten of him. A hundred. A thousand. A thousand Danny Willses are running amok in Jeffreys Bay. It's like the movie *Being John Malkovich*—except John Malkovich has become Danny Wills. 'I've just felt like a frothing little grommet, to be honest,' he says. 'I haven't been in a final for ages and if there's any wave where I can do it, this is my spot.' He's hurt his ribs while pulling on his wetsuit. He can't breathe, feels as though he's been stabbed. His problem is that he knows, he just knows, Fanning will score a minimum of 15 points. He'll get an 8 and a 7 or a couple of high

7's and 15 is just about the minimum for a man surfing with such a robotic fervour. Someone needs to push him into needing 18's and 19's. Someone needs to start forcing him out of his comfort zone. He's reaching semi-finals on his ear.

'I used to want to blow everyone away,' Fanning says. 'I used to want to get a 9 on every single wave. There's still a bit of that in me, but I know you don't need that all the time. I watched Kelly a lot last year and he kept just doing what he needed to do to get through. It doesn't matter how you get through your heats, you've just gotta get through them.'

The difference is that Wills hopes to do well while Fanning expects to. Fanning's a self-deprecating man. He's spent the first phase of his career calling himself a kook and looking at the world rankings with genuine disbelief. But he knows now that he's good. What a tremendous realisation to have. That you're good enough. Fanning beats Wills by almost 3 points and he's in the semi-finals again and somebody stop him.

DAMIEN HOBGOOD: Arrives saying he's glad to be flying under the radar. He loses to Payne in the second round and he's no longer even on the radar. See you later, alligator. He will not be No.2 in the world at the end of this contest. He will not be world champion at the end of the year. He will suffer a knee injury and he will not be mentioned again.

TAJ BURROW: One of the most harrowing and uplifting and emotionally draining weeks of his life begins with incredulity when he's told a shark has taken a liking to the look of Mick Lowe and security measures have been put in place. 'I saw a bloody great white,' Lowe says. 'It looked like eight feet. You could just tell it was a shark. It was so thick. It was coming down the point and turned in the wave. I saw how big it was. Phil McDonald caught a wave and while it was feathering across from Boneyards, I saw it in the wave. It did a U-turn and headed back. It was no dolphin. It had a girth on it like *this*. I know what I saw.' Lowe tells the two Brazillians in the next heat, Bernardo Mirando and Raoni Monteiro, they might have unwanted company. Asked how they took the news, Lowe cackles: 'They've just shit themselves.'

Burrow grabs his contest singlet and thinks they're pulling his leg when he's told of the hastily devised procedure for the surfers to follow if they see a shark. It's a three-step process. Step 1 will involve Burrow calmly waving his arms at the marshalls to alert them to the possibility of drama. Step 2 will involve Burrow pointing at the water so it's perfectly clear why he's decided to turn his back on 6-foot J-Bay in favour of returning to the beach. Step 3 will involve Burrow calmly paddling to shore. Interesting plan. Dare we suggest a more likely course of action for Taj Burrow upon the sighting of a great white shark would be to ignore this carefully devised three-step plan in favour of GETTING OUT OF THE FUCKING WATER AS FAST AS FUCKING POSSIBLE? Just a thought.

'The beach marshall gave me my singlet and told me to do the signal if I saw a shark and I was like, "What!?" We know they're out there. We just don't want to think about it.' Oh, god!

Burrow needs a 6.84 to beat CJ Hobgood in the first round. Snap, gouging turn, a drive down the line and he gets clobbered at Impossibles as his board lifts like a hydroplane. He loses to CJ, but rebounds by racking up 18.33 in his second round against Damien Fahrenfort with a perfect 10 for a wave that includes *five barrels*. He's fast and polished and edgy. He comes out of his first tube and there's another and another and three more of the sons of bitches. 'It just lined up for this pipe and kept getting more and more hollow. It's pretty hard to get a 10 these days. When you do, you know you've earned it. It gets the confidence up.' Confidence,

This is professional surfing: warp speed, effortless balance, critical manoeuvres and the aggression of a wild animal.

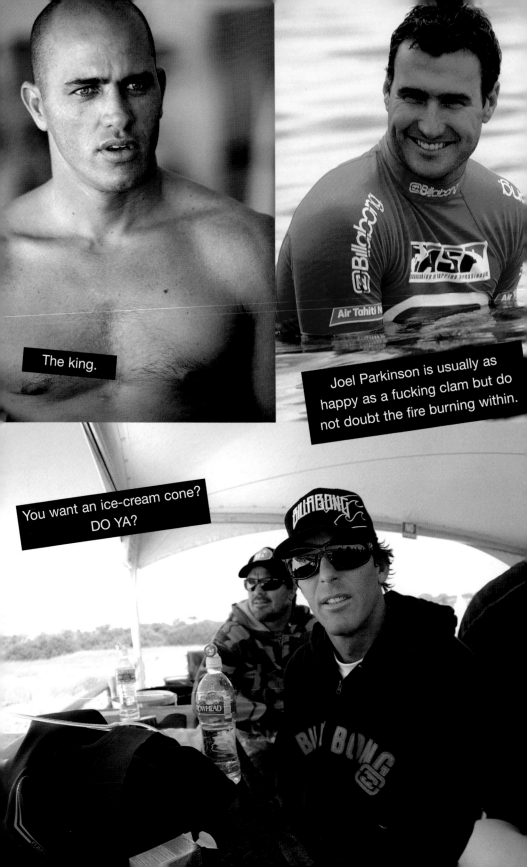

The king.

Joel Parkinson is usually as happy as a fucking clam but do not doubt the fire burning within.

You want an ice-cream cone? DO YA?

Slater and Irons, the two most ruthless surfers of the modern era with their combined eleven world titles, put the squeeze on Fanning before the Rip Curl Pro at Bells Beach.

Mick Fanning and his right-hand man, Matt Griggs, at Bells.

TAHITI

Teahupo'o, Tahiti, circa 2007: any chance of a *ka-boom*?

CHILE

Chile was a black-and-white photograph, that harsh.

Andy Irons wins the Rip Curl Pro Search: *'Vive ce Chile!'*

J-BAY

Jeffrey's Bay, South Africa. You will come here again.

Raging Bulls aren't supposed to have short-back-and-sides haircuts. Mark Occhilupo walking through the aloe gardens of Jeffrey's Bay. Thanks very much—and thanks.

J-BAY

Taj Burrow and his laptop. You can find all sorts of interesting stuff on the internet. The good, the bad and the ugly.

Taj Burrow's victory at Jeffrey's Bay was a triumph of mind over body on a marathon last day of heats—and with a whole lot of personal drama happening in the background.

TRESTLES

For the man on the left, it was an attempt to win a ninth world title. For the man on the right, it was a privilege.

FRANCE

France is a romantic movie.

Good things happen to good people. Amen to that.

Mark Richards says Slater threw Fanning the 'Are you worthy' test at Hossegor. This was Fanning's reply.

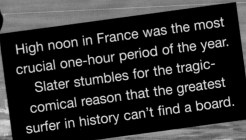

High noon in France was the most crucial one-hour period of the year. Slater stumbles for the tragic-comical reason that the greatest surfer in history can't find a board.

SPAIN

Numero uno after another dawn patrol, and another disappointment, at Mundaka.

They can have it this year ...

BRAZIL

A relaxed Taj Burrow and a freaking-out Mick Fanning just before the title goes on the line at Imbituba, Brazil.

Fanning with the Celtic Irish cross hanging from his neck, Dragon sunglasses hiding the anxiety in his eyes, footage of his last heat in his hands, the music of Tool burning his brain and an exercise ball just before it gets a workout in Brazil.

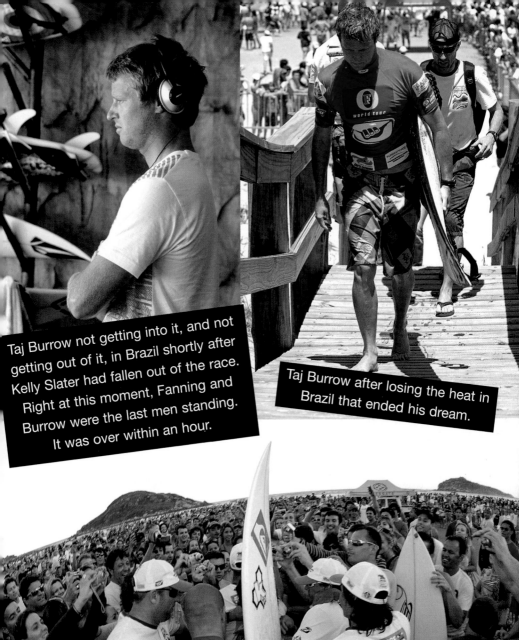

Taj Burrow not getting into it, and not getting out of it, in Brazil shortly after Kelly Slater had fallen out of the race. Right at this moment, Fanning and Burrow were the last men standing. It was over within an hour.

Taj Burrow after losing the heat in Brazil that ended his dream.

Excuse me, sorry, sorry: Kelly Slater gives up on running the gauntlet in Brazil, preferring to walk. Slowly.

Holy crap—Mick Fanning the moment Kelly Slater starts losing his heat against Kai Otton in Brazil, meaning the world title is just a heartbeat away.

The world champion with the author at Imbituba, Brazil.

I can keep this? Mick Fanning and the holy grail, the Association of Surfing Professionals world championship trophy.

Mick Fanning and the gauntlet.

confidence, the never-ending search for Taj Burrow's confidence. He can see the waves from his bedroom. He can see himself on them. One of the joys of J-Bay is that no matter where you stay, practically everyone can see the waves when their heads hit the pillow. And when they first open their eyes at dawn. Burrow's pad is not suffering from a lack of a view.

Burrow wipes out against Padaratz and the Brazillian runs over him but it doesn't matter because Burrow is becoming untouchable. Padaratz wins a paddle-battle back to priority and again, Burrow could care less. He keeps winning. He watches the waves and he's in that frame of mind where he starts getting these images in his head of holding up the trophy in the twilight of the final afternoon. He imagines himself ripping, and then he goes out and rips. Clarity can come at the most unexpected moments. It's a Billabong event and Burrow has a large support crew. He's going to need them. He likes to muck around on his laptop in his quieter moments, checking emails and the internet to see what's happening in the real (and unreal) world. And to his absolute horror he's about to discover that the internet keeps no secrets.

ANDY IRONS: He's livid about the latest round of Slater retirement rumours. 'Don't let him fool you,' he says. 'I'm sure he wants to get all the hype by saying he's going to retire and this and that, but he's as hungry as ever. You've got to have Kelly here. He's an eight-time world champion and to have him leave through the year would be disrespectful to the rest of the guys on tour. He's had a couple of bad results but I started with a thirty-third and I'm third now. As soon as he gets a couple of results, he'll be back in the top three.' Irons is equally fired up about speculation he's lost his most valuable attribute: mongrel. 'I want to hush the critics and all the people saying I'm over it and not hungry. The fire is still blazing. It never went away. I get two throwaways so I can get another thirty-third and still be alright—people don't understand that. Just because I started with a bad result doesn't mean it's going to haunt me for the rest of the year.'

He's announced his engagement. 'I'm more mature and more relaxed now,' he says. 'Just waiting for the golden retriever and white picket fence.'

He's super-trim. He wears bug-eyed sunglasses. 'I don't like the morning,' he says after beating Warwick Wright in the afternoon. 'You're stiff, tired, cold, Devil Winds, it gets very bumpy, the swell's dropping fast, so I'm glad they did it this afternoon, my body is warmed up. I've been awake for a long time, loosened up, got worked on. I'm definitely more of your afternoon-kind-of-guy.' Perhaps Andy Irons is a harmless soul who's just blown off course a few times. Perhaps he won't always be running with the wolves. Perhaps he's mellowing. 'You don't want to take it too seriously,' he says of a tour he takes as seriously as anyone. 'Just seriously enough. We're not curing cancer here. We're paid to do what we love and that's rare in this life.'

He slides past Fred Patacchia into the last eight to face Morrison. He casts his eye over the draw. 'Anything can happen,' he says. 'Willsy is surfing really good, me and Kelly are on the bottom half, Dean has been surfing great, Bede is ripping. Hopefully there are more waves and we get the opportunity to bring out the big guns.' He produces a water pistol to Morrison's bazooka. Morrison gets barrelled and if Irons is going to win he needs to do the same. His knees are super-low and he keeps twisting his head but he can't get in. Entry denied. Morrison won't budge and Irons loses by a point-and-a-bit and a whole lot of momentum has just been swept up and blown away by the Devil Winds.

Morrison has done Fanning two straight favours, beating Slater in Chile and Irons here. Mates, eh? You'd bleed for them. 'I got lucky,' Morrison says. 'That's all I can put it down to—luck. I'll take it any way I can, but it's a bit of a humbling win.'

Irons is gone. You'll refuse to believe the snake is dead as a world title contender until someone of appropriate authority pulls out a calculator and tells you he's become a mathematical impossibility.

JOEL PARKINSON: Might do a turn up here, what's over there, why not duck inside this bit, what next, how about a floater—he looks casual but he's right on his rails. Joel Parkinson is an exceptional surfer. He never falls. You honestly cannot remember one fall. In sections where even Slater will be swinging his arms like windmills and spreading his feet to keep his balance, Parkinson is leaning against a pole having a smoke. You're convinced he gets underscored because he makes it look so easy. If Slater looks on the verge of falling but makes it, he'll get high 9's because of the miracle recovery and because it's Kelly Slater. Same goes for Fanning, Irons and Burrow. But Parkinson doesn't do miracle recoveries. He doesn't need to. Maybe he should. Billabong's worldwide advertising campaign for *Trilogy* ranks the headline acts in the following order: Parkinson, Irons, Burrow. Read into that what you will.

Parkinson sits up near Boneyards because he can. The wave is so fast from up there but exocets like him can keep up. Parkinson is in round three against Trent Munro. He feels ill with food poisoning. The dreaded northwest breeze is becoming a gale. Parkinson is sick and the waves are flukey and there is the unmistakable stench of an upset. Parkinson wants to dominate from the start. He gets an 8. He's as good as home already because there aren't many 8's coming through. One more grin-worthy wave and Parkinson can go back to bed. He's paddling back out from his 8 and the hooter sounds for the start of the heat.

He's jumped the gun. His wave won't count. So he goes and catches another. Problem? Long floater. Floaters can slow you down but Parkinson speeds up. A big foam-ball climb. You cannot overstate this: Joel Parkinson is supreme. He's looking every bit as good as the guy he's traded so many blows with behind the old lava rock—Fanning. And Burrow. And Slater. He beats Munro. 'Yeah, I got a little bit sick this morning, not too bad,' he says. 'The doctor gave me a shot, which turned me round real quick. I felt a bit weak paddling, but when I was on the wave I felt fine.' He rides his last wave so far he'll need a taxi back. 'I don't think there are too many kinks in my repertoire right now,' he says. 'This wave has suited me from the first day I ever came. I just fell in love with it.' Parkinson's next round is against Taylor Knox. 'I wouldn't be out here if I didn't think that I could win,' Knox says. He is a mercurial type who can have his barnstorming days, but they're few and far between. Knox says over his dead body will he let Parkinson paddle straight to the inside and get the first wave. No matter what, no matter if he has to paddle to Cape St Francis, Knox says he will not let Joel Parkinson take the first wave. They paddle out and head up the point and Joel Parkinson gets the first wave and he's into a ball-tearing quarter-final against Taj Burrow. It's the cruellest of draws—for both of them.

TAJ BURROW V. THE CRUEL WORLD: The man is a dude. He has all the toys and creature comforts of the well-healed twenty-first century traveller. Slick Billabong threads with endless supplies of jeans and retro T-shirts, a black iPod, mobile phone with global roaming, tonnes of DVDs for when he escapes to his room to watch movies. And a sleek MacBook Pro computer for 'smashing emails'—as he puts it—calling home through Skype, cutting digital movie footage of all his surfing lessons, both free and in competition. And checking out the internet. The internet tells you all sorts of stuff about news, sports, celebrities, anything. His girlfriend of two years, Cheyenne Tozzi, a high-profile Sydney model, is a celebrity, and if you hit Google, there's no shortage of photos of her. A new batch has just started doing the rounds and Burrow, while mucking around on his beloved laptop in his spectacular J-Bay house midway through a contest which could make or break his year, stumbles upon them. The new pictures show his girlfriend hanging out with another guy and he immediately feels sick to the stomach. His girl is doing him no good. She's cheating on him.

Take the deaths of loved ones out of the equation and there are few more gut-wrenching moments in your life than the instant you realise your partner is being unfaithful.

Burrow and Tozzi started seeing each other when Tozzi was seventeen. She's making her mark in Los Angeles and New York. He's a pro surfer whose office is the globe. She's been in LA with renowned vixen Paris Hilton and her notorious band of cohorts. A gorgeous nineteen-year-old Australian girl is attracting loads of attention. She's young. She wants to impress. She wants to be cool. One mistake. You can't take that shit back. Especially when some germ with a camera is watching your every move. Maybe he's not a germ. Maybe he's a seeker of truth. Maybe he's doing Burrow a favour. Pictures are taken of Cheyenne Tozzi cuddling up to American Brandon Davis. He's the grandson of American oil billionnaire Marvin Davis and the ex-boyfriend of Hilton, Lindsay Lohan and Mischa Barton. He's a classy guy, as evidenced by his description of Lohan as 'firecrotch'. He appears greasy and covered in sweat in every photo you've ever seen of him. Tozzi and Davis are photographed at a restaurant called Nello in New York. He has a cigarette in his right hand. His left arm is around Burrow's girl. Her head is on his shoulder. Next they're photographed in their swimming costumes in the ocean in Miami. His arm is still around her. Then they're snapped holding hands walking along Madison Avenue in New York; her with the cigarette this time. Photos can be misleading. You can put your arm around someone for a split second for a happy snap, go your separate ways but leave the impression you've been having a raging affair for the last fifteen years. Burrow has no doubt about the tone of these pics. She really is doing him no good. Slater has been through the same ordeal. He was having his third fling with Pamela Anderson when he had a stopover in Fiji. He bought a magazine to pass the time and the cover story was about his girlfriend and her new guy, Marcus Schenkenburg. With the proof: intimate photographs. She hadn't told him. Good riddance to bad news.

Burrow is crushed. Can't sleep for days. Breaks down in tears more than once. You remember being cheated on. It's harrowing. You curled up in the foetal position for weeks, months, you can't remember. Taj Burrow is in Jeffreys Bay, South Africa, and his girlfriend is running around with some jerk on the other side of the world and he has to ignore all that to go surf a crucial heat against Joel Parkinson in the quarter-finals of the Billabong Pro.

He tells Tozzi to go to hell. *Respect.*

Nobody outside Burrow's very exclusive inner sanctum knows until one of the biggest-selling newspapers in Sydney, *The Daily Telegraph*, runs the photo of Tozzi and Davis on its front page. The story runs the day the J-Bay contest is completed and the secret is out.

'I lost my mind,' Burrow says.

BURROW V. PARKINSON: 'Sometimes, two in-form guys come together and it's anti-climactic,' Parkinson says. 'I hope it's not like that. I hope it's climactic—and I hope I win. It only happens in that one half an hour. It doesn't matter how you've prepared. It's just mind over matter. You just have to tell yourself you're good. You're out there, you're strong, you feel fine.'

Burrow and Parkinson have one common thread: a lack of a world title. It's ridiculous to criticise them for that but it can't be ignored, either. Both have made extraordinary successes of their lives. If Parkinson ends up 35 years of age without ever having bettered a world ranking of No.2, what are you going to do? Go to his sprawling mansion on the other side of the Kirra hill and sit on his leather lounge as Monica makes a cup of coffee and his beautiful daughters run around and watch his widescreen plasma TV and play with his dog and look at that permanent 100-watt grin on his face and sit there and say, 'Joel, mate, where did it all go wrong?' Same for Burrow. It won't be wrong if they never win a world title. But it won't be right. Decades from now, when the future generations are trying to get their heads around how great these two used to be, they'll hear all the stories and attempt the appropriate comprehension but in each case they'll always come back to the one all-defining question: Was he a world champion? Yes will mean they were great. No will mean they were something less. It's cruel. But it's just the way it is.

A heartbroken but resolute Taj Burrow sits near a happy-as-a-fucking-clam but purposeful Joel Parkinson. If Parkinson wants the inside, he can have it. The beauty of the blockbuster heat is that there is no script. It's the beauty of all sport. There are good guys, bad guys, villains, heroes, underdogs, rats, complete rats, humour, justice and tragedy. It's real and unpredictable drama and not even the leading players know the final act. Absolutely anything could happen in the next half hour and you know it and they know it and every person freezing their nuts off at J-Bay knows it. Send Burrow and Parkinson out a million times in modest four-footers and they'll have 500 000 wins each. But as Parkinson says, all that matters is this one. This half-hour. And as Slater said back on the Gold Coast, one move in one heat can be the difference between a good year and world-title madness. The whole thing swings on minutiae. It's the pressure. Pressure makes you do things you wouldn't normally do. Pressure is the difference between landing a floater and missing it. Pressure is surfing better than you can.

Parkinson opens with a 9.17. He adds a 7.33. Burrow goes all 9.33 on him. This is not going to be anti-climactic. Parkinson leaves the first wave of a set because the second wave looks better. But it's not. Burrow is on the first and he gets an 8 under Parkinson's priority and nothing makes a pro fly into a white-knuckled rage more than giving away a big score under his own priority. Burrow's board moulds into a curl. The 8 gets him home. The 8 which Parkinson could have taken for himself. It's another fifth for Parkinson which, given the standard of his surfing throughout, is incomprehensibly unjust. He dunks his head in the water. 'That was tough,' Burrow says. 'It was a really heavy heat. He opened with a 9—he does that every heat. It's a tough way to start. For me, anyway. I just surfed my guts out.'

There's more where that came from. On this day and in more ways than most of the people here—including Parkinson and Fanning—realise, Taj Burrow is proving beyond all doubt that he is made of stern material. He's in the semi-finals and a man-on-man clash with Mick Fanning.

KELLY SLATER: He's spent most of the last fortnight in his new home in Florida. Straight after his hasty departure from Chile, he's been bombarded with emails, texts and voice messages congratulating him on his career. It'd be funny if they weren't so serious. Reports proclaiming his retirement from the Australian news wire have been run by newspapers, magazines and websites all over the world. Slater Quits! Post mortems on his career have begun. The mourning has been incessant. For Slater, it's akin to being at his own funeral. He knows now how everyone will react when he really does go: the surge of praise, thanks and adulation. The irony being the morning after Slater retires, he'll probably go surfing. He's going to quit the tour, but he'll never retire from the sport. He'll still be prominent. He'll return for a few events at his favourite locations on the invitation of his sponsors. He will not lose money. Thomas

Victor Carroll became surfing's first millionaire in 1989. His seven-figure contract came five years *after* he was world champion.

Slater is wearing a green T-shirt. His last words at Arica weren't a farewell. They were: 'Even though I lost, I feel like I put on a good performance. That's what we get paid for. That's why we do this. But to lose, that's the fourth event that Mick has bettered me and it's going to be hard to catch him now. If he stays somewhat consistent at all, he's going to be hard to catch. If he were to better me in just two more events this year, I don't think I could catch him. That's a fact of life and that's the reality of where we're at right now. At this point, it's not feeling like a world-title year for me.' Slater looks strong, though. Vibrant. He looks like himself. You know when you feel like *you*? Maybe you imagine it. Maybe you just want it to be true. Maybe you want to see the king return to his pomp. Just once. But he appears to be fit and firing. He jokes about having something caught in his hair. It's been a long time since Kelly Slater had anything caught in his hair.

'I think for any sportsman, any athlete, thinking about retirement, it's tough to actually say, "That's it". I think all through your career you're thinking about it. How you're going to do it, and when. But the way it was supposed to have happened in Chile—that's the worst possible way I can think of for someone to go out. I'd never do it like that. But I guess I'd be lying if I said I didn't suffer a little bit of burn-out there. I felt like I really had to drag myself to get to Chile because I was really wanting to have more of a break, more personal time, just down time. But this, J-Bay, you've got to love this. I want to win another event. I'm still tied with Tom for career wins. Those precedents are set so you can try to push yourself to get to them. I've always been real focused in that way in my career.'

Asked about coming from behind—a long way behind—to win the world title, he says: 'Maybe I'll come around. I'm going to stick with it. I enjoy that challenge. Two wins would probably put me back in the game pretty solidly. I had a couple of years where I came from behind late in the season to win and they were some of the most exciting and glorious wins of my career, the most incredible feelings.'

He practises in the white wetsuit. Kelly Slater is feeling outlandishly good when he pulls out the white wetsuit.

'I don't even have to worry about keeping pace with them right now,' he says of Fanning and Burrow. 'I need to make a final, I need to make semis. It would be nice just to finish ahead of them in a couple of events, but I need to put away a win or two, realistically two wins, to put me back in the game. About fifty per cent of me feels like I'm taking the year off in some way, but you know it might feel different if I win a couple of heats along the way. So far, I haven't. Maybe that's why I feel the way I do.'

Slater downs Luke Stedman to reach the quarter-finals against Dean Morrison. 'I had a good heat, I got in sync,' he says. 'I just need to keep playing my game and step it up a level from that heat and I should be fine. I'm just going to focus on performance from here on and not really worry about it. I would expect that if I could get something going, it will be in these next two events.' There's the revving of an engine.

Slater rarely loses to anyone twice. Julian Wilson is still buried in the sand at Snapper. 'He got me the last time, so it's payback,' Slater says of Morrison. He's good to his word, but only by seven-tenths of a point. A man of a certain age is tiring. 'It's not killing me yet,' Slater says. 'I'm going to try to get my breathing pattern right, get my energy back up, but I started getting tired in that heat, my legs were going on me.'

J-Bay used to verge on hippiedom. People with wild hair, long hair, dirty hair, bare provisions, no possessions, drenched in surf. J-Bay's point is now filled with houses, bed-and-breakfasts, holiday homes of the rich and famous, apartments. There's the Country Feeling Clothing store and the headquarters for Billabong South Africa. Hundreds more houses are spreading inland. It's still off the beaten track, but no longer feral. You wish it was still feral. There's a local surf tribe but sightings are rare when the tour invades. The Jeffreys Bay Underground wear white rash vests with their insignia on their wetsuits. Stay away.

FANNING V. BURROW: This is it folks, over the top. 'Taj has been ripping all week,' Fanning says. They'll be the world No.1 and No.2 in that order after the final regardless of results in the meantime. It's gloomy and grey but glowing. Burrow has sent a mate at *Stab* magazine a text message expressing in no uncertain terms how he feels about his ex. Little things keep going wrong. Slater's late 9.53 against Adriano de Souza in the quarter-finals has been enough to snatch him a ten-grand Nixon watch for the highest heat score (19.23) of the contest—from Burrow. Burrow tells Fanning he can't believe he didn't win the watch. Fanning sits motionless. Says nothing. He doesn't so much as look in Burrow's direction. He's thinking, *It's only a stinking watch, who cares.*

Burrow does his one-millionth tail-slide of the week. Fanning takes off and you know he's going to get busy. They're both at the height of their powers. Every turn is completed with the finality of an execution. No matter how recklessly they throw themselves into their kamikaze hacks, they never fall. Fanning doesn't always finish his manoeuvres because he's already into his next. He lands a late floater on the bricks without tearing his hamstring clean off the bone and he's going like a locomotive. He claims it. Fanning has started fast. He's paddling out fast. He's doing everything extraordinarily fast. Every wave is ridden as though his life depends on it.

Burrow is in no mood to stuff around. Basically, given the surrounding circumstances, everyone can go and get fucked. We're only ten minutes in and this is something else. This is the best heat of the contest. This is one of the best and most electrifying man-on-man sporting contests you will see. Parkinson is all class and Slater is Slater but this is as riveting as anything you could hope for. How good is *all* sport. Burrow is going faster than the fastest surfer of all time. Burrow tries to get air. He gets air, but not a landing. There's nothing in it. This should be the final. You know what they should do? They should re-seed the surfers after every round, not just the first three rounds. It's a bit rough to have Burrow v. Parkinson in the quarters when there are six other surfers still alive. And it's similarly rough to have Fanning v. Burrow in the semis while the two other semi-finalists, Slater and Morrison, are both lower on the rankings. Fanning needs a 9. He doesn't make his last floater. He doesn't get the 9. Burrow is through and he's into the final and Cheyenne Tozzi can go up in smoke and maybe this won't be such a bad day after all.

'Taj has surfed insanely the whole event,' Fanning says. 'He's surfed so good. He just looks really sharp.' Fanning still doesn't know about the drama.

THE FINAL—BURROW V. SLATER: Slater wants to get the final underway ahead of schedule. He says it's time to go, even though it isn't. He's running to the water before Burrow has left his house. Now Slater is out in the water. Burrow still hasn't budged. ASP officials suggest he hurry up, but he holds his ground. The final isn't due to start for another 20 minutes and that's when Taj Burrow will be starting, thanks very much. Slater can issue a federal court order for all he cares. He ain't moving. He's in no mood to be told what to do. Not today. What a stand-off. In Slater's defence, the break between the second semi-final and the final is for the benefit of the second semi-finalist, to give them a breather. But Burrow has already been told the starting time, and it's not yet. Slater leans back on his board and kicks his feet in the air. He keeps looking around for Burrow. More attempts are made to expedite the process but Burrow stands firm.

'I was in the first semi and won that so I went back to my hotel room, got all warm, had a hot shower and started jumping round to get ready for the final,' Burrow explains later. 'We were staying right on top of Supertubes. Kelly won his semi-final. He's come in and he's pretty cold and he tells the organisers he wants to go again straightaway. He's telling them, "Let's get this thing going. I want to go, I want to go, Taj is ready, let's go". But I wasn't ready. I'm up there watching him run across the sand and I'm thinking, "What's he doing? He's too early". I thought I might just let him sit out there and chill. It was pretty cold. He was getting *really* cold, I think. I wasn't going to rush, no way. They were pressuring me to go out, but I just wasn't ready. We were about twenty minutes away and I wasn't going to go till I wanted to. I'm sure Kelly understands. I learned that trick from him.'

Martin Potter once told Slater: 'You remind me of me. You see a lip and you just want to smash it.' Here and now, fuelled by raw emotion, Burrow is doing the smashing. Pent-up emotions need to be released. Burrow ran out of gas in the final against Fanning last year but he's a different species now. You can't manufacture a miracle—the world championship—but you can position yourself for one. You can get yourself fit enough to mount a charge. Today's schedule is identical to the last day at Bells and Snapper—four back-to-back heats. Two hours of surfing won't kill anyone, but it's a mental battle, all that full-blown concentration. Exhaustion makes you think in curved lines. Burrow has a healthy body and a healthy enough mind. He can't do anything other than concentrate on the immediate task at hand: belting the crap out of J-Bay's rights.

Some Day

Slater's first wave is stiff and cold. He falls on his second turn. It's looked like a lot of effort. A man who can twist into more positions than a rubber doll is rigid. Slater's second wave is better than his first in that he makes his first *two* turns before he falls. He tries again. The roundhouse cutback isn't sharp and he drifts too far behind the pocket. He's scoring 2's and 3's. Shaun Thomson is commentating for Slater's next wave and tells a worldwide audience: 'He does a huge—ahh—kind of a—and a—reverse—um.' Slater's reverse um ends up a 360 or 720 or something and he's just flinging himself around and it smacks of exhausted desperation. He ends up on his stomach, gets back to his feet then goes down head-first again. He's out of sorts, or knackered, or too cold, or too flustered, or all of the above. Burrow catches four controlled waves to Slater's haphazard twelve. Slater follows a good carve with a failed floater. It's as though he only has the energy and momentum for one turn.

Burrow is travelling at a greater velocity, hitting each section with a greater purpose. Stop the fight. Burrow's moves are more critical. Slater's *condition* is critical. Burrow is feeling no pain. For the first time today, he's feeling no pain. Perhaps Taj Burrow is stronger than he thought. Burrow stands on the bricks. He grabs his leg rope and yanks his board back the way you pull the leash of a disobedient dog. You pull hard because you're at the end of your tether. *Come here. Come the fuck here.* The boy next door has gone a little bit hard core. He paddles back out with another dose of urgency and Slater's wave looks like a slow-motion replay of what Burrow has just done. His batteries are running low. The last resort is a tube. But he falls again. You've never seen *anyone* fall so often. A teasing little shack closes out on him. Burrow is playing the game, forcing Slater into waves he doesn't really want. Taj Burrow is out-Slatering Slater. He's a formidable sight when he's in no mood. Slater kicks out of waves to keep priority, beating Burrow out to the take-off zone, but even then he doesn't get the waves he needs. If the right waves come, he can win. He drifts up and down the point in vain hope. Nothing doing. Burrow picks off the gems. He's measured and calculated and controlled. He's as energetic as he was when he blazed his way to a 10-pointer nine days ago. A lifetime ago. A lot of things ago. He nails the end section. Nails the final. Nails Kelly Slater to the wall.

'It's an embarrassing finish,' Slater says.

Burrow nods. At the end of his most decisive wave, the most courageous single performance of the year for all the crap going on that no-one really knows about, he just nods. 'Last year in the final against Mick I was absolutely fatigued,' he says. 'I was wrecked on my last wave. I could've gotten the score I needed. I sat down and thought, damn, I could have won that if I was feeling a bit more fit. I'm trying to do what it takes. I feel good.'

Not *that* good.

And so Taj Burrow embarks upon the walking of a tightrope which will determine whether he fulfils his prodigious talent by becoming the champion of the world, or falls flat on his face. There are those among us who would give their eye teeth to finish second in the world and have it described as some sort of failure but normal rules do not apply to Taj Burrow. There's something amiss if he finishes his career without a crown. There are few more unfortunate words than *what might have been*. Burrow has thrown the title race wide open. A surfer with unrestrained natural talent and worldwide popularity is back to No.2, with a bullet. Fanning leads by the same margin as before the event, but this time his lead is from Burrow rather than Damien Hobgood and there's no doubt which one of those two he regards as the more serious threat. Burrow is unpredictable with unrestrained natural gifts but Fanning still has nothing worse than a third. Burrow has two victories and Fanning only has one and that will bug Fanning. He hasn't started going backwards, but he's no longer streaking ahead. You pull out a piece of paper and scratch down their results when the throwaways are taken into account. Fanning has a first, second and third. Burrow has two firsts and a third. On adjusted ratings, Burrow leads.

Burrow leads.

'I had it in my head that I had a first and a third, but then a ninth and seventeenth,' he says. 'The whole event I was thinking, "Win this thing and I'll have first, first, third". I was going, "First-first-third; first-first-third". I just kept thinking that.'

There's a hint of muscle along Burrow's arm which never used to be there. He's no Charles Atlas but he's in good nick. The fleshy face has thinned. Imagine the satisfaction he feels right now—of deciding after last year's loss to Fanning in the J-Bay final that his biggest road-block to the world title was his lack of supreme fitness and that getting into shape might, just might, get him through four back-to-back heats rather than three. And then he comes out twice in a year, in the hallowed halls of Bells and Jeffreys Bay, and blazes through those four back-to-back heats to win the finals of two of the most prestigious contests on the planet. And he's done it by beating Joel Parkinson, Mick Fanning and Kelly Slater in successive heats. 'I felt fine,' Burrow says and he sounds surprised. 'I felt *totally* fine! It's a great feeling to know I put in the work and it actually paid off. I feel amazing! I had a pretty tough draw, but if you start getting hard guys early you just gain momentum and confidence. It was a pretty gnarly draw but it all ended up working pretty well.'

It's sunset. Burrow is clapping and grinning *before* he's even introduced to the thousands of people who have resisted, momentarily, the temptation to go and find somewhere (or someone) warm. Slater is rubbing a sore spot just behind his left shoulder. 'I love it here,' Burrow says. 'Every time you get a good wave, the crowd just lights up. You finish a good wave and everyone flares.' The rest of Burrow's victory speech can be paraphrased as: YEEEEEEEEEEEEEEEEEW!

'To take down those guys today—it was no easy run. It's going to be pretty sick for the rest of the year. It should be exciting. This win is huge for me. I love coming here and I always feel comfortable. The water's kind of the same temperature as home, the weather's pretty similar and any kind of right-hander like this gets me pretty excited. Billabong's run it for so many years now and it's an event I wanted to do well in. It's all come together. I'm so stoked to have won two events. There's a huge carrot dangling in front of me for the rest of the year.'

Slater climbs into a jacuzzi. He's spent. He's finished with 6.17 points—comboed by Burrow's 16.5. Kelly Slater doesn't get comboed. 'The mind even got tired out there,' he says. 'I don't know the last time I surfed four heats in a day. The waves weren't that big, but I didn't eat much food. I wanted to try to not put that energy towards digestion.' Exactly how much energy goes into digestion, we do not know. 'I should have just tried to eat a bit more food, a bit more sugar.' Slater's scores on the final day have been a 16.17 against Stedman, 19.23 against de Souza, 13.83 against Morrison and 6.17 against Burrow. 'I peaked in the quarters,' he says. 'It's just . . . I got so tired. I went paddling up the point, going, "Don't go that way, you can't make waves from that far up". But I went anyway. I didn't even listen to myself. I was just tired mentally and physically at that point. Taj put it together. He made me sit out in the water and wait a bit at the start, which I was kind of bummed about. But it paid off for him.'

Still, it's the beginning of a revival from Slater and he says: 'This is the first contest in a few events where I felt I have finally hit my stride. I thought I was going to make the final on the Gold Coast. I felt good at Bells, but just couldn't put it together. I've only won one out of the last five, or two out of the last six, finals that I've been in. That's a little frustrating but I guess it's something for people to talk about. If I let it get to me, it'll put a little pressure on me, but sometimes it's the thing to get you going. I was thinking in the water, "Maybe a second is the thing to bring me to life instead of winning". It'll get me more motivated for the next one.'

Remember those words.

'Taj has streaks and sparks,' Slater says. 'He just never seems to get the engine into full motion and high gears. He tends to struggle with his consistency, and already this year he's had a first but a couple of throwaways. He needs to get fifths, thirds and better from now on to keep himself in there. Andy is probably kicking himself right now. Mick is just so consistent. He slipped his way to third in this event and barely broke a sweat. I've got to get seconds and better. It looks like a few people are shaping up to be in it. Mick is still the runaway guy, but me and Taj have made a move here. I imagine both of us moved up a spot. I definitely got myself going in a positive direction, and it's just playing catch-up now. I'll probably be somewhere near Andy, so it will be a little more interesting from now on. If Mick doesn't get a result at Trestles.'

Remember those words, too.

They've had good J-Bay, but not great J-Bay. Once in your lifetime, just once, you want to ride a board with a lightning bolt on it like Jerry Lopez in *Tubular Swells*. And once in your lifetime, just once, you want to ride a chest-high right-hand barrel like Wayne 'Rabbit' Bartholomew, in the same movie, at Burleigh Heads. You're not entirely sure there's a better single piece of footage than this: Rabbit with his hands in the air then clasped behind his back as he sways into a luminous curve, the sun ricocheting off his back. You want to do both those things, just once.

Burrow says: 'I am so happy.'

Periods of your life ignore personality and concentrate on character. Everyone has a personality, not everyone has character. Taj Burrow has proved in no uncertain terms that he is blessed with vast amounts of both. His heartache hasn't come from the death of a family member. He hasn't lost an older brother he worshipped and wanted to travel the world with, but if you've ever been through anything remotely similar to what Taj Burrow has just been through, you'll appreciate the endless reservoirs of intestinal fortitude required to get through it. He deserves all the credit and respect in the world. He's a good man, Taj Burrow. Cheyenne Tozzi is quoted again in the newspapers. She says she's still in love with him. Tell someone who cares.

10

Homage

The three-day Coolie Kids Memorial contest in remembrance of Sean Fanning and Joel Green is held at Snapper Rocks in August. Whales have joined the surfers on the final morning of all eight previous contests—and they arrive again this year. They slap their tails and blow water through their spouts. They show off. Go figure. On the morning of the anniversary of Sean's passing, the actual day, Mick wakes to the sounds of two kookaburras who have taken up permanent residence in his backyard. They moved in the same day he did. They've been named Sean and Joel. You can walk right up to them and they do not want to leave. Go figure. Mick hits a hole-in-one at a charity golf day held in Sean's name. Go figure. He's in the final of the memorial contest with Parkinson and Occhilupo. 'I've never seen this before,' he says, 'but a dolphin and a turtle came up to me together. The dolphin wouldn't go away. I ended up just talking to it the whole day. I don't know what it was or who it was.' Go figure. Maybe it was Sean? Or maybe it was just a dolphin.

11

The king

The plot thickens.

Fanning and Burrow are so good, but this is where it all began for Slater. Fanning and Burrow are so good, but this is where Slater won his first professional event as an eighteen-year-old rock star wearing stars-and-stripes board shorts. Fanning and Burrow are so good, but this is where they're going to get that wholly uncomfortable feeling of someone truly dangerous breathing down their necks. 'This is the first point break I ever surfed in my life,' Slater says. 'When I was twelve I'd come here every afternoon with my dad and brother. I've always loved this place. I've had a connection with it since that very first time. I look at this wave, and I just feel like it's right for the way I surf.' Fanning and Burrow are so good, but this is the place where every sporting cliché regarding pride and desperation will apply. Fanning and Burrow are so good, but, yes, this is the place where the eight-time and defending world champion will throw the kitchen sink. Think the king isn't up for the fight? Think again. He says a lot about the title race in the days before his opening heat, but nothing more ominous and telling than this: 'It's not over.'

'Just incredible waves,' Slater says of his first tour win at Trestles. 'We were surfing in trunks because the water was in the seventies, there were these light offshore Santa Ana winds, it was five feet and a south swell. I couldn't have—you know, sometimes I look back at things that have happened in my career and I couldn't have scripted them any better. Sometimes things just happen at exactly the right time. It was a big prize back then. It was an event I had really worked for years to try to win. I was starting my last year at high school, I was just turning pro, I'd just signed my contract with Quiksilver, everything really climaxed in that one moment. This place holds fond memories.'

An old man sits in the zoo that is Los Angeles airport. He's exhausted and alone. There's nothing more sad. No matter what happens for the rest of your days, you hope you are never alone. Aggressive people, busy people, shouting people, irritable people, angry people, confused people. What kind of hell is the City of Angels? It's hot, crowded, too big, too heavy, too claustrophobic, too fake. T.S. Elliot wrote: 'The first condition of understanding a foreign country is to smell it.' You smell plastic cheese.

Travelling is a humbling experience. You realise you're just one in six billion people milling about. No more, and no less. You need lunch so you squeeze onto a crowded plastic bench. You order fish and chips, water and a coffee. The waitress adds up your bill but doesn't charge you for the coffee. You stand there fearing the retribution of not telling her: bad karma. You honestly believe you'll be punished for robbing this sticky little joint of $3.50 for a cup of coffee bound to taste like sewage. But you do it anyway. Does this matter? Maybe karma is just your own peace of mind. Or maybe everything is completely independent of everything else.

Maybe that's good. Maybe that's soul-destroying. You drink your stolen coffee. People are trying to escape. Caged animals. You wonder what everyone is thinking. When we're all just walking around, what are we all thinking? You'd love to know.

There are blue signs, green signs, red signs, white signs. The purple signs will take you to the car rental office but there are no purple signs and your luggage keeps falling off this fucking trolley and you still can't find the purple signs and you hate this country but then you see the purple signs and God Bless America. Into a hire car and you swing south onto the ten-lane Highway 1. You go past Laguna Beach where they wear knee-length shorts and loafers into day spas and country clubs. Steroid-pumped men with obscene muscles strut around bare-chested and covered in oil. You see the fattest man you have ever seen in your life. He's three men. He's wearing knee-length yellow shorts, long white socks, mountain boots and a bow tie. He says he likes to be noticed. Rollergirls in tight pants skim along the footpath. A black guy shoots hoops on a beachside basketball court. Palm trees line the freeway.

You ask for directions. 'What you'll be doing is going to the corner of Christianitos Road and El Camino Real in San Clemente. What you'll be doing then is parking in the car park and going down the path. Then you'll be walking for about half an hour and what you'll be doing then is standing on the beach and walking down to your left to Lowers.' What you're doing now is thinking this bloke is being a smartarse by talking in future tense, but he's not. Every one of these lunatics is doing it. What you'll be doing tonight is going to Carl Jnr's for dinner for his Original Six Dollar Burger, which somehow ends up costing eight bucks. What you'll be doing then is paying fifty bucks a night for your room in San Clemente. What you'll be doing then is going round the fucking twist if everyone keeps talking this way.

You park at the corner of Christianitos Road and El Camino Real and it's doubtful you have ever been more dispirited. What a dive. A tarred car park is surrounded by a barb-wire fence. You cross the road and go down the path. Thick dry scrub to the left and right. You walk through rocks, broken glass and trash. Ashtrays have more natural beauty. A sign at San Onofre National Park says beware of the bears because they try to eat children. It's signed by the governor of California, Arnold Schwarzenegger. *Hasta la vista, baby.* You can see the ocean, so there's a start. A helicopter flies above the contest zone. The path goes under Highway 1. Serenity now—please. It's so loud. You keep walking, and walking. It's a mission and you're convinced someone is pulling your leg. Is this Trestles? *The* Trestles? You reach the train tracks and the car engines become a distant hum. Blown-out sandals are on the edge of the path like bombed-out cars on a desert road. About 50 metres to the north is the County Line. You're in the OC. And you're on the sand. An Amtrak train blasts its horn. The waves are shithouse: windswept, small and lifeless. This cannot be Trestles.

But it is.

You get a few waves. They're so devoid of power it's like riding a cotton wool ball. If you weren't right in front of the VIP tents at the contest site, you would honestly believe you were in the wrong place. The line-up is bloated with backwash, the kind of large ripples you get when a speed boat leaves a wake. You paddle against the rip to stay in what you've been assured is pole position: the area between the F and S on the FOSTERS sign. The water is freezing. You can't see any semblance of the magic or whatever it is that has made Trestles so famous. Walking back across the bowling ball-sized cobblestones that form the pathway to and from these virtually non-existent waves, you doubt it's possible to have a less enjoyable surf. Cold. Backwash. Weak waves. Trestles, on first appearances, appears to be the greatest possible let-down.

A sign halfway along the path has a diagram showing its five different breaks. The mocked-up picture makes the place look like J-Bay. The breaks are Cottons, where President Nixon's old house is perched on the cliff, Uppers, Lowers, Middles and Church. The contest is at Lowers. Walking, walking. You wonder where Slater keeps his eight world championship trophies. You imagine one of them is a doorstop.

Parkinson yells, 'Look at that set, whoa!' Sarcasm can be the truth. Walking back on sunset, there's a light brown hat sitting on the ground near the train tracks. A boy is with his parents. He looks at the hat and says: 'I should take it home, but there's probably a bomb in it.' When did kids starting thinking like that? Large power lines span the scrub. You can hear them zapping. A giant American flag hangs limply over Carl's. It'll be September 11 soon.

The king's first heat is against Cory Lopez and Dane Reynolds. 'Lopez' is Latin for 'wolf'. Your flight from Sydney to LA has shown the cartoon *Surf's Up*. It's the story of a legendary surfer who rediscovers his powers in the nick of time. Perhaps it's an omen. Perhaps it's just a cartoon. Slater plays himself in *Surf's Up* and his work doesn't appear to involve much more than saying, 'What's up, dude?' Reynolds was in nappies when Slater came good. He's qualified for the 2008 tour and, along with South Africa's Jordy Smith, he's surfing's next megastar. They both hit the accelerator about the same time they hit puberty. They're talented and cocky. Reynolds has previously beaten Irons at Trestles and fears no-one at a wave shaped like a half-pipe. Not Fanning, not Burrow, not Parkinson, not Irons; no-one frightens Reynolds here—except Slater. If Reynolds cracks the lip, he knows Slater is going to bash it. If Reynolds gets big air, Slater will get bigger air. A hack will be followed by a power hack. Guaranteed. You can't beat someone you worship. No matter what Reynolds scores, Slater will score more. Slater knows, Reynolds knows, Slater knows Reynolds knows and Reynolds knows Slater knows he knows. Reynolds posts 16.3 for the third highest score of the opening day. His score would've beaten Fanning. His score would've beaten Burrow. His score would've beaten anyone—with the exception of Slater.

Fanning's 9.8 is the best of the day. He beats Pancho Sullivan and Sunny Garcia. 'I need to better Mick, Taj and Andy,' Slater says. 'I need to get ahead of them in this one contest. I need to do it now.'

Slater can't help himself. He's still insanely competitive. He's been that way since he was two years old and hassling his older brother, Sean, for the deep end of the bathtub. He's been insanely competitive since Jack Johnson and the rest of their gang in Hawaii played a game in big waves called 'You Won't Go' and the king couldn't help going. He'll wonder about how much he cares, then bluff Shane Beschen into a crucial interference call at the US Open at Huntington that triggered world title number four. A jam-packed beach at the home of American mainland surfing decided Slater was an A-grade prick and let him know all about it, but he was prepared to be public enemy No.1 for a while because he *had* to win that heat. And who cares now? No-one even remembers. It was a must-win heat so he did what he had to do to win. Coming up: another series of must-win heats. Slater and Fanning are in round three but Burrow, Parkinson and Irons are taken to the gallows of round two.

You can't sleep. You're back on Highway 1 at 2 a.m., going north because you want to visit Huntington. This is about the only time when it won't be crowded. You go past the Rip Curl store in San Clemente and there's a massive poster of Taylor Knox on the front wall. Are they having a laugh? No Mick Fanning? Anyone seen the world rankings? You drive through the night in your American jeep with your American radio station playing American songs and every second corner post has an American flag and you don't stop until you get to Huntington. And there's the famed pier. But you know, it's just a pier. A Ruby's Diner is perched at the far end but at this time of night, the gates are locked. There are those lifeguard towers you see on *Baywatch*, fifteen beach volleyball courts, restaurants between the highway and the sand and Duke's Barefoot Bar. There's a lot to be said for a barefoot bar. Huntington has shopping centres, pizza shops, Coke machines, ATMs, concrete and commercialism. Across the road from the pier is The Surfers' Walk of Fame. The inductees have left their foot and hand prints in the pathway, and carved a message. Layne Beachley's says: *Live. Laugh. Love. Surf.* You put your feet and hands over hers. She has little hands and little feet. Occhilupo writes: *Get Down Low And Go Go Go.* Mark Richards' is *Surf For Fun* and he has drawn a smiley face. Andy Irons' suggests *Enjoy Life.* Slater was inducted in 2002. He was wearing a red-and-black flannelette shirt and black pants as he left footprints that appear right now to be a little bizarre. He has the weirdest feet. You take off your thongs. His heel is the same size as yours, but his toes are spread so wide it's as if he has an extra couple of toes. It's as though his feet have been squashed and spread. His foot is a V. His message is this: *Everything Is Possible*.

You drive back to San Clemente and you're thinking, yup, everything is possible. The most valuable thing there is, a life—*a human life*—can slip through your fingers like running water. What if Sean Fanning had left the party one second earlier or later? What if that one second would have changed every other circumstance of that night and what if he was still alive and on the tour and ranked No.1? What if Mick had jumped in the same car as Sean Fanning and Joel Green? Would he have died, too? Or would his mere presence have made everything different? What if . . .

Trestles is right up Taj Burrow's alley oop. 'I love Lowers, it's so good for getting loose,' he says. 'If you have good boards and you feel confident, it's the kind of wave you feel invincible on. It's so playful and you can do anything you want. I feel pretty good—I feel like, in a way, I've cracked the code to winning events.' But his opening loss to Hawaiian Fred Patacchia spells DANGER because as the highest ranked surfer in round two, he'll get one of the wildcards. He doesn't want to be drawn against Reynolds. Anywhere else in the world and Burrow could feel at ease. But Reynolds at Trestles is a threat to anyone because he spends more time here than the cobblestones. It's high-performance and new-age—and so is Reynolds. And even worse, Burrow is carrying a knee injury which he's trying to cover up. It's serious and infuriating and worrying. He doesn't want anyone to know. He doesn't want to give Reynolds or anyone else cause for optimism. And he doesn't want the judges to get it in their heads that he's holding back because he's hurting. He wants everyone to think he remains as unbreakable as he was in South Africa.

'I've fucked up—done something stupid,' Burrow says. 'It's a grade-two tear of my MCL. I've been really lucky with injuries. I haven't had anything major apart from a broken foot. I've been really lucky with my knees. They bend and twist and get in all sorts of positions, but I've never done any damage to them. It wasn't like it tore off, but it's separated and hurts like hell. It just blew out. I landed in the wrong position—it was bad.' He hasn't really fucked up. Just been unlucky.

'I was having a bit of a break at home in WA,' he says. 'I'd been going flat out. I'd just won J-Bay, had a big night there, went to Bali for a Billabong shoot, had a couple of nights there and really good surf. Went to G-Land in Indonesia and got really good waves—got hammered a bit out there, copped a couple of beatings, but the surf was really good. I was doing so much travelling, it was all just a blur. They were good times and I loved it but I needed to slow down. So I went back home and that's where it happened. It was dumb. I was just mucking around on a jet ski with some mates.

It was all such a mad flurry and I guess getting hurt was telling me that I needed to slow down for a while. I ended up sitting on the couch for a month doing rehab. I've never felt pain like it. I got my physio to fly straight over that day. Had the MRI and the whole deal—needed the full rehab even though it was the best-case scenario for what I'd done. But it was painful and the hardest thing is to get your head around it and try to convince yourself to get back in those same positions. Your body just doesn't want to go there even when your mind is telling it to. It's hard to get confident with it again. I have to tape it for every surf. It's punishing. We tape it up—then rip the tape off after every session. It's really thick tape and we pull it off and there's blood everywhere. It's so frustrating.'

Burrow is telling himself things don't feel right and he'll probably get the hardest draw of round two and even before the re-seeds are done and the ASP printer spits out the schedule, he's thinking, *I'm going to get Dane Reynolds, I'm going to get Dane Reynolds*, and the names are bracketed for the second heat of round two and those two names are Taj Burrow and Dane Reynolds. He has two lay days to sweat on it. And try to fix his knee.

The second lay day is September 11. Morning radio presenters with no passion in their voices replay recordings of the most harrowing emergency calls. Why don't newsreaders show their emotions? Why do they pretend they don't care? Just once you want to see a newsreader break down in sobbing tears about a sad story. People on the recordings are screaming about the need to get air into their lungs before jumping out a window on the 25th floor. Fanning has been to Ground Zero in New York. He was struck by the sadness of the place, the silence. He read the names of the deceased. One of them was Jack Fanning. Mick's grandfather is Jack. The American Jack Fanning died in a lobby of the World Trade Center's south tower. He was 54 years old and the head of the New York Fire Department's hazardous material unit. That May, he had testified to a senate subcommittee about America's lack of readiness to deal with a terrorist attack. He had virtually predicted his own death. His only remains were a crushed white battalion chief's hat. He is survived by an autistic son whose mother, Maureen, could only explain the tragedy to him with two photographs. One was of the father. The other was of the smoke-filled Twin Towers. The autistic son cried, 'No! No! No!' The son's name was Sean. Sean Fanning.

Today, right next to the Trestles car park—you'll go for a paddle, there must be a wave *somewhere*—is a 56-year-old disabled man in a wheelchair. He says his name is Mike and he's from Laguna Beach. A roll-your-own cigarette hangs from cracked lips. He's tied the Stars and Stripes to the fence behind him. There's dust everywhere. He waves at cars. They salute. He says he doesn't want to talk about why he's doing this. Then he does. 'I killed seven men in Vietnam and this is my penance.' His teeth are yellow. He tells you to do nothing but follow your heart, even if your heart keeps getting it wrong. And he says you only have one life, so you might as well live it. Or not. He says it's up to you.

The king's third-round will be against Rob Machado. What he would give for his little mate Reynolds to beat Burrow. If Slater is going to make a move, he has to start now. His mother and brother used to tell him he could fall into a pile of shit and come up smelling like roses. He needs to do it again.

Example 1 of Kelly Slater falling into a pile of shit and coming up smelling like roses: In 1995, Sunny Garcia took a virtually unassailable rankings lead into the Pipeline Masters. Garcia is a barrel-chested multiple Pipeline winner. Slater was a distant third and needed a thousand stars to align. He was curled up in his unit at Cocoa Beach in Florida just before leaving for Hawaii. The phone rang. A girl he used to date, Tamara, was on the line.

They were no longer together and her call was unexpected. She needed to talk—urgently. Things are serious when someone needs to talk urgently—and in person. It would take her five hours to get to Slater's place. In the meantime, he called his mother. Judy freaked out as only mothers can. She feared the worst. She thought Tamara had AIDS. Slater suspected something else. He was right. Tamara was pregnant, and she was going to have the child with or without Slater's support. Slater was only 23 and still a kid himself. They decided to combine parenthood and friendship without doing it all under the same roof. Slater was going to be a dad. His head was spinning off its axis when he went to Pipeline for some Garcia hunting. Machado was second on the rankings. Slater sensed the tour wanted a new world champion—anyone but him after two straight triumphs. He's no fool. He knows a vibe. He was in the same position he's in now with Fanning and Burrow. He needed to win, but also needed them to lose. The first 999 stars aligned when a person nobody had seen for a while came from nowhere to win the trials. Marco Jay Luciano Occhilupo was making a comeback.

Occhilupo was the lowest seed in the main draw because spending four years on the couch eating fried chicken had done nothing for his ranking. He would be drawn against the highest seed—Garcia. There were no second chances at Pipeline. The loser of every heat was eliminated. Occhilupo feared for his safety if he won. Bare-fisted Hawaiian locals do not always take kindly to someone beating one of their own, especially when a world title is up for grabs. Occhilupo needed a security escort to the water. He feared he would need a body bag if he won. He kept finding barrels—couldn't help it. Garcia kept falling—couldn't help it. Occhilupo built a formidable lead and was therefore unlikely to leave the North Shore alive. He panicked. He sat on the shoulder and started guiding Garcia onto waves, but Garcia was too far behind. Occhilupo won a heat he tried to lose. Slater raised an eyebrow. Here we go. Occhilupo reached the final. Slater and Machado squared off in the semi-finals. The winner of their heat would be world champion. They laughed, high-fived—and Slater won. Would they have laughed and high-fived if Slater had lost? He beat Occhilupo in the decider and a man previously covered in shit was smelling like roses all over again.

Taylor was born the following year. She had a serious infection and spent ten days in intensive care. None of Slater's family visited the hospital. He took two years to reveal in public that he had become a father.

Example 2 of Kelly Slater falling into a pile of shit and coming up smelling like roses: In 1996, Danny Wills won back-to-back events to take the rankings lead. But Wills stumbled and his best mate, Mick Campbell, was No.1 going into Pipeline. The Australians were one–two and only a hair on Campbell's chinny-chin-chin separated them. Again, Slater was third. Campbell lost to eighteen-year-old Bruce Irons, failing to make a single take-off while recording the worst three-wave heat score in tour history: 1.9. Wills reached the fourth round. Just two more wins would have made him world champion. You forget how close he came to the peak but he went down the gurgler and Slater ran off with the closest title win in history—a measly 38 points. See ya, wouldn't want to be ya.

Most career prize money: Kelly Slater. Most world titles: Kelly Slater. Youngest world champion: Kelly Slater. Oldest world champion: Kelly Slater. Most WCT victories in a year: Kelly Slater. Most tour wins: Kelly Slater and Tom Curren. Most points in a heat: Kelly Slater. The record for the man who holds the most records: Kelly Slater. He's a 175-centimetre, 72.5-kilogram phenomenon. He's been on tour for twelve years. His finishes have been: 1, 6, 1, 1, 1, 1, 1, 2, 2, 1, 1. That's magnificent. This is a privilege.

Decent little lefts and rights greet round two and the first three heats are bellringers; Irons versus Garcia, Burrow versus Reynolds, Parkinson versus the big-arsed Jordy Smith. The car park is full at 7 a.m. The real stuff will be over by breakfast. The path is crawling with people. The place has come alive. The walk takes ten minutes less. Lay days have given you the chance to look around, but you're not here to look around. You're here to watch heats like these. You're in full stride. There's no train. Marching along the sand past people with their bikes and prams—yes, prams—you see Garcia. Strapped tightly to the right ankle of the 2001 world champion is his leg rope. Strapped to his left ankle is a GPS tracking device so his parole officer knows exactly where he is.

Garcia is under house arrest for tax evasion. He's spent most of the year in the big house, and needed a special court order to compete. 'My life is in fucking crisis,' he says. Sunny Garcia has a lisp. Sunny Garcia does not beat around the bush. He's working as a bouncer at a downtown San Diego bar because he's banned from competition surfing apart from this fleeting cameo. He fails to see the logic. 'They want me to pay back all these taxes,' he says. 'So it makes no sense to have me sitting in the house not allowed to surf. They're allowing me to work as a bouncer in a nightclub but they're not allowing me to surf. I can make thousands of dollars surfing for a month, or I can make hundreds of dollars working as a bouncer. I'm not saying the legal system is unfair. I've paid my dues. I went to jail, I did my time. But I don't understand how murderers and rapists can walk the streets and here I am from an issue with taxes, and I've got this friggin' GPS strapped to my ankle. I'm trying not to make any noise. I'm trying not to complain and just ride it out but—why? I just don't get it. I'm grateful the judge allowed me to come down here and surf. You're not going to get one complaint out of me about that. Trestles is better than where I've been. Ultimately, if I'd paid attention to what my CPAs and everybody else was doing, I wouldn't be in this problem. But I still believe there should be some kind of a law that holds CPAs accountable. I'm not an accountant. You can give me papers with all these numbers on them and I don't know what the fuck they mean. Ultimately, that's why I was paying this guy thousands and thousands of dollars—to do my taxes. I hope he drops dead.

'It's really not fair. My accountant goes on with his life making lots of money and meanwhile, here I am, fucking crisis. I've lost my wife, I've lost my job, I've lost my dignity. And now I'm not allowed to surf apart from this week. It's worse for me to be out of prison and not be able to surf. I'd rather be in prison. I mean that. I know I can't get out when I'm in there. I can't even *look* at the ocean. I can just wait for my time to be up. It's a very humbling experience. It's not that I mind doing the work—it just doesn't make sense. You guys want money? Allow me to make some money. Allow me to surf.'

Garcia is naked from the waist up. Across his collarbone is a tattoo: *Death And Taxes*. 'I got it just before I went to prison,' he says. 'It's just a joke. It's my way of laughing at the system. It hasn't been easy for me, this whole experience, and I'm just trying to work out ways to get through it. I want to get back on the tour. I can still mix it with these boys. I have a gym in my garage. When I'm not working, I'm training in my garage. But it's hard. The light at the end of the tunnel keeps getting smaller. I'm getting more impatient. I'm on the door at Stingeree. It's a club across the road from the Convention Centre in San Diego. People come up and say, "Oh my god, has anyone ever told you that you look like Sunny Garcia?" I'm like, "Yeah, people tell me that a lot".'

Garcia rides his first wave with the unabashed joy of a laughing child. Irons is yet to move a muscle. He's slouched in the way you slouch when you're watching a boring TV show and you can't even be bothered turning it off. Garcia launches eight backhand blasts and this is more fun than the clink. But he's more at home in 15-foot Sunset than 2-foot Trestles. The waves aren't overly inspiring for a six-time winner of The Triple Crown in Hawaii. He smacks the lip, bloodying it, each smack more pronounced as if he's saying what (smack) kind (smack) of (smack) crap (smack) little (smack) fucking (smack) waves (smack) do (smack) you (smack) call (smack) these and his last smack, the one coinciding with THESE, is the biggest smack of the lot. And then the ocean goes flat and hundreds of people behind the cobblestone rocks are looking at each other a little uneasily. Is this as good as it gets?

Fifteen minutes into the half-hour heat, and Irons is *still* waiting. You'd suspect he's fallen asleep if not for the incessant flapping of his gums. It's kind of comical. Some surfers would give their left testicle to make the world tour and surf a heat against Sunny Garcia but Irons doesn't give a rat's toss bag about the result if the waves aren't good. It's his loss and will cost him. A left comes through. His blasts are fewer, but more ferocious. He has a 7.83 to Garcia's 6. But Garcia has priority. He can milk the clock and end up with two waves to Irons' one. With twelve minutes left, Reynolds gets into his wetsuit for his clash with Burrow. Three cameras are on him. And the eyes of Burrow.

Irons goes left, lands a backside air reverse and that's that, then. He's an uproariously funny bastard. Not funny ha-ha, just funny in his unpredictability and openness and honesty and the way his heart pounds on his sleeve. You're either with him, or against him. Garcia has always been with him. 'Me and Sunny talked a lot out there,' Irons says. 'It's really good to see him—it's been ages. We've surfed a lot together over the last ten years, but we started catching up a little too much. I started thinking, "Wait, I've got to surf a heat here. I've got to get back in the game right now".' Garcia has to paddle in because the waves have done a runner. It's belittling to be forced to paddle in after losing a heat, but life could be worse. Four walls, wash basin, prison bed.

And then Taj Burrow, world-title aspirant, appears. He laughs with an official. He ruffles up his already ruffled-up hair. He jogs up the beach with a slight limp which would be more pronounced if he wasn't trying so desperately hard to cover it up. You've never seen so many Firewire boards. There are Firewire shortboards, Firewire malibus, Firewire everythings. Nev, old boy, it's looking good. Reynolds has been grabbed by a voluptuous Israeli girl who wants his photo and more. She holds Reynolds' arm and whispers good luck. He says thanks with an I-have-abso-fucking-lutely-no-idea-who-you-are expression and runs after Burrow as if he wants to be saved. 'The next two are the heats of the day,' Irons says. Thanks, Scoop. Burrow's knee is heavily strapped. Still, nobody knows.

Burrow goes left and gets a 5.5. Reynolds goes right but the wave runs out of puff before he does. Irons cranes his neck. Reynolds goes left and detonates with a 7.5. The day heats up. Quick exchanges, Burrow playing catch-up, getting close but not close enough. It's a frustration dream. Reynolds is *right there* but then he's gone again and Burrow's knee hurts and it's messing with his head. With 30 seconds remaining, Burrow tries a big backhand air and he's getting all Montaj on Reynolds and the orange paint on his board spins like a firecracker and if he lands it he's home, but he falls so he's going home. Or straight to France. Burrow is out of the one contest this year he was convinced he was going to win. He has a shower and goes upstairs to the surfers' area. No-one makes a noise. The ramifications of this result are immense, but everyone is so ho-hum about it. Burrow could not afford another early loss. He still stays quiet about his injury. Right there, with that unsuccessful air, his campaign threatens to go up in smoke. Unless Fanning self-destructs. The ninth at Teahupo'o is now one of his best eight results. The commentator says, 'And Dane Reynolds goes into round three,' with all the astonishment and urgency of a sleep-in. You feel like running up to the tower and grabbing the microphone: 'DON'T YOU PEOPLE GET IT? TAJ BURROW JUST LOST. DON'T YOU SEE WHAT THAT MEANS?'

An hour later, you're having a coffee at Captain Mauria's in San Clemente. Chairs and tables are on the footpath. The main street is Del Mar. BMWs and Chevrolets fill the diagonal parking spaces. You eat a Bombay Melt and you're thinking, Burrow has lost. Taj Burrow has lost. Fanning has moved further ahead without even turning up. You recall Burrow standing next to the shower for a second and staring at the ground. He's feared the worst, and it happened. For an instant, his face collapses. He looks away. A young wildcard with bum fluff on his chin has done him over. 'I feel kind of bad,' Reynolds says. 'I was almost rooting for him— Taj is just about my favourite surfer. I've always picked out his heats and watched him really closely. I'd be psyched if he won a world title. But I wasn't going to roll over and just let him win. It's strange to have taken him out. Just goes to show things can happen any-which-way in the ocean. That's how it seemed for Taj. Every time I had priority, the sets would come and even when I picked a small wave, it would run away. I don't know. It all just unfolded for me. That can happen out here. You never know when it might be your day.' You have never seen Burrow act petulantly after a loss and you doubt you ever will.

'Tomorrow is going to be a big one,' Reynolds says. Tomorrow is Reynolds versus Fanning, but the wonderkid thinks he's drawn Slater. 'I always really feel like it's an uphill battle against Kelly,' he says. That's great boy-o, but you're up against Fanning. 'It's overawing, really, when I'm surfing against Kelly. I just want to not get comboed. I don't want it to get embarrassing.' But Dane, dude, you're not against Slater, you've drawn Fanning. 'It's embarrassing when that happens, getting comboed.' BUT YOU'RE AGAINST FANNING. 'I never beat him.' Who, Fanning? 'Kelly. He gets the best punts of all time in heats against me. It happens every single time. I want to get him one time, just once. I think he goes hard against me to prove his point. Kelly is . . .' You don't want to walk away, but you have to. Can somebody please give Dane Reynolds a copy of the fucking draw? Parkinson needs 6.67 to beat big-arsed Jordy Smith with an unlucky thirteen minutes left on the clock. Another upset is looming. Burrow is watching. His right elbow is on the table, his face resting in his hand with a rueful, distant look. What could have been . . .

Thirteen minutes have become thirteen seconds. Seven seconds, and Parkinson takes off. Snap, snap, snap, more backhand snaps, but they're not enough. The judges can write down letters instead of numbers: GONE. The big South African man-child with buttocks the size of 76-ounce steaks has beaten him. Burrow has patiently posed for a photo and signed an autograph on his way back from his loss. Very decent of him. Parkinson will be doing no such thing. He runs through the crowd. He's wild. He knows what this loss means. He throws his board to the ground in the shower. It thumps and bounces and cracks on the concrete. He hurls his singlet away. He storms up the stairs and gets into his black jeans. Five ASP judges would be in caskets if looks really could kill. Parkinson storms to the judges' tower and tells them exactly what he thinks of them: not much. 'You're getting it wrong,' he says. 'You've been getting it wrong all year.' He puts on his backpack, grabs his two boards and leaves in a rage, head down the whole way, not so much as turning an eye to the iodine sky.

'It sucks for Taj and Joel, but it's kind of good for me,' Fanning says.

One of the big plasma TV screens is showing Bede Durbidge getting out of the water after thumping Luke Munro and unless you're grossly mistaken, there's a booga hanging from his nose. And unless you're even more grossly mistaken, there's a whopping great black-and-white sticker on his board. Can't be. Surely not. Don't joke about Bede Durbidge having found a sponsor. The cameras turn elsewhere and you run down to see it for yourself. And there's Bede Durbidge, the face of MADA. He has MADA stickers and MADA hats and what the hell is MADA? Its website says: 'MADA is not a name. MADA is not directly defined. MADA is a movement.' A movement? Bede Durbidge is being sponsored by a movement? 'Finally,' he says. 'It's great. At last I've got some support again. It makes things so much easier. The deal is for a few years—it only happened in the last week. They're the coolest people and I hope I'm with them for the rest of my career. Things were getting really tight. I'd been eating into my mortgage and I didn't have much money left at all. I've got two houses at Currumbin and I would've had to sell one in October if I didn't get a sponsor. It's the best timing. Awesome.' You take back a little of the sympathy you previously held for Bede Durbidge. Two houses? Still. Good on him. MADA make clothes.

'That's really bad for Taj,' Durbidge says about the demise of the world No.2. 'He didn't need that.'

Trendy SoCal dudes have their caps on backwards. Few sights in America hold the comedic value of a Southern Californian man with his cap on backwards and a nose so sunburned it's about to peel clean off. Dude, turn your hat around. The tide is fuller and the waves are amping up for Fanning–Reynolds and Slater–Machado. Machado has developed this cult following and a reputation for being some sort of spiritual surfing guru with supreme skills. But you don't get it. You just don't get the whole Rob Machado thing. The crowd has swelled to 5000, maybe more, whistling every time the Fanning–Reynolds match-up is mentioned. Karissa is sitting in a small temporary stand. She doesn't shout, she doesn't jump up and down, she doesn't gesticulate or make a scene. Half an hour before Fanning and Reynolds come out, the swell picks up another notch. The atmosphere rises. Showtime. Taylor Knox walks over and raps Fanning on the knuckles. He takes a front-row seat. Fanning dances on his toes. Behind him, studying him, looking him up and down, is Kelly Slater. Watching him like a hawk.

Fanning wrings the water from his red singlet, his board wedged between his knees. There is no expression on his face. The Cladough ring on his right finger is blinding. He runs past women's world No.1 Stephanie Gilmore without seeing her. They're both from Snapper but he doesn't even know she's there. He doesn't see anyone until he gets to Karissa and Griggs. For the last half hour he's given the impression he cannot get in the water fast enough; that the opening hooter will be the flick of his switch. The hooter goes and Fanning is straight onto a left and he hammers it. This is the world No.1 and this is why and when he blasts his last turn, his new-found American audience goes silent as though he's arrived on shore in possession of a severed head. They stare at him in silence. He swings around and goes back out. It's a 7. Nothing wrong with 7's.

But right behind him, Reynolds has lucked out. There have been nothing but lefts all day but he's paddling into the biggest miracle in an ocean since the parting of the Red Sea: a right. He takes off like a boy on a billycart with no brakes. His first two turns provoke the biggest crowd reaction since Kerr's ridiculousness on his last wave at Snapper. The wall forms perfectly. He rides it all the way to the cobblestones in front of a manic crowd. They're going ballistic. Three judges give him a 10. Drug test them for hallucinogenics. It hasn't been *that* good. His total is a 9.93. The heat is supposed to be fought out in short lefts but Reynolds has been given a long right and there will not be another. Reynolds' score is called and Fanning immediately falls as if he's fainted. Fanning can't match a 9.93 on the lefts. He needs a right—but there are none. He could stand on his head and not get a 10. Not that standing on your head is a 10. There are no barrels when you go left. The face isn't as steep. It's a physical impossibility to smash the lefts as severely as the rights.

Fanning keeps going left because he has to. He thumps six verticals: 7.83. The wind picks up from the north and the waves are going bad and it's all going pear-shaped. He needs the waves to get better, not worse. They're getting worse. Reynolds goes left and lands a reverse air and you can hear Slater, normally so introverted, talking manically in the background. Taj is out. Parkinson is out. Fanning is out unless he uncovers a 9 in this land of 7's and 8's. Fanning attempts the same air that Reynolds pulled off. He doesn't make it stick. He scampers back out and tries again. No stick. He's doing everything he can: floaters, hacks, reos, tail-slides, everything. But it's over. He's out. Mick Fanning is out.

Slater doesn't have to walk to the guy handing out the singlets for the competitors. The singlet guy takes it to him. Welcome to America.

Irons bolts out the back of the surfers' tent and laughs like Dr Evil: *phwoar-haw-haw*. Darth Slater is going a bit hyper. Fanning really is out. He's coughed up his worst result in a year. Slater strides to the water's edge to begin making the most of this unexpected opportunity. Karissa is slumped back in her chair, legs crossed, arms folded, as Slater walks past. She doesn't look peeved. She just looks a bit sad. Slater isn't as intense as Fanning. But he's not as casual as Burrow. He's\somewhere in between.

Fanning's reaction to the loss is more Burrow than Parkinson. He's pissed off, but holds it in. Some clown asks him for a photo and Fanning politely says no. He throws his singlet away. He kicks an advertising sign in quiet frustration when he thinks no-one is looking. He goes to the corner of the wooden viewing deck, his back to everyone. He shuts his eyes and grabs a steel rail as if he's holding himself up. 'I really feel like I did nothing wrong,' he says. 'Dane's whole heat was that one wave. There was one good right and good luck to him for getting it. That's just what can happen out there. When someone starts with a 9, it's pretty hard to catch up and I guess I just wasn't able to do it.' He starts raving about Reynolds. He's on auto-pilot. The title race is brought up and that's when Fanning trips on his words. 'I don't . . . I don't know. I don't know what to say. It's all been going great—until now.'

Reynolds is going through the same routine. Goes out, flares, comes in, has the voluptuous Israeli girl fawn all over him, hands back his singlet, goes home. He admits he was over-scored with his high 9. 'I don't know if I'm retarded, or what, but I thought it was about a 7,' he says. 'A 9—that was news to me. Everyone seemed a bit excited. I didn't think I'd surfed it that great.'

Jordy Smith says of one of his scores against Parkinson: 'I did one good turn and got a 7. I thought it was, like, a 4.' The men with pencils. Who are they to judge?

Slater pulls off a 360 against Rob Machado as though he's celebrating Fanning's departure. Machado is a cool dude with an affro but he doesn't look so cool when he's face-planting after an ugly turn. Machado is the owner of big and funky hair and a slow drawl like he's perpetually stoned and everything is right on, man, groovy, and supposedly he's good enough to ride a bed post, and he wears a headband and that's all well and good but after watching him surf for a few days, all you can remember is the sight of him digging a rail and doing a face-plant. You'll honestly never get the Rob Machado thing. It's their first man-on-man heat since their Pipeline showdown for the title in 1995.

The commentator has finally twigged to what's going on here. He's screaming that with Fanning, Burrow and Parkinson having bitten the dust, Slater can start making a charge towards world title number nine. You look at Fanning as he prepares to say goodbye to Knox and walk the mile. He's putting on his Blues Brothers-style sunglasses. Slater can make a charge? Tell Mick Fanning something he doesn't know.

Everyone who walks across the cobblestones looks clumsy because it's like walking across a pile of ten-pin bowling balls but Slater glides along as smoothly as one of the supermodel girlfriends he's taken on the rebound from Leonardo DiCaprio. 'I couldn't think of a better time for that to happen,' Slater says as Fanning hits the road. 'You know, I think I might be a little bit more intense if Mick was still in this because I'd have no choice but to win the event if I was going to start catching him, but it does take the pressure off. I know if I lose my next heat, a ninth isn't going to do anything for me. I need to go out and surf freely and look at it the right way. I need to get at worst a third to put myself in striking position through Europe. If I were to win here and better Mick and Taj in France, I'd probably be right in the hunt.' Eight of the top ten are out, and Irons hasn't faced barge-arse yet. It's carnage. 'To tell the truth, I could kind of feel it coming,' Slater says. 'This is probably the hardest place to beat the wildcards because you get real performers with a lot of contest experience. If you surf at a spot like Pipeline, they surf incredible Pipe but they don't have a whole lot of contest experience. People like Dane and Jordy and Rob can just blow this place up.' Dane and Jordy, anyway. 'I was picturing this round being one of the harder rounds up until the quarters or semis,' Slater says. 'I'm glad I've survived the wreck.'

To the possibility that Irons will lose to Air Jordy, who's being courted by Nike with rumours of a $5 million deal, Slater says: 'That might put all the pressure back on me. Everyone will be looking at me, going, "Is he going to capitalise on that?" That's EXACTLY what we'll be doing. Look, whatever happens, however you want to look at it, I'm starting to like this situation.'

Irons is an arrow. He's slender. He has one of those clearly defined and elongated faces. His board looks as skinny as a dart. He has sharp features from head to toe, nose to tail. Jordy Smith—6'2" of prime South African beef—sticks out his gargantuan glutes and bludgeons a left for an 8. Let's not worry about the incrementals.

Some Day

It's 8 and a bit, but let's just call it an 8. The VIP tent is full to overflowing. Oversized cans of Fosters and Red Bull fill a fridge which never empties. There's seafood, fruit, rice and four widescreen plasma TVs. The place cannot fit in one more person. Irons' posse is loud. He squirrels onto a decent left and yells at the judges. Then Smith finds a Reynoldsesque right. Kids, eh? Smith is working it, working it, looking for a punt to launch from. The Big Ship Jordy is speeding, now he's airborne, now he's landing with his oversized tail pointing to the shore, spinning around and completing a 360. He puts his hands in the air like he just don't care. How good is an ice-cold beer on a hot day? Irons is out. 'These waves are shit, man,' says one of Irons' clan. 'They're just shit.' Slater's support crew give stiff high fives like the nerds at the school dance. Nine of the top ten are gone. The only one left is the king.

You expect Irons to come in, throw his 22-board quiver in front of the next Amtrak and then torch the joint. Light a flamethrower and toss it at the wooden judges' tower and tell them all to get fucked and he'll see everyone in Hawaii in December when there will be waves of genuine consequence and then we'll see who can get through their heats. But he places his board carefully in the rack in the way a bespectacled librarian adjusts the books on her shelves. Left, right, back to the left, back where he started from. In the shower, fast becoming the barometer for mood swings, he shrugs and says: 'Didn't capitalise. It happens.' He's strangely OK.

Reynolds, looking like a schoolboy in black shoes, black pulled-up socks, dark paints and a collared shirt, talks with Slater. The old bull and the young bull. They disappear into the shadows of the day's close. Garcia stays behind, staring at the ground. He's in deep thought. 'I don't want this to end,' he says.

Judy Slater was a tomboy who worshipped the sun. She'd spend her days in a chair on the beach smothered in coconut oil while her kids built sand castles. They were bored to tears soon enough. Slater's eyes drifted to the sea and a life changed. A quizzical look from the boy. He was five. He stood there and watched the waves for hours and he did not know the rest of his life would revolve around the water. All his friendships, opportunities and satisfactions would stem from an association with the sea that was only just beginning. What a photo that would make now. A five-year-old Kelly Slater standing on the sand as waves rolled up to his feet.

The king's fourth round is against Fred Patachia. The queue at the Coffee And Doughnut House is ten-deep. The contest will be won by nightfall. Another stretch of four straight heats for the winner. Who needs coffee? Who needs fried dough smeared with eight tonnes of sugar and cream? Alright, but make it quick.

Hummers are parked illegally, daring anyone to book them. It's hotter than Hades—you could throw a match into the brown scrub on either side of the path and start a raging inferno within seconds. And then you see the waves. They're on. Trestles is on!

You've spent the first six days clueless as to the reasons this place has been awarded such infamy. But now you're sliding along a curvy 200-yard right and the walk along the path has gone from being a pain in the neck to a quaint attraction; the rumbling trains have changed from an eyesore to an idiosyncrasy. The cobblestones look amazing in the sunlight. And on the seventh day, there is surf.

Slater comes out of a deep sleep. He's been dreaming about waves, their shapes and how he fits into them. He is agitated, anxious, tense, abrupt. Chewing his fingernails. You've never seen him so uptight. When Mick Fanning and Taj Burrow present you with a gold-plated invitation to join them for the deep end of the world-title race, you still have to accept it. There's a rugby league coach back in Fanning's birth place of Penrith who has a coffee cup on his desk which says: What Would You Do If You Knew You

Could Not Fail? Slater is so on-edge that he's *early* for his heat. He beats Patachia in a canter. Here comes the kitchen sink.

Steve Slater worked at a club in Cocoa Beach called The Vanguard Lounge. In 1966, Judy was working as a secretary in Washington DC. She went with a friend on holidays to Cocoa Beach. It was a stone's throw from Cape Carnaveral. The Americans were embarking on the *Apollo* space project and astronauts were among the biggest celebrities in America. Judy was at The Vanguard Lounge with a captain from the Special Forces. He wanted to take her for a walk along the beach. She said no. When he grabbed her and said a more forceful yes, the bouncer intervened. The bouncer was a surfer, swimmer and fisherman. He drove her home later that night. The bouncer was Steve Slater. The next year they married.

Kelly was eight when trouble started brewing at home. Every time his mum wanted to throw his dad out, Kelly would cry until she relented. He went to a contest with Steve. They stopped on the way home so Steve could have his 'two beers'. When two had become three, four, five and six, Kelly asked his dad if they could go soon. Steve yelled at him to stop his complaining. They didn't get home until the following day.

The king's quarter-final is against Taylor Knox. They've always been firm friends. Knox is square-jawed and likeable. There's also something a bit vulnerable about him. When Knox took his daughters to Disneyland earlier in the week, Mick and Karissa tagged along. When Knox went to a San Diego Padres' major league baseball game, Fanning was his sidekick. Knox is a veteran and Fanning says, 'Let's go, grom,' and Knox laughs like you do when a mate is taking the piss. Only mates are *allowed* to take the piss. Slater and Knox usually chat during their heats. This time, nothing. Slater is a whir of activity. He has Knox comboed. You're reading *To Kill a Mockingbird* and there's a line in there about courage: 'It's when you know you're licked before you begin but you begin anyway and you see it through no matter what.' Knox is licked but soldiers on.

The waves are molten glass with divine and curvaceous rights. No barrels, but the walls are sublime. Knox is furious at being comboed. Why do some people only get going when they're angry? He beats the crap out of the first lip he sees. He bashes the next. Clobbers the third. Clubs the fourth. Every time it looks like closing out, Knox gathers just enough speed to keep beating, bashing, clobbering and clubbing. He finishes with an up-yours to no-one in particular on the beach. And the judges give him a 10. If Slater is beaten in the quarters, Fanning's loss will not have been such a disaster. 'I was so fucking mad when I took that wave,' Knox says later. 'I just wanted to hit it as hard as I could a couple of times.'

A ten. 'That was scary,' Slater will say. 'I'm thinking, "Lucky I've got my two good waves already".' Slater has a 9.73 and an 8.5. 'I'm thinking, "OK, he's got a 10. I've got my 9.7. I've got to outdo his next best by more than .03." I timed when I got my waves real good because that put the pressure on Taylor. The pressure was still on him. He got his 10, but he still needed an 8.6. It's no mean feat to get an 8 but he did already have a 10, so I knew he could do it.'

With two minutes left, Knox takes a wave in the mirror image of his 10. But he's not as angry as he was before. Slater is paddling out right in front of him. Knox's first hack is the biggest of the contest. Jesus Christ. He'll get an 11. 'I was stressing,' Slater admits. 'I was paddling straight at him and it was such a good wave it could have won him the heat. He flared up on it, did two turns, the second turn was insane, too. I started paddling really slow, going, "No, no, what's he doing?"' But right when Taylor Knox had the chance to beat Kelly Slater, he blew it. 'He dug his rail,' Slater says. 'And I was, like, "Yes!". I wanted to claim it myself. You've got to have a lot of luck go your way.'

Knox could have slayed the dragon. No, no, no. There is no worse feeling than being underwater after a fall. It's too late to make amends. There's nothing you can do except float around like the piece of trash you are. 'I could hear the crowd when I got my 10 and I was so pumped,' Knox says. 'I was back in the heat, but I still needed another big score. I knew there was going to be another chance. An 8-point ride was definitely doable. I picked the right wave and... I don't know what happened. I got past the hard part and lost it on the easy part. I'm a little perplexed right now about why that happened.'

Here's why it happened. Taylor Knox choked. No shame in it. It's the reason why Greg Norman can hit the green with a thousand straight nine-irons then miss the one time he needs to hit it stiff to win the US Masters. It's why Andy Roddick will go three months without missing a forehand then belt one into the grandstand at five-all in the fifth against Roger Federer. It's the moment when an athlete has to ask himself: Can I really win this? Do I *deserve* to win this? It's not always easy to take what you want. Knox didn't really expect to beat Slater. He hoped he had some sort of chance but spent most of the heat trying to salvage pride. When the serious business of actually winning began, he became immobilised, hypnotised, paralysed. 'I'll try not to beat myself up too much about shoulda, coulda, woulda,' he says.

'You know, that's up there as a heat for me,' Slater says. 'That was probably me at my best. I probably paddled about a mile in that heat. Some of those rides were two hundred yards long and I got, like, seven of them. I was looking at that heat as being against the hardest guy I would have to surf against today.' Which doesn't say much for anyone else left in the draw—Troy Brooks, Pancho Sullivan, Jeremy Flores, CJ Hobgood, Ben Dunn and Tom Whitaker. 'These conditions suit Taylor as much as anyone else in this contest,'

Slater says. 'He's not known for having the highest scores, but when he's on, he's on. He has this sort of air of being unbeatable when he's really on. He doesn't get into that mode a lot, but I thought he was getting into that mode today. His board looked good under his feet, the waves were coming up, there was more power. I didn't want to leave anything to chance. I played it just right. It was pretty magical. The fog blew off, the swell was hitting, the tide dropped in, the wind backed off, it got glassy again, that blue water, the rights turned on and the sun came out. It's a relief because I'm at the point now where I'm definitely going to be satisfied with the result here regardless of what happens for the rest of the day. Having Mick and Taj and those guys bomb out wouldn't have helped me unless I'd come this far.'

Slater acknowledges the Fanning–Knox mateship: 'There's a lot of irony there. Taylor is my best friend on tour—one of my closest friends, full stop. He's always been a really loyal friend. I've had a lot of heats where everyone is pulling the voodoo doll out on me, but Taylor has been the lone voice rooting for me. But he's travelling around with Mick Fanning now. They're on the same team and I could see it in his eyes—he really wanted to beat me. Part of that was for himself and our little battle against each other, but maybe a part of that was to help out Mick.'

Steve Slater's cancer spread to his lungs. He couldn't eat. He was fading away. Slater lost to Parkinson at Snapper Rocks in 2002. He was planning to stay in Australia until Bells, but Judy rang and said he should hurry to Florida if he wanted to see his father alive again. Slater called Al Merrick and told him his father was about to die. Merrick asked Slater if he wanted company, and the answer was an emphatic and grateful yes. Steve Slater had never met Al Merrick, who has always been like a second father to Kelly. Steve and Judy Slater told each other they loved one another, and Kelly heard previously untold stories from his childhood. Steve told Kelly to appreciate his life every second that he still had it. And he told him to go and surf. They had three weeks together at the end.

A bird swoops and as it veers towards the national park, its left wing skims the water ever-so-softly.

The king's semi-final is against his conqueror from Bells. Whitaker speaks of 'knocking over the yanks'.

'When an Australian is in the race and he's leading, or a couple of Australians are leading, you know you can help them out if you beat guys like Kelly,' Whitaker says. 'It's going to be one of the best heats of your life, but it might also help bring the title back to Australia. It's about time that happened. Beating Kelly at Bells, maybe there's the added bonus of helping out a mate. It feels good to help someone out.' But Slater wins handsomely. 'I owed you that,' he tells Whitaker. Another win, another lunge at Fanning. 'I can't think of a better scenario given the position I was in a week ago.'

The king's last hapless victim is another of Fanning's stablemates at Rip Curl, Pancho Sullivan, in a bloodbath of a final. Fifty grommets paddle at him when the siren sounds and he says 'Party Wave!', wanting them all to ride to shore with him, but they hold back and let him go alone. Slater stands on the stage with California in the palm of his hand. 'It had been a somewhat lacklustre year before this,' he says. 'I surfed well in the first event but didn't make the most of it. I had contests here and there where I didn't pace myself and peak at the right times. This time, I've peaked in the right heat, against Taylor. I could feel that heat was really going to

be the climax for me. I knew, for sure, I wasn't
another heat that good.'

Slater has finally broken Tom Curren's record for the
wins at the place where they both secured their first.
is in every word, every movement, every joke, every la   , every
handshake. 'It'll be nice to be able to sit down and look back on
this one,' he says. 'To be able to steal that record from Tom, it's a
lot of years of hard work, but part of me is kind of sad. I was kind
of dreaming that me and Tom could stay on the same number
forever. That would have been kind of neat, but someone else is
going to come along and better what I've done. Jordy is the great
white hope right now, him and Dane. Those guys have big careers
ahead of them and a lot of years to go. Somebody can always set
a standard, but somebody else will come along and set a new
standard. While I've got the time and the desire, I'll stay around
and do what I can. I could potentially throw in the towel right now
and feel great about it—but I won't. This is very meaningful for
me. It's a beautiful day.'

All the gushing talk is about a ninth world title and Fanning's
alleged stage fright and how it's one thing to lead the ratings but
another to keep it and Slater keeps nodding and he says: 'I'm
definitely feeling pretty good about it all right now. I've almost
gotten as many points as possible in the last two events, a first
and a second. Before that, I had two events where I didn't even
want to be there, which was a bummer. I just lost my focus there.
I don't feel like I was intensely focused this week, either, but I
was just really calm and happy and enjoying it. After this, I've got
the chance to capitalise.' On the failure of Fanning and the rest
of the top ten to even reach the fourth round, Slater says: 'I'm
totally astounded.' Three days ago he expected it to happen. Now
he's astounded? 'To have those guys lose like that, I mean, honestly,
there's no way I could have drawn up a better possible scenario
for myself. It's the best possible situation. I told myself to just

concentrate on where you're at right now. Don't concentrate on the big picture until it's over. I just kept thinking, "Don't get ahead of yourself. You haven't won a contest in over a year. Just take your time". Getting second at Jeffreys kind of pissed me off. But it made me hungry. That's two contests in a row now where I've bettered Mick. All of a sudden I've had a couple of good results and it could be a momentum shift if I work it the right way. I've just gotta do the right thing with it. If I'd had the year Mick has had so far and then all of a sudden he'd caught up with me, I'd probably be a bit frustrated right now.'

You grab that quote and give it to Fanning. You cross paths near the portable toilets. Cross paths, not swords. 'Kelly was never out of it,' he says. 'He's a gnarly surfer and always will be. As soon as everyone lost, he really turned it up and surfed amazingly well. There were no surprises in that for me. I knew he'd make the most of it. That's why he's got such an incredible record and why he's got eight world titles and the rest of us have none. I had such a good roll for, you know, a year or so. It was bound to stop somewhere and I guess it had to be here. It's alright. It's done. I'll just start again and regroup and keep going and try to go mad in France.' Fanning heads for two of the more spectacular regions on the planet—the Bay of Biscay in France and the Basque country in Spain.

You doze off down near the cobblestones and you can still see Slater at the top of his waves, that mesmerising pause right when he gets to his feet but just before he sets off, when he seems to have all the time in the world to look left, look right and look left again before purring into motion. And you keep seeing that desperate look on Slater's face when he looked into the live webcam and said, 'Hey, wait, wait. Can I just say hi to my daughter?'

You're on your way to the after-party at the OC Tavern. There's a bar called The Rib Trader on the way. You take a look inside. The smoke is so thick you can't see six inches in front of your face. You go in. There's a band doing a George Thoroughgood cover. Rough as guts. There are orange and yellow lights and a guitar riff goes for five minutes and knocks you off your feet. The guitarist is one ugly critter. His eyes are jammed shut, his back is twisted, his lips and tongue are skinny like a lizard's. He's wearing a black baseball cap with the words 'Big Su' on it. You get a Budweiser. It's a place for the beaten, downtrodden and defeated. On the wall, there's a picture of the owner's son. He's standing in a trench holding a gun. He's at war. Is that what a father wishes for his son? That when he grows up, he'll go to war? There's something tragic about that photo, and this entire bar, but you can't leave. You stay there all night and hear all their tales of woe. Jones says he feels eighteen in his heart but then he looks at his haggard 67-year-old face in the mirror and he knows he'll never be eighteen again.

12

Omens

L iz could *feel* trouble.

'I was worried about Mick and Sean, as unexplainable as it was at the time,' she says. 'A few months before he died I heard a big crash—at the same spot on Boundary Street. There were always accidents there but this time I was panic-stricken. I couldn't see it properly but I had to run down to the site because I just felt that it might have been Sean in his Mini Cooper. I had to go and make sure it wasn't him. It seemed illogical but I had to go. I ran about three hundred metres and saw that it was another car. I went back and told a friend that it wasn't Sean. But from then on I stayed really anxious without knowing why. I had fears but no real reason to have them so I just asked the boys to let me know where they were at night and if they stayed out, I wanted to know they were safe. They always did that for me.

'The night of the accident, I was supposed to stay in Brisbane but at the last minute I wanted to go home. I just couldn't stay. Thank God I didn't. Sean and Mick were going to a friend's party.

I remember the last thing Sean said to me. It was cute. He kissed me and said, "How do you like the smell of my new deodorant, Mum?"'

And then came a deep grief no-one should have to know.

'Mick came into my bedroom and woke me, screaming that Sean had been killed,' Liz says. 'I don't even know what time it was. My immediate thought was that he must have been stabbed. I got up and went out to the hall and saw all these men standing there. They were plain-clothed police and two older friends of my boys. It was shock beyond words. I can't describe it. It didn't feel real. Mick wanted to go down to see Sean but I couldn't let him see anything. I didn't want that to be the last thing he remembered about him. I didn't see Sean before the funeral because I couldn't face seeing my beautiful boy without his life force. I wanted to remember his kiss.'

13

High noon

QUIKSILVER PRO
LA GRAVIERE/SANTOCHA/LES BOURDEINES,
HOSSEGOR AND SEIGNOSSE, FRANCE

Sometimes in this world, you have to fight to get back what someone else has taken away. Sometimes in this life, you have to march in and take what you believe to be yours. Sometimes, you have to just storm into a room and holler: 'This is the way it's going to be.' There's an American preacher called Reggie Dabbs. He's a huge black man with a booming voice. The veins on his neck, temple and forehead pulsate uncontrollably when he delivers a sermon. In 2007 he'll preach to 1.2 million American high school kids. When a fight breaks out, and a gun is produced, he will offer to take the bullet. He's been going to Australia for fourteen years in an attempt to lower the spiralling teenage suicide rate. For some reason, you think of Mick—not Sean and Liz, but Mick—when you hear him bellowing a sermon with all the sweat-laden passion it is possible to muster. To paraphrase Reggie Dabbs, with the capital words shaking the walls: 'My best days are in front of me, not behind me. If last year was good, just you wait and see what this year is going to bring. You know how I live? Man, if I drop dead tomorrow, it's all good. Don't even try to resuscitate me. You know why? Because to be honest with you, I'm living each day as if it's my last. This is my last sermon, and I'm sweating so hard I'm gonna sweat myself all the way out the building. Tomorrow, if I'm still alive, I'll preach another sermon like it's my last. When I get up, it's my last breath. It's my last breakfast, my last lunch, my last dinner. If you don't live like that, YOU'RE MISSING SOMETHING. You can think you're out, but you can tell yourself you're in. You can think you're dead, but you can tell yourself you're alive. The world can say no way, but you can say MY WAY. You know what we all get to do? WE ALL GET TO CHOOSE.'

The beauty of France for Fanning isn't in the snow-capped Pyrenees. Or the lure of the French Riviera. The beauty of France for Fanning is in having to wait only a heartbeat after his Californian catastrophe for the chance to make amends. If he'd opened the door marked *rankings* in such welcoming fashion at J-Bay—Kelly, maaaate, come on in, make yourself at home, you know where everything is—he would've had six weeks to stew on it. Six weeks to dwell on the worst result of his career. Six weeks to say to himself, *I didn't do anything wrong...did I?* Six weeks to try convincing himself, *I'm not going to blow this...am I? Shit, maybe I'm already blowing this.* For all the permutations and adjustments to be made after taking into account the throwaways, and just the inherently unpredictable nature of this moveable feast of a tour, there's one stone-cold fact in all of this: Kelly Slater knows how to benefit from the competitive misfortune of others. He relishes it like a vampire relishes the sucking of warm, thick blood. He knows how to win a world title. Mick Fanning does not.

'Having Mick lose at Trestles only helped because I won it,' Slater says. 'If you're in the Tour de France and some guy bombs out one day, you've got to have a good day to take advantage straightaway. When I went for my seventh world title, I really intently watched Lance Armstrong in the Tour de France that year.

I learned a lot from him about being competitive, about how to strike and win. If you want to be the top guy, you've got to be able to make something happen at the right times, no matter what position you're in. You have to be able to pounce if the opportunity is there. I'm hoping I can make that happen. I'm just trying to get to the line.'

Burrow's right knee is coming good thanks to round-the-clock treatment, but now his other knee has been tweaked. It's only a niggle, but niggles mess with your head as much as a snapped tendon. 'I was devastated at Trestles, but it panned out pretty well,' he says. 'Besides Kelly still being in it, it's like the event never happened. Apart from Kelly, no-one did anything. It's crunch time. Someone is going to get on a roll, and I want it to be me.'

Everything is Slater, Slater, Slater. All the talk, all the hype, all the posters, all the newspaper stories, all the magazine covers, all the billboards, everything. There's an exhibition being staged with a new heat format—devised by Slater. When Fanning departs the toll booth at the entrance to Hossegor where you pay 1.50 Euro to get through, he sees posters of Slater. So many times, when he's listening to the commentary, he'll be hearing Slater's voice. Fanning and Karissa have a couple of days of travel, packing and unpacking, the buzz from being in a new place for a new event. Fanning doesn't have time to think too much. Which is a blessing. Rolling stones gather no moss. There's not enough time for his mind to drift to places he doesn't want it to go. There's not enough time to *think*.

The main street. Women have ruffled hair, jeans, loose-fitting shirts and knee-high leather boots. Smoking kills, but it can also make you look very fucking cool. Hossegor is an attractive town. The single-storey brick Office de Tourisme boasts of 130 shops, restaurants, pubs and nightclubs within walking distance. The main attraction is the towering, three-storey Cafe de Paris. It looks magnifique from the outside but inside is neither here nor there.

It's bare and grubby. There's a bistro and a bar downstairs. Lunch costs 11 Euro. There's seating outside behind a plastic curtain where backpackers trawl the worldwide web. It's really pretty average but then again, fill a mausoleum with friends and you'll have a good night. It's the people, not the place. Everything is understated. Skinny people wear thin-rimmed spectacles. They take small sips from their tiny cups and puff quickly on slim cigarettes. Motor scooters zip around. A couple are arguing in the far corner, yelling with their faces close. She bursts into tears before an embrace so passionate it takes your breath away.

Opposite the Cafe de Paris is the Quiksilver store. It looks like a ski chalet. Slater, Slater, Slater. There's no escaping him. Another poster of him. The shop is right by the traffic lights on Avenue de la Gare. You stroll in. One of Slater's 6'5" boards is in the window. And one of his wetsuits. There's a 5-metre-wide shot of him from Hossegor last year, sitting on the shoulder of an epic right-hander, looking back towards the shore. Al Merrick boards are everywhere. Slater's FCS K-3 fins are next to a different model bearing Occhilupo's name. Slater's are sold out, bar one packet. Occhilupo's rack is full. Slater, Slater, Slater. An entire wall is covered with a shot of Slater in a trench coat. He looks like a mugger. Something called Boardriders TV is on a flat screen—showing Slater catching waves. DVDs are on the shelf—and they have *Letting Go*, the story of how Slater won the 2005 world championship. There's a token poster of French surfer Miky Picon but in reality this whole shop, this whole town, this whole event is being billed as Slater, Slater, Slater. Anyone round here heard of Mick Fanning? An ad for Quiksilver says: 'Our Roots Run Deeper'.

It's a five-minute drive from the Cafe de Paris to the beach at Hossegor. Trees line the streets. It's all so tidy. Gardens are immaculately kept. Black-and-white signs keep saying HOSSEGOR and they remind you of the signs in Tahiti saying TEAHUPO'O 10. Sports fields are on either side of the road and they're mostly for football. Margaret River in Western Australia has a similar feel. You're on a small two-lane road. Brown leaves line the footpath like you're driving through a romantic movie. Up and over the Canal de Hossegor. There's a fisherman in navy overalls. A golf course to the right, prim and proper. White homes have blue borders around their windows. More motorised scooters on your tail. Then beach. When the endless sand bars around Hossegor are working, you'll get more serious shacks than you'll know what to do with. Seignosse and Les Bourdaines are down the far end of Avenue de Tulipes.

Keep a secret? It was in Hossegor last year that Fanning and Parkinson sat down, gritted their teeth and vowed to end the reign of Kelly Slater. The king was running away with another world title and enough was enough. Two men who had known each other for thirteen years decided he had to be stopped. And if no-one else was prepared to do it, they would. They looked each other in the eye and made a pact that Slater's eighth world crown would be his last. They took immediate action. Parkinson won the next event— Hossegor. Fanning was in the final with him. Slater's lead in 2006 was already so vast that he wrapped up the title in Mundaka the following week, but Fanning and Parkinson remained good to their word. 'It didn't matter if it was going to be me or Mick,' Parkinson says. 'We just wanted to stop Kelly winning world titles. But, yeah, I wanted it to be me.'

Fanning recalls: 'Joel and I were sitting ninth and eighth in the world at the time. We were like, "You know, we can't just let him keep beating everyone like this". We sat there and said, "Right, whatever it takes, let's just go out there and smash whoever is out in front". We did it from the next event. We just wanted to work together to get ourselves as high as possible on the ratings. We've been best mates for such a long time. Now I'm out in front, he's probably making a pact with someone else.'

Slater, Slater, Slater. France has provided some scares. One of them was only brief; the other far too long. His first world title in 1992 coincided with Occhilupo losing his mind. At the Lacanau Pro, Slater was walking down the street on his way to a game of pool. He was carrying his own cue. Occhilupo saw Slater and tried to run him over on his push bike. Having failed there, he jumped off his bike and assumed his best karate stance. 'You got a karate stick, huh?' Occhilupo yelled. 'You wanna go? I'll go ya right now!' Occhilupo buried his boards in the sand and they were run over by a beach tractor. He would point out to sea and ask directions back to Australia so he could start swimming home. He was off the tour by the end of the year.

In 1991, Slater was staying with a group of Australians at a place where extra-curricular activities with obliging females were conducted in the loft. One of the Australians had spent the night up there with a woman. Slater climbed the stairs to check her out the next morning. She was 40-odd and large. Feeling lucky, punk? Next to her, a pram with her baby in it. In her hand, the latest ASP rankings. Anyone on the list could have their wicked way. If they wanted. It was an especially big if. No, no, no, said Slater. I'm not ranked. And that was expected to be the end of it. Except the woman wouldn't leave Slater alone when he returned the following year, marching in front of him, hollering his name and yelling, 'I love Kelly Slater!' It was embarrassing. She was a nutcase. She followed him to Australia in 1993, found his unit and slept outside in her van with her child. Back to France, and she camped on his not-so-welcoming mat. He couldn't leave without stepping over her. She wrote $E=MC^2$ on his door in lipstick, whatever that meant. He went to the airport. There were no flights for a few days. He slumped in a chair as his stalker fired off photographs from point-blank range. He wanted to hit her, but didn't. The police escorted her out. Next night, she turned up at a bar he was at. That's when he snapped. Slater poured a beer over her. She slapped him across the face. He grabbed her by the arms and begged her to go away. She returned with six Frenchmen and attitude. She was telling the men about the American insulting French women. Slater was in a phone booth when the men started pushing and shoving him. Tom Carroll and Ross Clarke-Jones pulled up in a car. Clarke-Jones went crazy, that scary-crazy which makes people run a mile, and the Frenchmen disappeared into the night. The woman stayed. Three years of aggro came out. Slater pushed her up against a wall. Right next to them was a 12-foot drop. He could have sent her plummeting over the edge. He admits it crossed his mind. Her son was bashing his legs and screaming at him to let her go, and so he did.

He never saw the woman again.

Slater beats Aritz Aranburu and Fred Patacchia in round one with a walloping 17.76. 'There are some amazing waves out there,' he says. 'Someone is going to score a 10.'

Fanning goes out and gets a 10. Run that up your flagpole and see who salutes. He rolls up his sleeves like you do at work when there's a lot on but you're kind of looking forward to it all. Any number of Slater's band of arse-kissers are proclaiming that Fanning is getting stage fright and he won't hang on now the race is down to the final few months. But in his first heat since Slater's revival, Fanning blasts 19.43 to flatten Mick Campbell and Marlon Lipke. Fanning barges onto four waves in his first five minutes and they're ferocious. He has his 10 and an 8.5 when Lipke has 2 points and Campbell has 0.23. It's brutal. 'I don't know if I've ever seen anyone surf that good,' Campbell says. 'He just had this *look*. He was a machine. I'm good mates with Mick and I know he's a great guy but that was like I didn't even know him. It was a bit frightening, to tell you the truth.'

Burrow comes last against France's wildcard Miky Picon and Kai Otton but his first rounds have become so routinely bad it would be more of a shock if he won.

Occhilupo becomes all misty-eyed when he beats Bede Durbidge in round two. Occhilupo has lost twelve of his thirteen heats this year in the worst streak he's ever had the misfortune to experience. 'I'd be lying if I said I didn't have a tear in my eye,' he says.

Parkinson and Irons remain long shots for the title. Parkinson downs Gabe Kling in round two. 'I hate the second round,' he says. 'HATE IT. That's the stressful part of our job. I'm glad it's over.'

Burrow scrapes through a terrible second-rounder against Lipke by 9.3 points to 8.73. The knee problems are still a major irritation. 'I didn't feel comfortable at all,' he says. 'The knee rattled me. It was a close one. Horrible times. I can only improve, I s'pose. I knew if I lost that one I wouldn't be finishing number one.' The early rounds come and go and Irons bombs out and his heart isn't in this and then comes high noon, the most crucial and telling one-hour period of the year.

Hossegor has a corso leading to the beach. If you've ever been to Manly in Sydney, it's like that. There's an ice-cream stand. A pub/restaurant called Rock Food has a green counter under French flags and the beer is served in plastic cups. You've been there ten minutes and your bare feet are covered in grime. You order an Occy: chicken wings, fries and sweet chilli. Want flies with that order? You get them. They're everywhere.

Slater, Slater, Slater. He's on another television. Across the corso from Rock Food is Dick's Sand Bar and the Hotel de la Plage. Dick's Sand Bar has photos of Fanning from years past. He looks to be having a fine old time. You could do a triple somersault off the balcony of the Hotel de la Plage and land near a little hole in the wall that is the clubhouse for the Hossegor Surf Life Saving Club. Standard dress: wind cheater. Further along, the sand-coloured Hossegor Surf Club. It smells of damp wetsuits. There's a boiling kettle to the left. On the sand, surfboats are face-down and sleeping. There's a cluster of hotels, villas, cafes and assorted other buildings, and then a long stretch of nothing but sand dunes and vacant property as if no-one can decide if they really want to build here or not. Men in slippers throw breadcrumbs to the seagulls. A sign at the surf club says: 'Leave The Ocean The Way It Is.'

Round three. Fanning will go the entire year without being beaten in round two—because he's the only surfer on tour who is never in it. An army of glamorous sunbathers usually lay about Hossegor like lizards on a rock. It's not the way they look, but the way they are. They laugh, smoke cigarettes and swim. They're free. But at noon on September 27 at La Graviere, it's cloudy and rainy when the clock strikes noon. Painted skies. A 6- to 8-foot pulse. Offshore wind and dredging waves. You start reading into everything, looking for hints, clues, smoke signals about who is going to do what and when and to whom. The business end of the year is here. No longer can Fanning play down his chances because you never know what may happen later in the year. This *is* later in the year.

Slater just yawned. What does that mean? He's bored? He's relaxed? He's been up all night? Out all night? My god. Kelly Slater has been out on the turps all night. Burrow is laughing out loud. He's up? He's going insane? Fanning isn't here. He's sick, he's . . . Are we going to Pipeline? Can it end here? Mundaka? Brazil? High noon begins with Kelly Slater's third-round heat against a Tahitian by the name of Mikael Bourez. You wouldn't recognise Mikael Bourez if you tripped on him. He's never been in a tour event. He starts with a couple of decent rides. Mikael Bourez is looking surprisingly good. And your mind starts whirring into another round of over-activity: Slater is going to lose. It's not his day. He's past it.

He's too old. He starts with a 1.07. Kelly Slater can burp and get a 1.08. He won't win a world title. He's going to get a 17th and the degree of capitalisation he's been banging on about since Trestles will be zero and Fanning will be world champion, but then Slater gets a 5.83 and he's back, baby, and he's going to be world champion unless Burrow starts ripping again but even then it'll be Fanning. No, it'll be Slater. Burrow. Maybe it'll be the mathematical possibility: Parkinson. There's a lot of moving water, a strong rip. Slater does a late take-off and ducks inside but the crumbling white rocks clip him hard enough to make him stumble and fall. The rocker bends under his front foot and his board breaks.

These high-performance sticks are not the ones you buy in the shops. They're as light as a feather. And they're flimsy. They're Formula One race cars compared to whatever you're getting around in. Slater is on the sand, frantically looking for his caddie. His tail pad is blue and black and shaped like a target. His caddie is nowhere to be seen. Being a caddie is not the hardest job in the world. You stand on the sand holding a spare board. It would seem to be fairly difficult to get it wrong. But Slater's caddie has managed it. Bourez is riding solo. He's starting to look *very* good. So much priority, so little time. Wherever Slater's caddie is, he's not where he should be, near the water's edge. Fanning is in the next heat. He has three boards. He believes one of them goes better in lefts. It takes a while to get your head around that. A board can be better in lefts? He swears on it. Bourez gets a barrel. The lip brushes his cheek. And in that instant, with Kelly Slater falling behind in a heat for the tragi-comical reason that the greatest surfer there has ever been can't find a board, the beach goes quiet. Mikael Bourez leads. Mark Richards and Tom Carroll are among the throng. Superman raises his eyebrows.

High noon.

Fanning is preparing to take on Miky Picon in the heat after Slater's. His pre-heat routine is as precise and methodical as a samurai preparing for battle. It's disciplined. It's planned to the last second. He waxes up. His board is studied in microscopic detail for the slightest irregularity. He stretches on his oversized rubber ball. He looks up when Slater's dire situation is being called over the loudspeaker. There's a look of mild surprise—gulp—but then it's gone. He goes back to waxing his board. Back to his own world. *Don't let anything in. Don't.* Fanning has shaved his head again and you swear on your mother's life that Mick Fanning is more formidable with a shaved head.

Slater is all over the shop. He doesn't swear, but where's his fucking caddie? Anyone got a board I can use? It's so ridiculous it cannot be true. Burrow rubs his hands together. Slater's caddie: great work, pal. Finally, the caddie appears and hands over Slater's spare board and the king bolts back out and moves up the point. There are only slim pickings. For Kelly Slater, there are desperately slim pickings. It's overcast and spooky and quiet at La Graviere, as cold as Bells. Surely he can't lose to Mikael Bourez. Surely the master of Heat Poker can't blow this hand. Six minutes to go, and he needs a 6.18. It's a shallow break and you're taking shallow breaths. Fanning is walking to the water and he's displaying the customary tunnel-vision, but inside, his mind is doing cartwheels. *This is it, this is it, this could nearly be it.* Bourez has done all he can. His cards are on the table. Beat that. All Slater needs is a 7. Momentum is impossible. When you've got it, you can't slow down if you try. Nothing bothers you and nothing feels impossible and riding a wave on a surfboard becomes as natural as taking a breath. But Slater has no momentum. This wave is no good and that wave is worse and who does Mikael Bourez think he is and all these waves are too mushy and bumpy and wrong. There are four minutes to go and the clock ticks so slowly but so fast and Fanning is sitting on the shore doing his meditation and his eyes remain closed. All Slater needs is the chance and they've been coming all his life and all his career—one wave when he *really* needs it to make everything alright again, to restore the order in his world. They're called 'Kelly Waves' on tour and they're his last-minute saviours. And here it comes, another Kelly Wave. He needs a 6.17.

Now, Kelly Slater has scored 10's at Pipeline and he will forever be remembered as the first surfer to poll 20 out of 20 in a heat, at Teahupo'o, and he's done all there is to do in this game and 6.17 is piffle and he is up. Nice, nice, good, sweet, amazing how many times Kelly Slater gets out of jail, milking it, and there's a rollicking little section out in front. Here we go again, the shit and then the smelling like roses. A burst of sunshine, right on cue. Slater's eyes bulge. So far, he's only done enough for a 5. But he sees another section forming out in front and there are definitely another 2 points over there—as long as he makes it. He's bouncing his board, *so* desperate, trying to get all the speed he can, the section shaping up in such a perfect little wedge that he will go 6.17 and beyond and Fanning will feel like he's been punched in the stomach because Slater has escaped with a victory that was so close to being a defeat. Slater will be into the fourth round and it'll still be game on and won't anything ever make Kelly Slater go away? Yes. The ocean. Slater isn't allowed onto the next section. The wave goes fat and the next two more crucial little points run off without him—he should have started pumping earlier, but it's too late now—and in that one moment, that single instant when this seemingly unremarkable La Graviere right-hander scoots away without Kelly Slater on it, both Superman and Mark Occhilupo begin to suspect that this is going to be Mick Fanning's year. Or Taj Burrow's. Slater has missed his chance by a millisecond. He watches the lost opportunity slide away with an incredulous look. *What? Where are you going?* He frantically paddles out to try again because maybe that wasn't the Kelly Wave, maybe that's still coming, but there's nothing up there and what the ocean wants, the ocean really will always get.

High noon.

Fanning's heat starts at 12.30 p.m. and he smashes his first wave beyond recognition. They'll need dental records. He takes another wave almost immediately and pulverises it so severely that the first wave ain't feeling so bad anymore. Fanning catches two waves in the first three minutes and his surfing is immense. Opportunities can be frightening. They can make a man run and hide, or they can make him better than he's ever been. Mick Fanning is not afraid to take what he wants. He catches waves like an addict needing another hit. One isn't enough. More, more. On the beach, a big flag: 'Fanning #1'.

His surfing is fast and vertical. There's no bullshit in anything he does. More and more he's been using this phrase: *Let's do this.* He's doing this right now. There's not so much as a glance in Miky Picon's direction. He's the Scarlet Pimpernel. Picon seeks him here. Picon seeks him there. The Frenchie seeks him everywhere. Fanning surfs with INTENT. Everything is done with such great intent. He latches onto nine waves in 30 frenetic minutes and it's 1 p.m. and by the end of high noon in the big sand basin that is the Bay of Biscay, Mick Fanning has blown Kelly Slater out of the water. They weren't surfing directly against each other, but they were. Slater still had enough of the bastard mongrel in him to win Trestles when Fanning bombed out and now Fanning is on his way to returning the favour.

Picon takes one late wave that very faintly threatens to snatch a victory that would have brought Fanning to his knees. The vocal French crowd and various other stickybeaks do their best to pressure the judges by reacting as though Picon has cured cancer. Fanning hears the roar. Surf crowds are more knowledgeable than you think. If someone needs a score at the death, they'll roar if they think they've done it. This was some roar. 'Yeah, that was a big heat,' Fanning says. 'I heard the crowd go crazy and thought it was a 9. I was ready to cry. Glad it didn't come to that. I'm out of here. I'm going to get ready again and regroup for the next part. I just wanted to get the win and get the roll on. It's a pretty big day. When Kelly lost, I knew that was a pretty good opportunity to space myself. But I can't get carried away. Taj and Joel are still in the event. I just have to keep focused and keep doing what I've been doing all year.' The gap between Fanning and Picon is immeasurable but on this occasion, it's six points.

'That heat of Kelly's—that's such a key moment,' Occhilupo says. 'Kelly had that wave and it could have given him the score he needed to get through and he's the kind of guy who would go on and not lose another heat all year. But it just didn't connect. If anyone could've made the score on that wave it was him, and he was, like, an inch off. He could have survived that heat and reached the finals so easily. That's all there was in it. One inch. That was so huge. And then Mick came out and made him pay for it.'

Fanning keeps an extraordinarily low profile throughout this event. He's nowhere to be seen when he's not in the water. He's been quicker to the draw and high noon is over and you're so stunned by the ferocity of Fanning's assault you need to go and sit down. Later, Slater is casually strumming a guitar with Tom Carroll. The joy of a varied life—one part goes up the chute and you can fall back on another. It's slow and small when Fanning returns to take on South Africa's Ricky Basnett in the fourth round. You keep thinking of reasons why Basnett will win but then Fanning goes out and smokes him.

Taj Burrow keeps chugging along. He's been craving the chance to dominate a heat after a succession of just-enough wins and he finally fires against Royden Bryson. 'I feel a lot better after that,' he says. 'I just felt like I surfed better. I spent a little time warming up. I've never had a sore knee before and it's still toying with me. Even in my first few heats here I was just a little bit tentative, just not really confident. I've been free-surfing as much as I can to get it feeling good. That heat makes me feel like it's working properly.

Some Day

I saw Kelly and Andy go down—I don't like to get the voodoo doll out on people but you see a few results like that and it makes you realise you can make up some ground. I'm starting to feel confident.'

Joel Parkinson is hanging on. 'My heats have been frustrating,' he says. 'Just ugly wins, I guess you could say. But I'll take that win any way I can get it. Andy and Kelly are both out but I don't want to think about that. I just don't want to. It's screwed with me a few times before.'

Parkinson and Burrow will meet in the quarter-finals. It's another vicious draw but another blessing for Fanning. His perfect scenario is for Burrow to lose to Parkinson before Parkinson bombs out in the semi-finals. The waves are small, and so is Burrow. Eddie wouldn't go in this. He wouldn't be arsed going out at all, but Burrow goes ape in the tiny stuff. Eight. The knees are coming good and so is his mood. 'Classic Taj,' Carroll says of Burrow's opening salvo. Parkinson fires back with an 8.83. 'Almost too relaxed for my liking,' Carroll says. 'I like them more on edge.' Burrow is 5'9" and 68 kilograms—the perfect build for rippable little French beach breaks. Parkinson is a bigger guy at 6 feet and 80 kilos, which is not too good for these dainty little French two-footers. Burrow sets off, bends and springs as if he's been fired from a pistol. Parkinson is more upright and takes more time to get moving. Just a bit. A little cavern opens up and he tries to go in.

'Get tubed!' Fanning shouts. 'Get tubed!'

Parkinson gets tubed. He celebrates with an air reverse. It's the kind of syphoning runaway barrel he's been getting all his life on the Superbank. His right knee is low on his board. He throws his hand out. It's not a macho first-pump, more of a *Got it*. His scores couldn't be more favourable if Fanning had bound and gagged ASP head judge Perry Hatchett and grabbed one of the pencils himself. Parkinson has 18.33. Burrow has an 8 and an 8.7, outstanding, but not outstanding enough in this exalted company. Parkinson can't shake the thought of Burrow's miracle comeback from a similar position at J-Bay—'You lose heats during the year that you never really get out of your system'—but there's to be no repeat here. Parkinson wins and another key result has gone Fanning's way. Momentum. You'd sell your soul for it. The weather had previously been cold with onshore winds and rain but with Burrow, Slater and Irons all out of the draw, Fanning takes a walk and conditions become pristine. Momentum. You'd kill for it.

'I'm pretty upset,' Burrow says.

Parkinson is not out of this. If he can win the event, then go deep into the draw at Mundaka, never say never. 'It was one of the biggest waves to come through,' he says of his heat-winner. 'I was in the right spot and it looked just like a perfect little Snapper barrel. It ran off perfectly and I just sat there in a perfect little spot. And I was able to get that little air section at the end.'

Fanning's quarter-final is against a complex individual who can match him for brooding intensity. Brazil's Neco Padaratz will attack Fanning with the viciousness of a pit bull terrier. Your mum sends a text: 'How's McFanning going?' Her knowledge of surfing is second to none. McFanning goes off like the nuclear bomb dropped on Mororua. Hammer and tong. He starts with a 9.5 and the crowd is going nuts in a way it hasn't been going nuts before. 'There's a little bit of fire there,' Carroll says during his commentary. 'He's ready for this.' A deep bottom turn. He lights up. The waves are disappearing but he already has a 9.5 and a 6 shoved down the back of his wetsuit and Padaratz has nothing but a 6.33. Padaratz is anxious, dazed and confused. Fanning's back foot is always adjusting, footwork no-one sees from shore, but he's up on his board, back a bit, back up again but not too much. Padaratz thumps the water. He's been beaten and even worse, not for one second has he remotely felt like he was a chance.

'Mick is full of heart,' Carroll says. 'I love the passion, the commitment to every turn. Wow.' And again: 'Wow.'

Padaratz is a shell of his former combative self and Fanning is hurtling into the semis. He's running up the sand. Catch me if you can. Padaratz says what Fanning dare not: 'This is his time.'

The last three heats are at Les Bourdaines. The paddle out can be a bitch when the waves are big, but they're not big today. Warnings at the start of the walk over the dunes say, *Plage Non-Surveillee*, but a lack of lifeguards will not be mattering. The red roof of the Les Bourdaines clubhouse doesn't stand out as much as the Allez Jeremy banner at the entrance to the first of two car parks. It's a little out-dated. Flores has been knocked out by South African Greg Emslie forever ago. The clubhouse is covered with graffiti and there's a small community of villas next door. A gravel road leads to a bullring under floodlights with rickety old grandstands big enough to fit about a hundred people. Since when do they have bullfights in France? The path to the beach is wide enough to drive a tractor through. There's wire fencing on either side, manicured grass at the front of the clubhouse and weeds embedded in the dunes. Further along there's a tennis club and putt-putt golf and one of Slater's favourite hangouts, the Cream Cafe at Seignosse. Wednesday night is open mic night and he's not against the idea of turning up and hogging a guitar for an hour-and-a-half. You peer through the windows. There's a drum kit and pool table but no Kelly Slater.

The first semi-final is Parkinson against Emslie. Fanning will follow them out against Troy Brooks. It's past 3 p.m. by the time there's a worthy wave. For five hours they've been on hold. Five long hours. There's the odd set limping through, sorry and pitiful. The swell is on life support and peaks at only 3 feet. Offshore wind and light rain. Parkinson goes out to face Emslie, a friendly man with a choir-boy's haircut. He's the hard-working type. Invariably, one of the first in the water every morning and one of the last to leave at night. He's constantly a little bit sunburnt. Emslie is light and skinny in the mould of Burrow. Parkinson has to escape another whippet. He won't sink like a stone but he's going to have his work cut out—again—to hit full speed. This is killing Burrow: little left and right shooters. He'd be chewing them up. He'd reached the last eight and polled a commendable 16.7 but he's still been rubbed out. Can't take a trick. The crowd is the largest seen in France for donkey's years. The tour will survive without Kelly Slater. It won't be the same, but it will survive. Judges tell the spectators to sit down because they can't see. The sand is damp and the locals are not entirely happy about getting their bony little French backsides wet.

Parkinson opens proceedings with a decent left: 5.83. You keep thinking the day will be decided by a Reynolds-at-Trestles-type right, just the one fluke occurrence, and Parkinson is on it now, racing along but the score sheets only say 6. The waves are as clean as a whistle and you know what, they're starting to look quite good. Emslie is a wave magnet every time he goes out. You've surfed with him at Trestles and he was on auto-loop. He goes left and his toothpick of a frame sends him top-to-bottom without his needing to pump. The judges hand him an 8 and they must be stoned. An 8? Parkinson was previously only a mathematical possibility of winning the title. Now he's only a rough chance of getting through this heat. The crowd is in their winter woollens and the free-spirited sunbathers with their devil-may-care cigarettes are but a memory. There are two waves in each set. Emslie takes the first and goes left. Parkinson takes the second and stalks him. A direct comparison is possible because they're both in the one slow-mo frame. Parkinson is in the pocket because that's where the points are. Emslie is hanging outside. With so much riding on this heat for Parkinson, the judges take their time, watching more replays than normal. There are few more important words in the criteria than the need to be 'in the most critical part of the wave' and so Parkinson is given 8.57 and Emslie is admonished with a 4.83.

But Emslie learns his lesson and pulls in tighter for a 7 and Parkinson is left needing a 7.77. The Phantom takes off, goes left, changes his mind and goes right, goes back left . . . stuff it. He doesn't know where he's going. Emslie lands a cautious floater and they give him another 8. Give us a break. Parkinson is getting frustrated. It's slipping away. He needs an 8.86. He gets air, but not much. Fanning walks to the water's edge. Another key result is going his way. Emslie has the lead and he can sit there and block Parkinson from waves then, when the 9-pointer comes through, *if* it comes through, he can take it because he holds priority. Parkinson bows out and shakes Emslie's hand and he remains a riddle that cannot be solved. Barring a bona fide miracle, another year is going to pass when Joel Parkinson is not the world champion. That can't last forever. Or maybe it can. Look at Burrow.

Straight off the gun, Fanning's onto a right and he has a 7 before anyone has taken their seat. They're hollering on the sand. Fanning's second wave is a 5.17 and Brooks is in combo-land. Fanning is catching everything in sight like he has to be at work in half an hour. Brooks is in no such hurry. He only wants two waves. Two belters. He waits out the back. Fanning wants a different board and gets one immediately. Griggs is a more reliable caddie than whatever bozo has been working with the king. Slater is told Fanning thinks one of his boards is better in lefts and he says: 'Are you serious? Humph.' There's a paddle battle, and Fanning wins it. But Brooks is about to be rewarded for his patience. While Fanning has been a whir of activity closer to shore, Brooks has bided his time. The risk is that he could sit out there all day and catch nothing but hypothermia. But the possibility is that he could come across the kind of curl presently rising above his head. It's the biggest wave of the day and it belongs to Troy Brooks. The result is an 8.5.

With fifteen minutes to go, a long time but not much time, really, just enough to make you famous, Fanning is after a 7.51 and now he's the one under pressure and Slater is starting to think maybe things aren't too bad if Fanning doesn't reach the final. Fanning keeps looking at his watch and why does time always start going so fast when you don't want it to? Then he hits the afterburners and gives a quick demonstration of *it*. His finishing burst is a slamming of his first on the table. There are eight minutes left. He's still behind. A third would be OK, but disappointing. He won't have done to Slater what Slater has done to him at Trestles. Eight minutes. Bang, bang, bang, fist-pump, out the back, onto another wave and he hasn't even received his last score yet. He's in a car no-one else has access to. There's an extra gear none of the others can find. Brooks' jaw drops to the floor. Those two waves were insane given the circumstances. Fanning was in trouble a second ago. He's not in trouble anymore. He's replaced a 6 and a 7 with an 7 and a 9.97. The latter should come with exclamation marks. Nine-nine-seven!! All these blokes can surf, but the great ones know when to. Maybe, just maybe, Mick Fanning is becoming great.

When the 9.97 is read out, and the crowd is making its almighty din, that's the moment when you look at Michael Eugene Fanning and think: world champion. Surely this bloke *deserves* to be No.1. He ends up with eleven waves, a broken board (the one that goes best in rights), a place in the final, a hug from Brooks and a ratings lead so huge the only thing that might be able to stop him is a broken leg or hamstring torn clean off the bone. Don't even think about it.

'I had him under pressure,' Brooks says. 'But that's why he's number one. He came back and smashed me.'

Fanning gets out of the water and doesn't look at a single one of the thousands of faces staring at him. He makes a bee-line for the surfers' area and says he doesn't want much of a break. When you have this kind of momentum you hold it like you do your children. He pours another round of water, the best of the brain foods, down

his throat, whacks his earphones back on (you will read his playlist
if it's the last thing you do), stretches once more on his exercise ball
and has Griggs whisper another round of sweet everythings in his ear.

Emslie agrees to start the decider earlier. The first South African
in a tour final since Thomson in the 1970s blows his first wave in
the way people blow it against Slater just because they're surfing
against Slater and they feel like they have to do more than they
can. Fanning starts with his trademark slice and he's building another
house. His first brick is an 8.5. The tide is filling in too much and
the waves are getting fatter and slower. Emslie is trying to do what
Fanning does, but he can't. That's no insult. Ninety-nine per cent
of the world's surfers would kill to do what Greg Emslie does. But
Fanning is faster. Fanning is steeper. Fanning is better. At the end
of the day, he's just better. Emslie tries an alley-oop for the first
time anyone can remember. See? He thinks he has to do something
he's never done before. Slater is on commentary duty. He's wearing
a navy blue jumper and sounds flat. 'He flows so well between his
turns,' he says of Fanning, and he almost sounds envious. Fanning's
second wave is fast and furious and a 9.93. Emslie needs 18.44.
He could sit out there till Christmas and not get it.

What a joyous feeling for Fanning, basking in the glory of it all,
surfing free of pressure, surfing in the knowledge he simply cannot
lose this final. Slater vows to keep fighting at Mundaka but he admits:
'It's really coming down to the wire. I have to be real about the situation
I'm in. I have to win two of the three events left. I've won those three
events before—but not in a row.' There may be no escaping this
particular pile of shit. What you'd give to see them go head-to-head.
'It's a funny thing with me and Mick,' Slater says. 'We don't have that
confrontational rivalry. Mick has had that with Parko in a way, and
I've had it with Andy. We've had some battles out there, me and Mick,
but not as passionately as you'll get in some other scenarios.'

Emslie limps in. 'I could see that Mick was in a pretty good
rhythm and I just didn't know how I could break it. He will be world

champion this year and he could do it for the next three years. That's the stage I think he's gotten himself to. I've beaten a lot of the top guys. I beat Joel and I've beaten Taj and sometimes you feel like you can break those guys. But against Mick, I didn't think I could break him. I've never beaten him and I don't know if I ever will.'

Mick Fanning has felt the full wrath of Kelly Slater's fury at Trestles—and turned that on its head. He's suffered his worst contest in a year—and responded with one of his best. His greatest fear was having a rampaging Kelly Slater coming at him in the second half of the year and it's happened, but he's pulled the dagger from his heart and recovered. He's fought to get back what Slater was threatening to take away. He's stormed into the room, the water, the contest zone and hollered: 'This is the way it's going to be.' He's competed like an impassioned American preacher lives. Every bone, every muscle, every fibre of his being has treated every wave as though it's the ocean's last breath. When he gets up, it's his last ride. It's his last take-off, his last barrel, his last 10. If you don't surf like that, YOU'RE MISSING SOMETHING. After Trestles, the doomsayers thought he was out, but Fanning told himself he was in. They thought he was dead, but he proved he was alive. The constantly judgemental surfing world said no way, but Fanning said MY WAY. You know what Mick Fanning did in France? He shook the walls. You know what he got to do? HE GOT TO CHOOSE. He's marched in and taken what he believes to be his. He's streeted away again and if Slater cannot haul him in, who can? 'There was no way anyone was going to beat Mick here,' Campbell says. 'I watched him the whole time. He had all that pressure on him but he came out and blew everyone away. That was as dominant as anyone has ever been.'

This is getting close. The only man who can beat Mick Fanning now is Mick Fanning. He wants this so much. The only risk is that he wants it too much.

14

Next

What happens when we die?

Seriously, what happens?

In this day and age, when we know everything about *everything*, isn't anyone trying to find out?

15

Rock bottom

BILLABONG PRO
MUNDAKA/BAKIO, BASQUE COUNTRY, SPAIN

A man is injured when a car bomb goes off in the 700-year-old town of Bilbao, just a 20-minute drive from Mundaka. You suspect the bomb was planted by the mustachioed guy you nearly dropped in on at dawn. You keep seeing him and he's watching with seedy sideways glances and you're convinced he wants to kill you. You imagine him puffing on a cigarette, slitting your throat under a single street light, then going back to his cigarette. You take a walk and accidentally-on-purpose get lost. Mundaka is a maze of alleys and narrow back streets where stone-aged men wear berets and smoke cigars and play cards on square tables and spit and cuss when they lose. A pebbled path leads to the tip of the windswept point.

There are chest-high weeds as though no-one goes out here anymore. It's quiet—*too* quiet. Vultures sit on the top of an abandoned monastery. They stare and fill you with unease. You imagine them gouging your eyes. Your walk becomes brisk and in circles. Circles never end. There's the rhythmical beating of a drum but you can't see anyone. You stop and spin on your heels, then push through the brown grass and hear the blood-curdling scream of a child. You want to run. You hurry to the monastery and it's frightening. The stone walls have three windows about 15 metres from the ground. The windows are large black circles—lifeless eyes. Giant wooden doors are protected by cast-iron gates. The gates have been welded shut and the windows have been blacked out and what's in there? The walls are stained and decaying. You touch the iron gates and have to pull your hand away as if you've been scolded and you really cannot understand why. Another baby cries and as God is your witness, you are hearing the screams of children without being able to see them. You leave and do not return. The last thing you see on the point is a metal cross forged to the jagged rocks.

It's not small and wooden, but it's a cross.

You should have taken Fanning at his word at Trestles. When you bailed him up right when Kellymania was going through the roof, you doubted he was as calm as he claimed to be. You thought it was talk, just meaningless talk, when he said all he could do was go to France and go berserk and get the wind back in his sails. You thought he was trying to convince himself more than anyone else. Back then, he said all he could do was win a couple of heats and see where that particular plan of attack left him. He looked relaxed, but you doubted he really was. He looked confident, but you thought it was an act. He seemed totally and utterly unperturbed by the arrival of Kelly Slater in his face and you didn't believe any of it. More fool you.

The narrow and winding roads of Basque country. Everywhere you look, it's fantastically lush and thick with green. Farmhouses are nestled at the foot of mountains. There are endless valleys, more mountains, more valleys, sheep and homes on the hillsides, the road traversing the steep cliffs with the Atlantic down below stretching forever into the darkness. Rain hits the windshield hard while impeccably dressed elderly women stand beneath umbrellas.

Sandstone buildings crowd one another as if there's only enough room for a hundred buildings in Mundaka but they've gone for 150. The doors of Hotel Mundaka are deadbolted. Your room key doesn't work. You sneak behind the front counter and grab the master key, but that doesn't work, either. You're locked in. Hotel Mundaka: you can check in any time you like, but you can never leave. You wander around the creaking wooden floorboards of the hotel but there is no way out. Your room has a view of the bustling street below and through a small window you can sit and watch the world go passing by.

You escape at 6.30 a.m. It'll stay dark until almost eight. There's the stench of prawns and raw fish from the harbour. Mundaka's roof is thick with stars. Mark Occhilupo looks over the bay. With his hood up and standing alone in the darkness, he's as calm and motionless as a monk. He's barely breathing, his eyes sneaking looks at the stars, the medium-sized hillside staring back at him. He's not smiling but it feels as if he is. In this half-light, half-darkness, he looks like a man at peace. His son, Jona, is in a pram.

The blackness peels away and Mundaka reveals herself as though the curtain is being pulled across a Spanish oil. The black turns into a melting pot of blues and greens. You're perched on a cliff at a rivermouth in the middle of the Urdaibai Biosphere Reserve. Birds of prey hover and dive into marshlands. On the far side of the estuary is Cape Ogono: more dense greenery, another S-shaped road leading back to France. The island of Izaro is right in front of the Ria de Mundaka and blocks more swell than it should. Lines are pushing through the rivermouth but the tide is too full for anything to break.

'Maybe manana,' Occhilupo says.

What?

'Maybe tomorrow.'

Yeah. Maybe tomorrow.

Mundaka has extreme tides as though every night is a screaming full moon. Laida is a beach at low tide but doesn't even exist at high. Contest director Mike Parsons appears and he's on his mobile phone. 'Flat as a freakin' lake,' he says. Thick fog fills the river like smoke trapped in a funnel. The moon, the stars, the early arrows of light, the chugging of the fishing trawlers heading out to sea, the earthiness, the ripples of struggling waves lapping against the rocks at the bottom of the cliff are all majestic.

Fanning's first heat is against Kai Otton and Manoa Drollet, but it's not at Mundaka. It's at the back-up beach of Bakio because Mundaka has no waves and that's the risk with this joint. You can be here for three months without getting a solitary wave. The first time you go to Bakio, sadly, is not the last. 'Where's my Dream Tour singlet?' Irons asks with as much sarcasm as he can muster. The small straight-handers are a joke. Irons is mocking the waves and he has every right to but the lack of oomph will make the results no less important.

'I just have to go for broke,' Burrow says. 'Mick did well winning France but it was a hard one to swallow. I really wanted to do well there. He had a good run to the final, and I came up against Parko. That was tough. The conditions probably suited me a little bit more, just because they were smaller rights, but Parko is good in anything and he just jagged this crazy little barrel in really small surf. And then he lost. It's given Mick a jump on everyone and there are only three events left but that can be enough. I'm just so hungry to win this one. I have to step up and win two out of three. I can do that. I'm going to go mad.'

Burrow is the most fit he's been since J-Bay. 'I've been thinking about the race a lot, all year, and now it's coming down to the end,' he says. 'I'm thinking there's three events and I've got to try to win them all. It feels like it's all gone so fast and we're down to the last run and the world champion is about to be decided. I'm like, how did we get to this point so quick? Mundaka can be great when it's working, but it gets a bit boring when it goes flat. I've spent a lot of time in my room banging keys on the internet. Managed to sneak to France yesterday and have a little surf. But when it's good here ... I snuck down here one year when I was in France and it was as good as it gets. Six to eight feet in the barrel from start to finish, fast and hollow and thick. It's fickle, but it's amazing. It's just hard to get a good day out there.'

Slater beats Spain's Hodei Collazo and Fred Patacchia without getting his scalp wet. Collazo is staying at Hotel Mundaka. You saw him at breakfast and thought he was the concierge. Finally, Slater and Irons agree on something—Bakio is a dud. 'You don't want to surf in waves like this,' Slater says. 'It's not all that different to Florida. Actually, I think Florida is probably bigger, maybe twice the size. Maybe we should have gone mobile to Florida.' Kelly Slater, comedian! 'If I'm here,' he says, 'I'm here one hundred per cent.'

Parkinson does a few half-arsed stretches that border on a comedy routine, then slays Cory Lopez and Gabe Kling. 'I was really hungry,' says Parkinson. 'I paddled and hunted. It's not over till it's over. I'm frothing to surf heats. I just want to surf more and more, keep it alive.'

Fanning disposes of Kai Otton and Manoa Drollet. On not losing an opening heat all year, he says: 'I'm proud of that. But it's not over until the fat lady sings. There are three events left. You can make up a lot of points in those three events. There's still enough time for these guys to catch me.' Ah, piss off. It's over. You think. Stick a fork in it, this pig is done. *You think.*

Burrow has lost to Mick Campbell then drawn Drollet in round two. It's like getting a bye because if there's one place where a Teahupo'o charger will be lucky to score a point, it's Bakio. You can bet on surfing and there are bucketloads of cash to be made. All you need is a reliable swell chart at the start of the day because certain heats, in certain conditions, are beyond any semblance of doubt. Taj Burrow and Manoa Drollet in 2-foot Bakio dribble is one of them. It's such a fait accompli that the pros have wagers about whether Drollet will reach double figures. He finishes with a grand total of 2.74 to Burrow's 16.5. 'The waves are good for doing airs and stuff,' Burrow says. 'I like fooling around in little waves. Hopefully I can get on a roll and get some confidence going.' Confidence, confidence, confidence, the never-ending search for Taj Burrow's confidence. 'I'm just getting warmed up,' he says. 'I had a dream last night that I won this contest and that everything opened back up again in the race. It was cool, a nice little dream to wake up to.'

Next morning, Occhilupo is back on the cliff with Jona. 'Mick has put so much time and effort in this year,' he says. 'Surfing and training—he's done everything he could possibly do. He's a good guy. We surf a fair bit together and we're quite close and I'll be proud to hand it over to him if that's what happens. He's not there yet, but he's getting closer. You could tell from the first day he was going to be dangerous. He's always been dangerous, but there's been something extra in him this year. He's the most focused guy on the tour right now, I'm certain of that. Even the heats he's lost, they haven't been poor heats.'

You're yet to hear a bad word about Mick Fanning and there's a perception he's proving you don't have to be a prick to win. Occhilupo isn't sure. It depends on your definition of prick. 'You know, you've still got to be mean in your heats,' he says. 'Sometimes there's a situation where you can block someone to stop them from getting the wave they need, and you've just got to do it. I find myself in a winning situation and I know if I just paddle over to the guy and block him . . . It's just common practice. Sometimes you don't do it and afterwards, you're beating yourself up because you know you should have. You've got to do it all the time if you want to win a world title. When you're in the water, sometimes you do have to be completely selfish about it all. It can be hard for someone like Mick if it's not always in your nature, but you've still got to do it. If you don't, other guys are going to do it to you and that's worse.'

The Raging Bull nestles Jona into his boulder of a shoulder. He's still one of the first guys checking the waves every morning. He still loves the tour but not even he can do it forever. 'I haven't really thought about next year too much,' he says softly. 'This has pretty much been my life.'

Occhilupo lives near the Fannings and he kisses Jona hard on top of his head when he's asked about the night Sean and Joel Green died. 'They were really sad times,' he says. 'They really were. Everyone stuck together when it happened, and they still do. Everyone keeps saying it, but it's true—you just have to celebrate their lives. That's what everyone does. It was such a sad one. It brought everyone closer together. Their lives were short, but they had good lives and I guess that's the way you have to look at it. Mick has such a good support crew of people around him now. There are a lot of people helping him, but he'd be stoked to do this for Sean. It would be an amazingly emotional climax to the year if it were to happen.'

Occhilupo is eliminated by Tom Whitaker in the second round. No-one celebrates when they beat Occhilupo. 'I don't even feel like I'm in my own body,' Whitaker says. 'I was so nervous about surfing against Occy at a location that is like one of his second homes. I'm lucky I even kept my board under my legs to get two good waves. I had four or five sleepless nights and the jelliest legs I've ever had in competition just thinking about surfing against him.' Not that it's at Mundaka. It's still at stinking Bakio.

But the swell is building. Hour by hour, the tide drops and Mundaka's bank starts to appear and it really is building before your very eyes. We're on. The sun is out. It's not warm, but it's not cool. The coastline is one of roughed-up rocks and stone paths carved into ancient cliffs. We're on. A disgruntled fisherman has to pull in his bait because he's been casting out near the contest zone. Kids are playing in the concrete courtyard of Mundaka College. Waves start breaking at low tide and there's an energy on the cliff. The energy of the ocean. It gets into your system. But no heats are held. We're off again. And back to shithouse Bakio. You drive through a forest of ten-storey trees that's like a scene from *Lord of the Rings*. A church is perched atop an island and it could well be the most magnificent building you've ever seen. There's peak-hour traffic in the harbourside town of Bermio. More straight-handers at Bakio landing like a deflated balloon. There's no crowd and no atmosphere.

Burrow quietly gets changed in the car park. He strips down from his blue hoodie and climbs into his wetsuit. It's just Burrow on his own with fast music coming from his rental car. It's a grey Volkswagon Passat, if you want to know. Registration number 3251ZH76, if you *really* want to know. His spare board, yellow wetsuit and black backpack are in the boot. Three empty one-litre bottles of water are on the passenger-side floor. White sneakers are under the glove box. Receipts are shoved into the compartment between the front seats. 'May as well get wet,' he says. Burrow walks to the sand and the only other creature within a hundred metres is a sleeping dog.

Irons loses to Hodei Collazo and a person of suitable authority pulls out a calculator and says he's no longer a mathematical possibility of winning the title. Irons isn't even pissed off. He's given up the ghost. One theory on Andy Irons: with his marriage not far away, he's finally found what he was looking for in *Blue Horizon*—happiness. And that's sucked the life out of his previously unrelentingly single-minded desire for computer points and cash. Another theory is that he's over the tour and suffering burn-out after nine straight years and needs a year off. *Another* rumour is that he has been in drug rehab with Lindsay Lohan.

You grab the finest espresso this side of Milan and wait for the call. Burrow goes round the sleeping dog and the closer he gets to the water's edge, the faster he walks. He breaks into a run and he's in. Surfers invariably run like the wind when they get near the water. They're so close to where they really want to be. Bakio feels like a ghost town. Hundreds of apartments hover over the beach but there's no sign of life in any of them. There's not so much as an open window. It's creepy. The whole day is called off and it's been a wasted trip and there still hasn't been one heat at Mundaka. Nobody wants to see the Bakio Pro. Burrow comes in. Cameramen ask him to do a 'YEW!' as if he's had the greatest surf of his life. He returns to 3251ZH76 and it's another lonely scene.

Drenched from the rain, bored stupid after standing around all morning, you realise the Dream Tour isn't always so glamorous. That the waves aren't always so flash. There's always tomorrow, though. Maybe manana. The beauty of surfing: there's always manana. Burrow grabs lunch at Atallya. He digs into a ham and cheese concoction next door to a church with rotting walls.

A heavy-set woman is selling fish on the harbour. She's wearing rubber gloves. Her shoes and clothes are splattered with blood and intestines. She guts and fillets the fish for each customer with a knife as long as her forearm. She has a fat neck and this is not a woman to be trifled with. You walk the streets. The apartments above the street have those tiny balconies with a metal railing and enough room for two people. Old men stand up there and smoke cigarettes in their white singlets and they squint when they look at you through a cloud of their own smoke. They stand there for hours. Days pass with no waves. There's not much to do at Mundaka. You attempt to swallow your own tongue.

Fanning goes to Bilbao, the biggest town in the Basque country, and pays his 12 Euro to see a Picasso exhibition at the Guggenheim

Museum. It's an astonishing building where paper-thin titanium panels shimmer in the light like a school of salmon. Paddle boarders stand in the middle of the rivermouth. Parkinson and Occhilupo push their thick 10-foot boards onto waves and float so far down the river they disappear. They're mischievous little kids with high-pitched giggles. You tell Occhilupo it looks like fun and he says, 'It *is* fun!' Forever young. The surf is no good again and the forecast is no good for too long. This is the pits. Parkinson, Irons and Burrow are in a restaurant overlooking the park where the European premier of Trilogy is underway. You expected more. There's great footage but it feels like an ad for Billabong. You could be wrong.

Lake Mundaka refuses to change. It's Groundhog Day. Every morning you wake up and get into the same jeans and T-shirt and walk down the same side of the street and go across the same park and see Occhilupo at the same spot pushing Jona in his pram and you go past the same security guards, who are sitting in the same seats, and the same pasty-faced workers are in the canteen and the same heavy-set woman is gutting her fish and the coffee is in the same plastic cups and the surf is flat again.

There are miniscule bursts of waves when the tide is just right at Mundaka and Emslie—who's usually parked in the breakfast bar of the Hotel Mundaka with coffee and his mobile phone—is out there with Fanning. You join them, climbing down the limestone rocks. You dive in and the water is warmer than you expected. You can wear board shorts here without turning blue. The rip is strong and you're on the bank in two seconds flat. The river goes for miles. Left-handers swing through and they line up perfectly. It's about four feet. You sit there pushing against the rip, non-stop paddling for most of it. People on the cliff start whistling and you know a set is coming. There are three or four waves to a set. Every one is a gem. Problem is, they're too few and far between. You get a few waves but the mustachioed local keeps staring daggers. You paddle into the harbour with the fishing boats. The lay days keep

coming. You have dinner. Old men with their gravel voices from
The Godfather drink wine and smoke cigars while watching Bilbao
play soccer on TV. An obese man in his twenties walks in. Giant
rolls of fat hang over his tracksuit pants. He can barely sit on his
stool as he takes his place right under the television. He turns
his head as though he can't hear anything. He squints as if he can't
see. One of The Godfathers pokes him and tells him to go and sit
in the back corner. The man is offended and screws up his face
in protest. Everyone in the bar starts hounding him. They tell him
to go away. When Bilbao score, he lifts his shirt over his head,
exposing his masses of flab to everyone, standing right in front of
the TV screen so they can't see it. His arms are spread wide like
the wings of an aeroplane. They hiss and jeer and tell him to go
back to his corner. They treat him like a freak. It's cruel. Eventually,
he goes back to his corner. He has Down syndrome.

Fanning keeps waking to the possibility of waves, but Mundaka
keeps denying him. You drive to Laga and there's barely a ripple,
but you surf it anyway because you're starved. Hours are spent on
the cliff looking at nothing. You're waiting for a pulse, waiting for
heats, waiting for Fanning, Slater and Burrow to settle this thing.
The wait is interminable and excruciating and the slowest of climbs.
If Fanning finishes two rounds ahead of Slater and Burrow, he's
the champion of the world. Get that? Mick Fanning is *this close*
to being the champion of the world.

'The waves weren't that good but there's a lot at stake out there,'
Parkinson says after beating Gabe Kling. 'World titles are up for
grabs. It doesn't matter what beach you're at or how good the waves
are, it's still on. It's still happening. People like Andy are starting
to fall out of the race and I don't want to be one of them. I'll keep
going to the death.'

Some Day

Fanning beats the concierge after trailing momentarily. 'He started with a couple of waves and got a 6 and I was like, "What?"' Fanning says. 'I couldn't get more than a 2 to start with.' A 9 sends Hodei Collazo back to reality. Reporters keep asking Fanning about the world title and he consistently refuses to tempt the fates. He keeps saying he doesn't even know the equation—if he finishes two rounds ahead of Slater and Burrow, the crown is his—but you're not too sure about that. He *must* know. 'I'm just taking it heat by heat,' he says. Say it again. 'Heat by heat.' Say it one more time. 'Heat by heat. I know that's what I keep saying, but it's just what I'm doing. I know that if I get the waves, I'll be able to get the scores.' There's confidence in that final statement. In Mick Fanning's mind, it's not a matter of him being able to surf well. He knows he can do that. The only real variable is whether or not he will receive the opportunity.

'He's so focused,' Burrow says of Fanning. 'He's at the stage where it's obvious he really wants a world title. He's showed that all year. He's just so strong. His fitness and his technique—he's like a robot. He'll paddle into a wave and just destroy it. It's tough to beat.' Fanning and Burrow have barely said a word to each other all year. They just don't mix. Burrow is asked if he's had much to do with Fanning and he replies: 'Not really. We don't really associate that closely. We haven't done any trips together, we haven't done anything together. We just travel and end up in the same places and see each other out in the water, I guess.' What about Slater? 'We text every now and again, talk some shit, have the odd session together when we're both around. But Kelly keeps to himself a fair bit.' Slater likes riding solo so much that he's not even staying in Spain. He's driving back to Seignosse every night. Mundaka locals take it as an insult even if that is not Slater's intention. He just wants to be where the waves are and they most certainly are not at Mundaka.

Slater is on his way out again. Hold the front page, hold the back page, hold every damn page. SLATER IS ON HIS WAY OUT. The first domino is falling. He needs an 8.34 with fifteen minutes to go. He needs to shed a pair of 4's. It's like a game of cards, Heat Poker, but the picture cards are out of the pack. Twos are no good. Tens are unbeatable. A pair of fours is barely worth the effort. Slater takes off but pulls out. His mind is a whirlpool. To try or not to try, that's the question. He's on the verge of surrendering and leaving Fanning and Burrow to slug it out. He's lost for inspiration and going through the motions and Tiago Pires doesn't exactly make his competitive juices bubble over and Bakio is an abominable place, but right when Slater is about to concede defeat to fall out of this contest, fall out of the chase, fall out of his dream of ten world titles without even getting to nine, his back stiffens. He becomes resolute. Kelly Slater doesn't always find his heart until he's forced to go looking. He tells himself he must try because that's what he's always done. He barges past Tires onto a wave and makes his final floater and he can argue against this point until he's blue in the face and you still won't change your mind: Kelly Slater exaggerates his landings in his most desperate moments in an effort to bump up his scores. He cons the judges. It happens so often that it cannot be coincidence. He comes in because he's broken his board. It's the same board he used on the final day at Trestles. He's running up the sand and unlike the Hossegor debacle, his caddie is right there. Good job, pal. Slater is still facing a second straight year-ending defeat but every paddle is screaming urgency because he's wasted time and he still trails what's-his-face Pires. With two minutes to go, Slater needs a 4.51. Not many waves coming through. Does Fanning know? You can't see him. Is he watching? Does he know how close Slater is to being booted out of the contest, the race, *everything*? Heat-by-heat and here's hoping Slater fucks up. *Don't let anything in. Don't.* Eight-time world champion Kelly Slater trails for 28 of the 30 minutes but muscles his way onto a beyond-late wave that gets him through by the skin of his teeth.

'There wasn't a whole lot of preparation for that heat,' he says. 'I've been sleeping a lot, the waves have been bad and it's been cold, rainy and windy. The swell has been pretty flat and the tides are high through the afternoon. I just seem to never get with the time over here. I'm still jet-lagged. I can't say I'm the best prepared surfer on tour right now.' On his mid-heat turnaround in attitude, he says: 'I think I just woke back up and realised that I was still in the world title race. Good thing I got a wave there at the end. But I don't think I'll worry about the big picture right now. It's stressful, really stressful.'

Hotel Mundaka is plying you with hot chocolate. You're having your umpteenth when someone says they've started round four at Bakio and they're going to run the first four heats. Fanning is in heat four against Luke Stedman. You jump in a taxi with 25 Euro in your pocket and tell the driver to floor it to the hell hole.

Parkinson needs a 9 to beat Phil McDonald. He honestly believes he's come close with a strong wave completed by a miniscule air reverse. Miniscule air is better than no air. He claims his wave because he really does believe he's snuck through. It'll be close. Definitely a 7. Probably an 8. Maybe even a 9. The judges give him a 3. Parkinson is fucking livid. He's the closest you've ever seen him to distraught. It's all over. Not matter what he says or does and no matter how badly he still wants to be in the race, he's officially out of the reckoning. He comes in and stands in front of the judging tower and gives them another gob-full. He's not hysterical. He's controlled, firm and passionate. Anyone who ever doubts if Parkinson cares should have seen this: he's on the sand in front of thousands of people telling the world of his frustrations at the inconsistent scoring system. Real anger is carved into his face. He's been given a 3. A good-for-nothing 3. He's suggesting in the strongest possible terms that it's bullshit.

There are nods of agreement. Tension grips the site. McDonald has deserved to win and feels no sympathy for Parkinson because he's in a dog fight to stay on the tour. But still. Fair's fair. It might not have been a 9, but a 3? Parkinson climbs the tower and lets loose. He tells the judges they're getting worse. You know where Parkinson is? He's where Fanning was eighteen months ago. Frustrated with his scores. Unable to find the logic. When Fanning was here, in Mexico after losing to Chris Ward at La Jolla despite being convinced he should have won, he went on to do something about it. Hatchett had said Fanning was too mechanical; that every wave was the same. So Fanning started surfing on his instincts. He solved his own problems. Time will tell whether Parkinson does the same. Later, he's hugging his daughter Evie on the Mundaka cliff. He looks genuinely downhearted. 'Yeah, shattered,' he says. But ambition is creeping to the surface. 'As soon as I lost I thought, "They can have it this year because I'm winning it next year". I've already got myself a bit of a plan. I'm trying to keep it to myself but I'm going to keep really motivated. I'm watching Mick do it and I can't see any reason why I can't.'

Fanning's problematic round-four heat against Luke Stedman is fast approaching and so is darkness. Matt Griggs is pacing the shore. The Parkinson-inspired drama has faded. It's the calm *after* the storm. The atmosphere is dial-tone flat. Griggs is anxious. Stedman takes the first good 'un. Fanning falls. None of this feels right. It's almost 7 p.m. Cold winds of change. Fanning falls *again* and these are as many falls as he's had in the past six months. Griggs stares at the sand. Fanning is being comboed. He's 12 points behind. Three crunching turns on a left and he's not being comboed anymore, just losing. He gets an 8.5. That seems generous. There's a smattering of applause from a lazy crowd. They're into their tenth hour of watching heats and they've just about had enough. Fanning again, at speed, but he misses a floater. Griggs is down on his haunches. It could be so easy for Fanning to lose this. Luke Stedman is an exceptional surfer. It's late and the life has been sponged out of this marathon eleven-hour session. The sun's going down and the crowd is starting to pack up and go home because they assume Fanning will win and they can see him tomorrow. Stedman's senses are on high alert. He can steal a huge win while no-one is looking. Staff pack up their tents and begin collecting their rubbish. It's like last drinks when the barmen start putting chairs on tables while you're still trying to have a good time. You have no doubt Stedman is going to pinch a win from the Spanish darkness. But the downtrodden vibe seems to make absolutely no difference to Fanning. He picks off a high 7 and stands calmly on the bank looking at Stedman during the countdown of five, four, three, two, one and that's another heat (by heat) polished off with neither fuss nor bother and that's another couple of nails in the coffins of Burrow and Slater.

'I'm believing in myself more than I ever have,' Fanning says. 'I'm just doing what I want to do. Doesn't matter what everyone else does, I'm just doing my own thing. If I can get three firsts for the year, the pressure rolls back onto those other guys. I just have to keep really focused.'

Fanning's quarter-final is against Knox. 'Mick against Taylor, I hate it,' Griggs says. 'I hate it. It's a tough one because Mick is going for the world title but it's just as important to Taylor. They're really close mates. They've become really good sparring partners, which you don't get that much in surfing. They've got a healthy respect for each other. Not so much for their surfing, but their attitudes towards life. They just get along really well and that's rare in this world. It's a pretty selfish world. Everyone is out for themselves.'

While Liz, Karissa, Gary Dunne and a few of Fanning's mates have come and gone as his travelling companions during the year, Griggs has been the one constant. He's a calm man and full of surf knowledge. 'My job is to help all the Rip Curl guys in any way possible,' he says. 'Getting fitter, getting stronger, a bit of diet, everything, just one hundred per cent support in every area whenever they need it.' Griggs is tall with blond hair. He has a square-shouldered-stuff-all-waist kind of build because he's a gun surfer himself. He's exceedingly modest. You've texted him a request for an interview. He's replied that he's only agreeing to the must-do interviews because he doesn't want too many distractions. And you're thinking, gee, you didn't realise he was in such high demand. Fanning rings five minutes later. 'G'day mate, Griggsy told me to call you.' You have to explain that no offence, Mick, but it's Griggs you want to interview. The pit boss hasn't thought for one second that anyone wanted to interview *him*.

'It's incredible for me to have Mick going for a world title but the biggest thing for me is the way he's kept his attitude,' he says. 'He's stayed a nice guy and not many people recognise that. A lot of people used to give him the advice of, "Mate, you've got to be more of a prick". They only told him that because it was their way of trying to do it. But that's not the way it has to be, and it's not Mick's way. To get the best out of Mick, we have to let him be Mick. We have to let him have his own personality and his own brand of surfing without trying to change him. It wouldn't work if we'd tried to turn him into a clone of someone else just because they were already winning contests. If we let Mick be Mick, he's going to enjoy it more and whatever happens, happens. He can do it his way and it just works better because he's being true to himself. You can't change anyone. Not really.'

Fanning is sitting nearby. Perhaps he can hear. 'We're in a bit of a rhythm with each other now,' Griggs says. 'I know his routines inside out. We've developed a few of them together but to be honest—and I really want to emphasise this—he teaches me a lot more than I teach him. I can't stress that enough. He's the one out there actually doing it. Just watching him is phenomenal. We can have the best plans in the world and talk all we want but at the end of the day, he's the one who has to get out there and actually do it. He's the one getting up at dawn to go surfing. He's the one getting 8's with five minutes left. He's the one going to the gym and staying fit. It's not like he's the only good surfer out here. Almost every guy on the tour has the talent. But Mick just has this awareness of what it takes to win and be the best. He just knows. He asks questions of me and other people around him but he ends up making his own decisions. He's firm with that. He wants to know every possible area of improvement and get everything straight in his own head. He'll get the advice—but then plot his own course.'

Fanning looks so calm. 'He's just very aware of where he's at,' Griggs says. 'When he lost to Dane at Trestles, he just sucked that up and kept going. He's humble enough to know that losses are part of the deal. He gets pissed off if he makes mistakes but he doesn't get too down on himself. He won't beat himself up over anything. He's young, you know, but he's pretty wise. He just doesn't worry. He accepts a lot of things that other people might find difficult to deal with. He just gets on with things. There's a reason why Mick is going so well right now and not all of it has to do with talent. It's in his head. It's in his attitude. I think Tom Carroll was probably the first guy to bring in this sort of professionalism, but Mick has taken it to another level. He just does it every day. If he loses the world title, it won't bother him. No-one will believe that, but it's true. He'll be disappointed, obviously, but he's going to be happy with himself at the end of this because he's done everything he can. He's having a crack at it and if it doesn't work, well, it doesn't work. He'll turn around and have another crack.'

Fanning is making shapes in the sand with his toes. Where does this calm come from? This never-ending calm? 'I could get spiritual with you and say he's an old soul,' Griggs says. 'He's had some experiences in his life, good and bad, and that's a big part of it, I think. But let's not get too deep and meaningful. He just has a certain wisdom in him. Even on the tour, he's a wise voice. I'm not sure if you're born with that.'

Adriano de Souza has a quandary. He's drawn against Slater in the heat after the slightly surreal Fanning–Stedman stoush. De Souza doesn't want to surf until tomorrow—as per the original schedule. Fanning's appearance in the twilight zone was supposed to be curtains for the day, but they've decided to tack on one more heat to the end of the program. When it's a 50/50 call like this, the decision is left to the surfers. *Both* of them. That's the protocol. But in this case, it's being left to Slater. The king has one opinion and a baby-faced rookie has another and there's only one winner. De Souza has the right to say no, and he does, but Slater has already paddled out J-Bay style. The organisers tell de Souza he has to surf. De Souza is an extraordinarily easy-going guy who shrugs his shoulders, goes out, gets beaten, comes in and shrugs his shoulders again. Heaven forbid Kelly Slater doesn't get his way twice in one year.

De Souza is chronically under-scored and Slater is suddenly full of pep and the Brazillian asks for the judges' scores of each individual wave to be called up in the press tent. Slater's 16.5 has beaten the 13.23 from de Souza, who leans in close to see the details of each wave. On one wave, his scores have ranged from 6.2 to 7.8. Two judges have watched the same ride and been a whopping 1.6 points in disagreement. There's something seriously flawed in that. On one of Slater's rides, the difference has gone from 8 to 9.5. So, one judge thinks a wave is a whisker from being perfection, a 10, while the guy next to him thinks it's only an 8, good but not great. Earlier, for one of McDonald's waves against Parkinson, the range has gone from 6.5 to 8.5. That's astounding and a source of discontent among a lot of pros not wanting to speak out because there's nothing to be gained from getting on the wrong side of the judges. They'll ride a 6.5 but receive a 6 for being a whinger. That's their worry. But take it as read: not all the surfers have faith in the system. De Souza rolls his eyes and calls his mother to tell her that he'll be home soon. It's properly dark now. Most of the crowd has left but a couple of hundred people have stayed behind.

Slater doesn't paddle in after beating de Souza. He goes back *out*. And herein lies the fascination of Kelly Slater. He's in the darkness catching waves with gay abandon. He's throwing himself into impossible positions on the off-chance he'll make them, and occasionally he does. The crowd is entranced as though a magician is pulling rabbits out of a hat and no-one is entirely sure how he's doing it. It's the best surf Slater has all day. He paddles back out *again* and it really is night-time now and you can barely see him. He starts skimboarding in the shore break, frolicking. He's on his own. Nobody on the beach leaves. Earlier, he's been giving barely half an effort in a heat of the utmost importance. By nightfall, he's having so much fun he doesn't want it to end. Eventually it does. A swarm of children follow the pied piper as he trudges through the soft sand. A man is knocked to his feet in the crush. Slater and his security escort keep ploughing forward, but Slater comes to a sudden stop when he sees a girl of about six stumbling backwards while she desperately tries to get her el cheapo little camera to work. Slater smiles and stops. He poses while she keeps fidgeting. Thirty seconds later, he's still posing. 'You OK?' he asks. She gets her shot and he ruffles up her hair. 'Well done,' he says. Kelly Slater is probably a good dad. He might not be around all the time but when he is, you bet he's a very good dad. That counts.

'Felt good then,' he says of beating de Souza. 'I was a lot more focused. I knew what waves I needed and I knew how to ride them. I got in a little bit better form.' He's studied the rankings points. 'If I don't beat Mick in this contest, I'm pretty much out of it,' he says. 'Right now I'm six heats behind him. I just need to keep moving along. It can happen. I feel pretty good, actually, a lot more lively.'

And then he drives back to France.

Mundaka remains such a fiasco they should never come here again. Fanning strides into Bakio. He sits alone. He says he's trying to lay low. He's succeeding. He's arrived wearing sunglasses and a hoodie. Only from the gait of his walk can you tell it's him. He's on the sand. He throws a tennis ball back to a crowd swarming on the promenade. It's a poor substitute for the Mundaka cliff, but it'll have to do. Fanning is chatting to Phil McDonald as Burrow shoots past Emslie's South African mate Royden Bryson to make the quarter-finals with Slater and if either of them reaches the semis, the race is going to a place the whole world should be: Brazil. It doesn't matter what Fanning does, the race will be alive and kicking and book your flight for Imbituba.

'I feel like I'm doing just enough to get through,' Burrow says. 'I feel like I haven't surfed my best yet.'

The quarter-finals will run in the following order: Bobby Martinez against McDonald, Fanning versus Knox, Slater against Jeremy Flores, and Burrow versus Bede Durbidge. Fanning loosens the buckle of a belt holding up baggy blue jeans. Griggs arrives with the big purple exercise ball. Knox turns up wearing a thick woollen coat designed for a Colorado winter and a beard fit for a three-month stay. 'It's not like you're really against anyone out there—just another colour singlet,' he says. That may be true, but some singlets surf better than others. 'Mick will go out there and do his thing and I'll do mine.' Knox has identical earphones to Fanning but the music doesn't get into his bones. He sits near Fanning and Griggs but he doesn't seem entirely sure what to do. Any other day, and they'd hug. Not today. Or not now.

Some Day

Burrow is on the promenade. He's relaxed. Taj Burrow always looks relaxed enough and that's the mind-boggling intrigue of his underlying search for confidence. On outward appearances, you could swear he's the most confident of the lot. Strangers hesitantly ask if it's OK to have a photo with him and he says yeah, of course it is, as if there's no way it could ever be a problem.

Fanning lies back on his purple ball. His feet are flat on the ground. He stretches so far his open palms touch the ground behind his head. He rolls sideways. Rolls the other sideways. Stretches his right leg and his left leg. He's getting sand on his jeans but stretches his arms and shoulders, wiping the sand away. Good to go. Nope. He's not. More stretches start with fifteen minutes left before his heat. Everything is becoming faster. He's walking faster, pacing the white surfers' tent, prowling. He's on his toes. He's swinging his arms around. Ten minutes. The blood is flowing, he's checking the waves, eyes darting around the tent, back to the waves, then he's jumping. He wipes tan-coloured sunscreen across his nose and cheeks. Durbidge walks in but makes no attempt to engage in conversation with his mate. Everyone knows the drill by now—leave Fanning alone. He grabs his board and flicks sand off it. He grabs his block of wax and studies it the way you might try to work out a Rubik's cube. He finds the cleanest side and waxes up. He's barefoot and you swear he's forgotten his wetsuit because he wasn't carrying one when he arrived. He starts taking his jeans off without a towel around his waist and you swear he's about to flash. He has his wetsuit *under* his jeans. Five minutes to go.

'It's down-pat pretty much to the last second,' Griggs says of Fanning's routine. 'We don't live in a consistent world in surfing. The ocean is always changing so he needs a dependable routine that he can take into whatever situation he's thrown into. When he puts those headphones on, he's in his own world. It doesn't matter what country he's in or which beach it is, he has the same music and the same check-list and it makes him feel comfortable.

Nobody needs to motivate him. He's motivating himself. He doesn't need me or anyone else by now.'

The music burning Fanning's brain picks up. He's playing air guitar. No-one else sees. He's throwing his head around. Must be some album and you're going to find out what it is even if you have to steal his iPod when he's in the water against Knox. He unzips his jacket, has a word with Griggs. There are more deep breaths as the nerves really start kicking in. Nerves are good. They mean you care. He's doing a drum solo, slapping his hands against his thighs, his head bobbing up and down. Now he turns the music off because his own switch has just come on. He folds up his earphones cord and places them neatly in his backpack.

Fanning beats Knox to the beach marshall for his singlet, two steps ahead. They say nothing to each other. Fanning beats Knox into the water, two steps ahead again. He smashes Knox in their heat, 14 to 6 in slop, give or take a few tenths of a point.

Slater is preparing for his heat. He just saunters around, killing time like he's in a supermarket queue. *Dum-de-dum.* That's pretty much it. 'Mick and I have always done things a little differently,' Slater says. 'He listens to music, I never do. I watch the conditions and try to get in tune with what's happening. He lets his thoughts develop differently. We certainly have different ways of approaching it. He shuts out the world while I try to think about anything but my heat. He has a little bit more support around him as far as having people close to him. His entourage now, that's generally more than I've had my whole career.'

Slater has a warm-up surf right next to the contest zone during the final stages of Fanning's bulldozing win over Knox. He's as close as he can be without being told to rack off. Slater again becomes the drawcard with aerials, and floaters. The crowd shuffles away from Fanning's heat to be closer to Slater's one-man cameo. When Fanning completes his last wave, Slater is studying him with squinting eyes. Flores beat Slater at Trestles so he's going to lose to him here. HAVE WE MENTIONED THE FACT THAT BAKIO IS AN ABSOLUTE FUCKING DISASTER? 'It would definitely have been an Australian title, no matter what, if I'd lost,' Slater says after disposing of the Frenchman to reach the semi-finals and therefore end any chance of Fanning winning the title here. 'I think surf fans around the world want to see the race continue for a little bit longer, no matter who wins it. Mick is in the driver's seat and we're just along for the ride at this point, trying to catch him. Sometimes it's hard to define exactly what you have to do in these situations but right now, I know exactly what I have to do. I have to go to Brazil and I have to win it. That's it.'

And then Burrow hits his straps. His 15.94 to beat Durbidge is the best of the quarters. Taj Burrow is back. He's in the semis with Slater. The race is going to Brazil. Ladies and gentlemen, we have a ball game on our hands. 'It's all coming together,' Burrow says. He's landed an air but received stuff-all points. 'I was just telling a few people that the judges aren't recognising airs,' he says. 'They think we're not making them, but we are. As soon as the wave dumps, it just stops. You're making the air as good as you can, but the judges aren't rewarding them. I've had a few and got 2's and 3's. The same thing happened to Parko. There was one where I thought Bede got an 8 and he got a 2. It's weird. I don't think the judges are doing anything wrong, but they can't tell from up there that the wave just stops as soon as you've made your air. You've made it as good as you can.'

The first semi will be Fanning and Bobby Martinez. The second will be Burrow and Slater. 'It works out pretty good for Mick, doesn't it?' Burrow says. 'With me and Kelly on the same side of the draw, one of us is going to have to get knocked out. We're all going for it. It's going to be tough—but Kelly is Kelly.' And Taj is Taj.

Thousands of people are roaming the streets and lining the cliff for finals day but the surf is so bad at Mundaka that the ASP and Billabong should never hold an event here again. Slater deserves better than this. He shouldn't have to defend his world title in conditions bordering on the farcical. They all deserve better than this crap. It's not like it's any great surprise. The 2005 event was abandoned altogether because the sandbank had disappeared. It was always going to be 50/50 if waves would come this year and they haven't. The two most important groups of people in all of this—the surfers and fans—have been robbed blind. The last three heats will be held at Mundaka only to save the embarrassment of going through the entire Billabong Pro Mundaka at Bakio. Burrow comes in from his morning surf. 'Can't say it's very good out there.' He's being polite.

'I could lose, I could win,' Martinez says, sounding dangerously fatalistic. 'I'm going to go out there fighting. Mick is winning everything right now, but I'm not afraid to lose. I've lost all this year. I've lost all my life.'

Fanning is the first surfer to traverse the cliff and he's about to be struck down by something he never saw coming. Just when he appeared to be moving so effortlessly towards another final he will be knocked off his feet by thoughts of the person making a lot of this possible.

Sean.

There's a stretch of sand eight paces wide allowing entry to the rivermouth. The water cameraman starts wading through the river. Fanning is paddling out and he can't think straight but he keeps going through the motions, telling himself to get over it, waiting for the hooter because that will be the signal to stop being so bleeding melodramatic. Or realistic. He's so wide of the bank and cliff that you can barely see him. He's out on his own about a hundred metres away from where he'd be sitting if Mundaka was humming. Instead, Mundaka is comatose. She's an immense disappointment for the twelfth straight day. Either give Mundaka a fifteen-year waiting period or give it a miss. Fanning sits on the elbow of the bank and waits for Martinez to join him. He waits for the resumption of his campaign and he waits for these unnerving thoughts to get out of his head. An ASP press release goes out saying: 'Clean three-foot waves are reeling through the contest area, creating the perfect canvas for the top three surfers on the Fosters ASP World Tour—Mick Fanning, Kelly Slater and Taj Burrow— and the defending event champion, Bobby Martinez, to unleash on.' Perfect? Unleash? It's comedy writing of the highest order. They're running the finals today because they have to. There's no point extending the waiting period because there's no swell coming anyway. Honestly, what are we doing here? Mundaka is back on the schedule for 2008. What a joke.

And still, Fanning cannot get his head right. He takes off on a simple wave but goes base over apex. He tries again and falls again. Mick Fanning could ride these clandestine little lefts with his eyes shut under normal circumstances, but no matter what he does now there's a sadness he feels that he cannot overcome. He latches onto a couple of half-decent waves because they're running 35-minute heats and that's a hell of a long time but Martinez has him covered from go to whoa. It's too late by the time Fanning recovers his senses. He suffers an incomprehensibly shaky loss of 14.17 to 11.67. He's still recorded another third and the world title should be feeling like an inevitability from here, but it doesn't. It's suddenly feeling extraordinarily difficult again. Mick Fanning is showing signs of unravelling. The night is darkest just before the dawn.

Fanning can't even get in. This has been the worst possible morning. He's been soundly beaten and his mind has started playing tricks and now he's stranded out in the middle of the fucking estuary. He has to paddle to a faraway sand bar and stand there like the village idiot until a jet ski finally arrives to rescue him. 'It was fun,' Martinez says. For him maybe. He takes three steps backwards as the media crew moves in. One more step and he's over the cliff.

Slater puts on his supersuit and hits the water to exact revenge on Burrow for the J-Bay final and take a small but important step back towards Fanning. There's so much at stake. Slater could move to within four heats of Fanning by the end of the day. Or not make any ground at all. Ditto for Burrow. It's such a let-down to have all these drama-charged scenarios about the world title and have such a polished gem of a heat between Burrow and Slater—but have to sit around like shags on a rock while they try to surf such pathetic waves. Fanning has coughed up his worst heat of the year at the most inopportune time: what Burrow so accurately called *crunch time*. You cannot win the world title at Snapper Rocks. You can only win it at Mundaka, Imbituba or Pipeline. Or lose it. Slater's nostrils flare. First, with the whiff of a chance. But then with anger.

He showers in the limestone cave then tries to put into words the frustration of it all. Burrow has been brilliant, genuinely brilliant, overcoming a crazed priority call in Slater's favour—which prompted a cry of 'Fuck off, judges!' from the gallery—to dish out a hiding of J-Bay proportions. Slater's final score: 4.93. The king has been in the water 35 minutes and his final tally is 4.93. It's the lowest score he's ever had for a heat, and not his fault. You can't ride waves that don't exist. The ASP and Billabong or whoever is responsible should hang their heads in shame. And issue an apology. They suspected this would happen. 'I'm bummed,' Slater says. 'It's so bad out there. I'm lost for words. If the conditions this year don't make Billabong re-evaluate coming here, I don't know what will. It's incredibly frustrating to want to perform and put on a show but not be able to. They should get out of here. It's not feasible to hold an event here. You need four good days for most events but here, you're always going to need eight because of the tides. It's too frustrating. It's a beautiful place and I love it but it doesn't have the quality of wave to allow fair heats. It just kind of goes against what we're trying to do with the tour as far as finding the best waves. Bakio isn't even an average beach break. I don't know, I probably need to decompress before I even talk. I'm just really frustrated. That was the worst and most frustrating heat I've ever had.' Which, of course, speaks volumes for Burrow's ability to dig through the rubble and find 14 points in the same 35-minute period. The same stupefying fall into an absolute pit of despair.

'I need a first in Brazil, and I need Mick and Taj to get fifths,' Slater says. 'I can't win the world title without winning the next contest. Taj and Mick have both won before in Brazil, so it's probably not the best circumstance for me. But anything can happen. I'll be there. I'll get two or three boards I really like, and I'll show up ready to go.'

Burrow comes in, guzzles half a can of Coke and vents. He tells chief judge Perry Hatchett the priority call for Slater was 'horse shit'. Hatchett goes as red as a beetroot. Burrow and Slater had both caught waves. Burrow was the first to be where he wanted to be; out wide on the edge of the bank. Slater kept paddling further up the bank to where it was virtually impossible to make a take-off because it was closing out. But because he was on the inside, he got priority. Burrow is yelling at Hatchett. 'So, if I'm sitting where I want to sit, I can't get priority the whole final?' They agree to disagree. And they can't even agree on that. Burrow storms off. He's in another final and gained on Fanning. Another little push, another shot in the arm, another reminder that Burrow possesses the kind of doggedness he's previously been accused of lacking. 'The plan was to win the next couple of events,' he says. 'So far it's all good. I knew I had to do something serious here.'

It's not humanly possible to make the take-off from deep on the sand bar—unless you're a goofy-footer. Burrow returns to his little spot on the outside but Martinez can sit where Slater received his controversial priority call. They're about 80 metres apart. They may as well be at different beaches. Martinez gets first bite at every wave and if he doesn't make it across, Burrow can try to latch on. It's beyond slow. A mate goes to Alitalia for a round of coffees and returns without having missed a single wave. Photographers stand with hands on their hips. Teeth are grinding. Burrow is so far away. He gets a 9 but can only back it up with a 6 and Martinez defends his Mundaka title by .28 of a point. See the importance of the scoring? Burrow is back in the race by making the final. He would've been right back in it with a win. But it came down to the judges having a difference of opinion of a quarter-point when we've seen they can disagree by more than 2 at any given time. Burrow's dream about the contest hadn't ended like this. But Martinez's did. Burrow is told Martinez also dreamed of winning the contest and he's replied: 'You're kidding, right?'

'I didn't even tell Cleo, my fiancée,' Martinez says. 'I didn't want to wake up. It felt so real and it's come true.' People are clapping because we have a winner and we don't have to go back to Bakio ever again. You're not entirely sure what you'll be doing next October, but you sure as hell won't be coming to the Billabong Pro Mundaka. But it just might pump. And then you won't be able to book a flight fast enough.

Martinez is given the purple felt Basque beret and is thrown into the harbour as per tradition. Burrow takes off his wetsuit. Girls giggle at a hint of butt-crack. He sits with his hands on his knees like exhausted people do in a sauna. His head hangs low. It's been a good day and was the whim of a judge away from being great. Fanning hands him a beer. He gives Slater one as well and for a short while, The Big Three talk quietly. When Fanning leaves, Slater grimaces like he's tasted battery acid and gives the beer away. 'I don't want that,' he says. Fanning squeezes Martinez's arm. 'Great surfing, mate. GREAT SURFING.' It's been great surfing from Bobby Martinez because Mick Fanning genuinely likes him. It's also been great surfing from Bobby Martinez because he's been the crucial difference between Burrow making a moderate move, rather than a full-blown horizontal dive, at a man who has officially become the hunted.

'I'm tired and a little frustrated, to be honest,' Burrow says.

'That was tough. It actually felt totally unfair at first because Bobby was taking these waves from deep that I knew I couldn't make. I couldn't sit where he was because you just can't make those waves on your backhand. They were just too small and too quick, but he was flying through them. I was thinking, "I'm doomed, I can't win this final. I can't do anything". Then luckily enough the tide came in a bit and the faces opened up. I had to go sit wide because that was the only spot where I could make them from. I just started my run a bit late. I got that 9.33 pretty late, and with my 6.83, I just needed more like a 7 or something. It was pretty tight and frustrating, really. I would have loved just one more chance, one more wave. But I can't complain. Second is great. I'm on track. I just need to place better than Mick in Brazil. Any event I go better than Mick is a good one. It's an insane race and it's still alive.'

Fanning is a bit hyper. There's no denying his loss to Martinez has been a shocker because a couple of those falls have been so stiff and rigid they cannot have been him. They defy explanation, but not for much longer. 'I'm fine with it,' Fanning says initially. 'I've known from the beginning of the year that it would probably go down to Brazil, maybe even Hawaii. I'm not worried. I'm just going to keep doing what I've been doing, just go surfing. It feels good to be in this position. I've been in the race at certain times in my career, but I've never been in the position that I'm in right now. It's exciting. I have a seventeenth to get rid of with two contests to go and those guys are keeping ninths so in the big picture, it's still looking pretty good. It's been a good month.'

Anxiety is described in your pocket dictionary as 'distress or uneasiness of mind caused by fear' and you think that good things can sometimes be as frightening as the bad.

16

No

Not now.
   The real and untold story behind Fanning's defeat at Mundaka
is that for the first time this year he's been completely overwhelmed
by his thoughts of Sean as he's paddled out towards the metal
cross. He's told no-one.

   'I can usually think about Sean and not get sad,' Fanning reveals
later. 'But it all just came out before that heat. I was trying to
ignore it, but I couldn't. It wasn't like I was nervous about the
heat. It was just one of those times when I guess emotions can
get the better of you. I was paddling out and this really sad feeling
just came over me. Sean was right there in my head and I couldn't
think about anything else.'

   Fanning goes home for three days before travelling to Brazil.
The world title race is banned from all conversation. As per normal,
he visits Sean's memorial before going to the airport. Sean's tree
is a native frangipani which did not flower for its first nine years.

But when Fanning visits the memorial ahead of the most important week of his life, the tree is in full bloom.

Fact is better than fiction.

17

The gauntlet

HANG LOOSE SANTA CATARINA PRO
PRAIA DA VILA, IMBITUBA, BRAZIL

There's a large Rip Curl billboard straight across the road from Kinka's Bar and Petisquera and it says one word: **MICK**. The band plays Bob Marley cover songs about how every little thing is going to be alright, but Fanning isn't so sure. He's stressing. Don't tell him the scenarios because he doesn't want to know. Don't tell him Burrow didn't make much ground in Spain, not really, and that his fate from here rests entirely in his own hands. Don't tell him that all he has to do is match Burrow and Slater at Praia da Vila and the crown is his. Don't tell him Slater falls out of the race if he finishes anything worse than first or if Fanning makes the semi-finals. Don't tell Fanning who isn't coming, who is, what he has to do, what the others have to do. Don't tell Mick Fanning anything about *anything* because he really does not want to know.

Before we get started, someone should go rescue Slater from the police. He's been questioned in Tel Aviv after shoving a member of the paparazzi outside the house of Israeli model Bar Rafaeli. The paparazzi are leaches. Slater's only regret should be that he

244

didn't shove them *all*. Burrow has attended the Sydney premier of *Trilogy* but excused himself early from the after-party. Parkinson and Irons have kicked on. Irons won't be in Brazil. He's had enough. He tells the ASP he needs to go home to prepare for his wedding. Of all the lame excuses. He's a beaten man and The Ballad of Andy Irons is over for another year.

'I reckon either Mick or Taj will win Brazil,' Parkinson says. 'I'd be so stoked to see Mick do it or failing that, Taj. It'll be good if it's an Aussie. Don't write off Kelly. He's a freak.' Parkinson has been tempted to follow Irons' lead and give Brazil a miss but he wants to be in the general vicinity of a funky little town called Imbituba if his mate becomes No.1. 'We've pushed each other so much,' he says. 'Even now we'll go home and surf together. He's definitely inspired me, and I hope I've done the same to him. Dean Morrison, too, we've all pushed each other along. I think we've gotten to where we are today because of that. Not that I'm taking any credit for what Mick is doing. Putting all the competition and competitiveness aside, when I'm fifty years old, I'll be proud to say I had the chance to surf with Mick Fanning.'

Parkinson was flying home from the Maldives the night Sean died. 'It was devastating,' Parkinson says. 'It cruelled everybody, especially Mick. It broke him.' Those three words and the way Parkinson says them will stay with you a while. *It broke him.* Of course it did. You haven't always paid that due respect. It broke him. You've heard about the brave face Mick developed when his brother died and how he was the rock on which everybody leaned. You've heard about him consoling half the Coolangatta community and how a seventeen-year-old aged ten years and became a man overnight. You've felt incredibly sorry for Sean Fanning because no-one deserves to be cut short like that. You've felt immense sorrow for Liz because the thought of losing a child remains incomprehensible and unfair. Parkinson says he has all the respect in the world for Mick, Liz and the entire Fanning clan but he looks gutted to be recollecting the night when everything went bad. Mick Fanning found strength after Sean's passing—but not for a very long time. When he slowly walked into his bedroom and stayed there for four days immediately after his brother had died, do not doubt for one second the magnitude of his grief.

It broke him.

'None of us can imagine it,' Parkinson says. 'It just devastated our whole town. It was a terrible time. Sean was Mick's big brother. He was the guy he looked up to. Sean was a couple of years older, and he'd keep an eye out for us. He was just always around. You'd go for an early surf and Mick and Sean would always be down there together. To this day, he draws on it. A lot of the drive and determination you see in Mick—I think it has eventually just made him a very strong man. He went through such a tough and horrific thing and you see him now and he's just such a mentally strong human being. But it broke him back then, I know it did. For Liz, to have one of your kids die before you, it can't happen like that. I think Mick gets a lot of his attitude from her. She's an unreal woman—she had to put up with us when we were kids. She'd come home from work and there would be twenty of us in her house.

'I got back from the Maldives and went down to the beach. There were a few mates around but they all looked a bit weird. I knew there had been a big party the night before. I kept asking everyone how they were going but no-one was really saying anything. I ran into this guy and said, "Maaaate, how was last night?" and . . .'

Five flights take 38 hours to reach Florianopolis followed by a two-hour bus trip down Death Road to Imbituba. There's an average of five fatalities a day on Death Road and right on cue, a car is crushed like a soft-drink can. The driver's head is slumped forward, his forehead is pressed against the steering wheel. The car horn blares until his head is pushed back. His eyes are still open and they look down Death Road. The signs say 60 but the message seems lost on the truck drivers hitting 140. There are rice fields, mountains, knee-high weeds and unnerving statues of horses' heads. One out-of-control truck overtakes on the left as another roars past on your right. You decide to stay in Imbituba until you *have* to go back to Florianopolis.

Cracks of thunder and lightning illuminate Imbituba as if God is flicking a light switch on and off. It's spectacular. A horse and cart takes a grubby man along the main street. The barber shaves beards with a glistening knife. A restaurant has no name. Garbage bins and benches are decorated with whales' tails. Every fountain has a statue of a whale. The storm reaches land and unloads gale-force winds. The ocean falls behind a cloak of rain squawls and thick clouds and the forecast is for 10-foot waves and the storm of the century. Cars have their headlights on at 10 a.m. It's that dark. Tents collapse. Trees bend. Half the contest site is either ripped to shreds or blown away. A powerline comes down. The streets are flooded. People peer through closed windows. No more cars on the road. Imbituba is a small town with a bus stop. Four dogs run in circles seeking shelter near Praia Hotel where a sign in the foyer says: HANG YOUR WETSUITS TO DRY INSIDE YOUR SHOWER. SUITS HUNG OUTSIDE THE WINDOWS WILL GET STOLEN. LIKE LAST YEAR. THANKS. ENJOY. The dogs hide behind the concrete wall next to the billboard saying, **MICK.**

Burrow and Slater know they need to finish ahead of Fanning or it's over. 'I was doing an interview at Fox Sports and some guys pulled the sheet out with all the numbers,' Burrow says. 'They were all talking about it, but I didn't pay much attention. I don't want to complicate it. I know I just have to do better than Mick. I have to win, and Mick and Kelly have to lose. It's full-on. All I can do is win it.'

Burrow is asked for an honest appraisal of his chances. 'I really, really don't know,' he says. 'I honestly feel really confident that I can win in Brazil. I mean, shit, I know I've got a chance. I'm going to be positive and go out there thinking about nothing else except winning it. If I win Brazil we go to Hawaii and it's all on. I'll go straight to Hawaii and just surf Pipeline every single day. I want that third win. That'll make things interesting. I'm going to do it. What Mick does is out of my control, but you're not being honest if you don't admit it's better for you if someone else loses. It's a hard one. You don't want to jinx anyone. It doesn't even work for me, anyway. The more I focus on what the other guys are doing, the more it does my head in and the worse I go. The more I want someone to lose, the more they seem to keep winning. You don't want to think, "Fuck him, I hope he loses". If you hear someone else has lost you can think, "Yep, that's cool". But you don't want to get too excited if they lose, just like you don't want to get too down if they keep winning. It's out of your control—even if you do want it to happen.'

His first heat is against Luke Stedman and Marco Polo. Fuck off. Stop making jokes. Marco Polo? Burrow has lost eight of his nine first-rounds this year and they've stripped away any possibility of the development of an air of invincibility. Everyone knows Burrow can cough up the odd bad heat because he keeps doing it. Burrow gets in no-man's land against those below him on the pecking order because he thinks too much. That's hell, when you think too much. As Fanning is finding out.

He sits at the pre-event press conference and appears on the verge of a coronary breakdown. He looks tense and gives only short answers to the local media. He's not in the mood to talk about the race. He's been talking about it all year. He just wants to finish it. His demeanour compared to the effervescent Burrow, sitting next to him, is chalk to cheese. A running joke among Fanning's friends is his propensity to tell 'Mick Stories'. He starts weaving a yarn and it sounds riveting and it's building to the big punchline—but goes nowhere. Fanning needs this particular story to go somewhere. He's travelled 178 548 kilometres this year and still hasn't gone anywhere, not really. Slater doesn't make the press conference on time. Cameras keep filming his empty chair as though he's going to miraculously appear. He arrives right at the very moment Fanning and Burrow are finished and start walking for the door. Coincidence? Not on your life. He's profusely apologetic and sits down alone (always alone) and proceeds to charm the pants off everyone in the room for more than an hour. 'The support here is as strong as in my home town,' he says.

Dave Rastovich has been protesting against the killing of dolphins in Japan. With the water thick-red with blood, Rastovich and five others have paddled into the middle of a killing spree and attracted worldwide publicity in the process. Slater says he's late because he's been up half the night talking to Rastovich. 'Ask anyone what their favourite creature is, and many people will say a whale or a dolphin,' he says. 'I think we have to look at the way we treat animals. I eat meat, too, but I think if we saw videos of cows being killed, I don't know how many of us would want to keep eating meat. We're growing cows for food. What if every animal treated the Earth the way we do? It's unthinkable to me that anyone would want to kill whales or dolphins. It brings out that instinct of the need to protect, and it creates that energy of what you give is what you receive. I'm becoming more aware of the effect I have with the choices I make.' Kelly Slater would save the world if he could.

'I'd like to think that Mick's not going to win the world title,' he says. 'But the reality is that it's going to be really difficult for me or Taj to catch him. I'd like to win the world title again before my career is over. If I win the title I'll do the tour again, for sure. If I don't, it's hard for me to say. I want to build a house and live a normal life on some level. The other day my daughter told me she wasn't happy that so many people know me. I asked her why and she said, "I don't know, it's just not good!" And lately I've been feeling that a lot. I just want to be anonymous sometimes and it's hard to do that at contests. The thing is, though, I love what I do. I love to surf in competitions. And right now, even in the position I'm in, if I were to win again it may be the best thing that has happened in my career. I love the challenge. I love being in that position.'

Heats start at Praia da Vila beach at 2.15 on a sun-drenched Saturday afternoon. Church bells chime. You're having lunch at Panificadora e Confeitaria. A petite woman on the next table has a tattoo of a butterfly on the small of her back. She's smoking a bong. The owners pick up your plate and order you to leave because they want to get down to the beach. It's hot as hell and people are burning their feet on the roads. There are eight in a car with a bare-chested man surfing on the roof. He waves his shirt above his head. Praia di Vila is a long stretch of coast with countless sand-bottomed breaks. Surfers hurry to shore, throwing their boards away and sprinting towards the contest zone. Cars are double-parked. Hanging from the third-storey balcony of the Pousada do Mirante apartment block—right near the billboard saying nothing but **MICK**—is a lone Australian flag. You reach the beach. The surfers have a chill-out zone. It's a viewing area with a bamboo floor and bean bags. The crowd is going ape. Clothing is optional. If you've got it, flaunt it. If you haven't got it, who cares, flaunt it anyway. An entire country is living as if this is all there is. A woman of Amazonian proportions wears a tiny bikini and six-inch heels while she walks on the sand. Throbbing nightclub music pours from loud speakers and everyone is drinking and it's chaotic and intoxicating and mesmerising and Brazil is magnificent and that's the honest-to-God truth.

'Your first few years on tour, some things go your way and some things don't and you can't work out why,' Fanning says. 'It's been the same this year. I was being comboed by Josh Kerr by eighteen points at Snapper but I got out of it. They're the times when you start thinking everything might end up going in the right direction. There have been times in the past when I've had the highest score in the heat for one wave but no other waves have come through so I've lost. There's no reason for that, it just happens. I guess sometimes things can start going your way if you hang in there long enough.'

Mick Fanning runs the gauntlet for the first time before his opening heat against Bruce Irons and Guga Arruda. The gauntlet is a full-blown sprint from the top deck of the contest area down a 30-metre runway to the sand and then across the beach to the water. Fanning's descent gives you more goosebumps than anything you've ever seen in sport. It's bedlam. He stands above a heaving mass of people like an Olympic downhill skier right before a no-holds-barred run into oblivion. Fanning bolts along a narrow path bordered by knee-high steel railings on either side, but the railings run out with a good 75 metres left to the water. It's open slather. It's the running of the bulls but Fanning is the bull. He charges. It's electrifying. No matter what happens, no matter how many guards are on offer, no matter how many times Gary Dunne worries about the need for more security, Fanning will have to run the gauntlet before and after every heat. He beats Bruce Irons and the gauntlet turns evil. It's OK when two girls are hysterical at the sight of Fanning and start crying and shaking, but then a man tries to tackle him as soon as he hits the beach. Security guards wrestle the man to the ground and lay into him with their fists. Fanning bolts again and the crush returns. The noise is a jackhammer. His hat and sunglasses are ripped from his face. He's pushed and shoved. 'What was *that*?' he says when he stumbles into the no-spectators area.

Fanning has won but he's been unconvincing. And then out comes Slater with the most scintillating heat of the day and his 18 points swamp Fanning's score by 3 and this is the most emphatic possible declaration that he's not prepared to relinquish his crown without a fight. It's a thorough demonstration of his powers and an insight into his ability to rise to an occasion. It's why he's done what he's done. If the decibels reached fifteen for Fanning along the gauntlet, they've hit 35 for Slater. Go beyond bedlam and you get mayhem. Go beyond popularity and you have a form of worship. Slater has to run from the masses and jump a nearby fence. 'People are going a little crazy right now,' he says. 'That's the best heat I've had since Trestles. I just haven't been in sync with it all since then. I got a third in Spain but I didn't surf very well that whole contest. Even after all that ground I made up on Mick at Trestles, from Jeffreys Bay until now we've ended up even.' Slater knows more stats than the statisticians.

'I've had a huge amount of support from Brazil since day one,' he says. 'They've been behind me since I first came here in 1992. It's like I'm from here, or something. The number of people who have come up to me and said, "I hope you get the ninth", and just people supporting me and shaking my hand, even out in the water, it's amazing. I'm trying to soak it all in because I don't know how many more times I'll be in this situation.'

Parkinson wins and he's the wildcard. 'I've come here without a goal, really,' he says. 'I had a look at the rankings and I can't really go up, and I can't really go down. Not having the world title hanging over my head, or any other crap to worry about, I'm just here to surf.'

Heats are called off after Slater's decisive victory. Burrow has to sleep on it. They've noticed Fanning's stuttering start against Irons. 'Mick surfed pretty well, but he didn't surf great,' Slater says.

'Beach breaks are a different story for him. Mick grew up in rights and point breaks, not left beach breaks. Hopefully someone can step up to the plate and at least keep him to a fifth so if I can somehow win this thing, I'll have a shot. I'm just trying to keep myself in there. He looked to me like he stumbled a little bit.' This whole thing still feels on a knife's edge. 'I can only do what I can do,' Slater says, 'and sometimes that has an effect on the other guy.'

Fanning is fretting.

'The emotions I've gone through the last year, I don't know how Kelly has done this eight times,' he says. 'It's so draining. My hat is off to him. Andy has done it three times, Mark Richards has done it four times, Tom Carroll and Tom Curren—it's such hard work. There have been times when I haven't been able to sleep and I've only been up to the third round. Kelly's mind must be an amazing place.'

Taj Burrow wakes at first light. The sun is hidden behind one of the two medium-sized mountains within swimming distance of Praia da Vila. The audience on the mud-coloured sand consists of one deserted bicycle with a collapsed wheel and a tennis ball. The gauntlet is no more. Burrow makes his way to the beach at 6.30 a.m. and sees what everyone sees first thing in the morning: Greg Emslie. There's none of the atmosphere of last night. Brazillians aren't leaving home at 6.30. They're more likely to be *going* home. The sun coming up is their cue to start leaving their throbbing nightclubs rather than being any kind of signal to get out of bed. These are not morning people. Burrow sits on a bean bag. His hood is up. He's watching the surf but it's not a Fanningesque inspection. He chats and wipes the sleep from his eyes. Slater is never a member of the dawn patrol. He's more likely to have a covert half-hour session just before dark. Sightings are rare, adding to the mystique. There's no familiarity. Burrow runs a white towel along the edges of his board like he's polishing a Ferrari. If only they went this fast. It's five past seven and Taj Burrow is in no immediate hurry. He casually waxes his board. Just chucks a bit on, really. He appears nothing if not wondrously relaxed.

Over the PA in broken English comes an order: 'Please clear the water—we start in fifteen minutes.' Luke Stedman is doing sit-ups. You can smell marijuana. Four guys have pitched a tent up on the hill and they're starting their day with a smoke. Burrow is jogging across the sand. They yell at him—Boo-Row! Boo-Row!— and cackle like hyenas. Boo-Row gives them a wave and they stand to give him an ovation. Fanning can block out thousands of these lunatics without so much as a glance in their direction unless someone is trying to tackle him into next week, but Burrow waves to a group of blokes off their faces in a yellow tent. He laughs and shakes his head. Another fan arrives. He's having a beer. Go health. Probably no worse than a double-shot coffee.

You're squinting into the sunlight. It's hard to see. Burrow gets the first wave and it's a belter. He's smooth and inverted. He does three power hacks and finishes like a gymnast at the end of a sleek routine. That's it then. Except it hasn't been Burrow. It's been the thirteenth-century-traveller-and-teller-of-many-exotic-tales, Marco Polo. And it's an 8. Burrow starts so slowly he may as well have stayed on his bean bag. He's spent more time in round two than his own bed this year and he's going there again. The thirteenth-century-traveller-and-teller-of-many-exotic-tales has him comboed. The pro-Brazillian crowd would be going ape if they were here. There's a comatose man lying face-first in the sand. You hadn't noticed. He'll be in trouble at high tide.

Burrow remains slow-moving. Then comes the kind of onslaught which won him Bells. And J-Bay. Surfer in red still the most dominant of colours, gets a 9.33. He needs a 6 to catch the thirteenth-century-traveller-and-teller-of-many-exotic-tales and does four gouging turns, but falls. He gets a 5.9. Would Fanning have fallen then? Slater? And then Burrow falls again for less than a 6 and now he's urgently tapping his wrist above his head because he wants the commentator to tell him how much time he has left. Fanning would have a stopwatch providing the answer down to a hundredth of a second. And then with 25 seconds left Burrow dissects an immaculate right-hander for much more than a 6 and he's escaped the hangman's noose.

'I had a really shaky start and felt a bit clumsy,' he says. 'I was burning up out there. It was so hot. I got the hottest head. I was in a bit of a fluster. As soon as I hit the water I thought, "Oh no, this wetsuit is too warm". All I wanted to do was come in and get my wetsuit off. I overheat a lot. I hate wearing too much rubber. I thought I was going to be in the second round again, for sure. But I was thinking, "OK, just relax, if I have another heat later today that's fine, I'll just wear my board shorts and I'll be fine".' Burrow turns up in Chile without booties because he hates wearing them. He goes out here in a wetsuit instead of boardies. Part of the enormous appeal of Taj Burrow is that he can make the same bone-headed mistakes as the rest of us, but then soar in a way the rest of us will never know.

'I didn't have a watch on—I wasn't sure how much time we had,' he says. 'I had my hand in the air for a time check but I figured I'd better stop worrying about that and just get a wave. I put everything I had into that 9 and then I needed my 6 and it shouldn't have been too hard because there are some pretty nice waves out there. So I got a 5.9. But I jagged that wide one at the end. The other blokes were too deep. I figured there were only a few seconds left. Mick and Kelly got through first, but I'm with them now. I'm feeling really good, to tell you the truth. I'm not really feeling any pressure at all.'

Some Day

The thirteenth-century-traveller-and-teller-of-many-exotic-tales is gutted.

Later in the day, an ugly onshore gale ruins the line-up and sends everyone running for cover. Competition is postponed. It's a wild and windswept scene and the contest site is at risk of being torn apart again and only one man remains in the water, pushing himself in waves no-one else wants to know about, looking for just an extra half a per cent because it must be in there somewhere if he just keeps looking and trying to be better than he was yesterday. That surfer is Mick Fanning.

Liz is at home on the Kirra hill. One minute she feels good and strong about it all, the next she's weak and sick with worry. 'It's very nerve-racking,' she says. 'Waiting each day to see if it will run. I never call Mick during a contest. I just text him before his heats. It's always the same: "Good luck, have fun, I love you". And then afterwards, "Well done, Micko, great surfing". There are times when I feel really positive and confident he'll win. But there are times when I have this surge of grief. How will we support Mick if he doesn't win? It doesn't matter to me if he's the world champion or not—I'll love him just the same. But I've been feeling for him, and how he'll get through if it doesn't work out. I've had so many people calling me to ask how I am. I talked to Karissa and my children and they were all so positive. Rachel has three children and we've had long conversations about how badly mothers want to protect them from disappointments. I've been walking around like a lost soul, just trying to be alone and keep calm. I've made a garden.'

Slater plays guitar on a small stage in a bar at Imbituba. He sings and taps his foot. 'I can't believe we're going nowhere . . .' His lyrics are from the heart. 'If I'm really happy or really sad, that's when I can write,' he says. 'You wake up feeling happy and the melody writes itself. If I'm feeling in the middle, I get this block and I can't write anything. You might be sad and depressed about your life, your relationships.' Can he sing? Verdicts range from no to not really.

ESPN Brazil is showing the contest live on TV. Occhilupo is asked for his verdict on the title race. 'I really hope it's going to be Mick,' he says. 'It'd be great for Australia and great for the sport. We used to get a lot of world titles in Australia and it's been too long for us. I won mine in Rio and I'd love to see Mick get his in Brazil. I hope he can—and I think he will.'

Standing next to Slater on top of the runway as he prepares to run the gauntlet—there's a string coming out the side of his red singlet and he says, 'What's this, my bikini strap?'—you see the genuine excitement on his flushed face and it's real and you wonder how anyone can give this up. His opponent, extroverted Brazillian Fabio Carvalho, is down below, thumping his chest, pointing to the Brazillian flag, whipping the masses into a frenzy. He throws himself into the crowd and they swallow him whole.

When it comes to world-title races, Imbituba has been good to Kelly Slater. In 2005, he held a narrow lead over Irons. His first heat was against Guillerme Herdy, who had been grinning like a fool for photos just before their heat. 'Keep smiling, bro,' Slater mumbled. 'Our heat's up next.' Slater decimated Herdy then went for a quiet dinner with family and friends. He gave the impression of being an individual in complete control of his emotions and destiny. Next morning, he had a staggeringly inept loss to Travis Logie. He was sincerely devastated and wanted to drive back up Death Road and get the first flight out of Florianopolis. CJ Hobgood talked him out of it. Irons caned Bede Durbidge and his next heat would be against Nathan Hedge. Irons could send the race to Hawaii by beating Hedge, who is as feisty as they come. He sat with Slater and said: 'I'm going to win this heat. I'm going to end this thing today.' Hedge sat out the back and waited. And waited. Slater couldn't bear to watch, pulling his jacket over his eyes. Tears were streaming down his face. Hedge won. Slater had his first world title in seven years—at the expense of Irons. 'Thank you Brazil,' Slater said during the presentation. 'I feel like a second brother to you.'

Fanning has a quick surf and a massage. He stays holed up in his hotel. There's a painting on the hotel wall of women carrying baskets of food as children fly kites. There are two swimming pools out the back. Banana chairs. Flowers in vases. 'I just want to get out there and surf,' he says. 'It's not just about this week. This has been building for three or four years. The waiting is the hard part. We got here the first week and it was flat. We went to Mundaka and that was flat. They're the things you just have to roll with. Mother Nature doesn't care about a surfing contest. It can be hard but then the waves turn on . . .'

The waves turn on.

Praia da Vila is clear with 2-metre swells right in front of the judging tower. A man rubs the stump of his amputated leg. Fanning has drawn the thirteenth-century-traveller-and-teller-of-many-exotic-tales in the third round. Fanning beats the thirteenth-century-traveller-and-teller-of-many-exotic-tales. 'Nerve-racking,' he says.

'I'll be straight about this,' Slater says. 'Very few people get the chance to win ten world titles. I'm happy with eight but if I get to nine, I'll go for ten.' If he hadn't quit for three years, he'd be going for twelve. Would, could and should. Ban them. Slater thumps Renato Galvao and Burrow takes care of William Cardoso and they're all through to round four with one day remaining. It will be a repeat of the gruelling schedule that saw Burrow win at Bells and J-Bay, and led Slater to victory at Trestles. And it will be identical to the four straight heats Fanning won behind the old lava rock in March. 'I started getting a headache out there, just thinking about it all,' Slater says. 'The situation is what it is. It's a long shot for Taj and I. We just need to keep putting up some numbers and getting through some heats. We're on the opposite side of the draw to Mick so there's nothing we can do to stop him. He surfs before me. I'm out of the race if he gets two more wins. But if he goes out in one of those heats, that's going to pump me up and get me inspired.'

Fanning says nothing.

He doesn't want to tempt the fates. You should not tempt the fates. You *cannot* tempt the fates.

A cameraman is already on the beach at 5.30 a.m. to capture footage of Fanning's arrival, but Occhilupo's heir apparent is unusually late. It's one of the very few occasions this year when he hasn't been out with the birds. It's after 7.30 a.m. when his white rental car finally appears. He surfs briskly. He claps Mick Campbell during the first heat. Fanning is more relaxed than he's been all week, but every now and again he tucks his knees up into his chest and stares at the grass. The rest of the pros sneak glances at him, then turn away when he looks in their direction. All eyes are on him, but nobody wants him to know. They want to wish him luck, most of them, but they don't want to freak him out. Everyone tries their best to act too-cool-for-school. Fanning has drawn Stedman again. He sits on the edge of his seat and slowly turns into the machine. His face becomes stone. The eyes glaze over. There's neither a breath of wind nor a cloud in the sky. His shirt is off. The Celtic Irish cross on the chain around his neck reflects the sunlight. Mick Fanning sits and waits. The gods contemplate his fate.

Burrow beats Ricky Basnett. 'Mick and Kelly get their heats in before me, so I've got to keep catching up,' he says. 'They're always one step ahead of me. I feel pretty good. I like it when there are lots of waves like this. You don't have to stress about catching that last wave. I get nervous when you only get to catch two or three waves in a heat. I want to keep catching waves. I want to keep moving. It's a long shot, but I feel really comfortable with it.'

Fanning picks fluff from black socks. He keeps licking his lips but his mouth stays as dry as the Atacama Desert.

Slater turns and takes one last disbelieving look at the ocean in the way you look at an old friend when they say the thing you thought they'd never say. He's been beaten by Kai Otton. And then there were two. The world title will be returning to Australia.

Slater marches up to Fanning and high-fives him. 'I used to be more worried about Parko and Taj just because they had so much natural talent,' Slater says, 'but at the end of the day, Mick just wants it more.'

Burrow is at the back of the room in a T-shirt. His headphones are on, but they're not covering his ears. He hides behind dark sunglasses.

Stedman is staying with Burrow. 'Taj has got a bit of cash,' he says. 'I might have to see what it's worth for me to knock off Mick. It'd be good to do Taj a favour. He's a good mate. So is Mick, we're all mates, but I want to beat him.'

Fanning trounces Stedman for the third time this year. He exhales deeply as though he's finished one piece of paper work and only a couple remain. He's asked for autographs, but he's torn. He wants to sign them, but he wants to get back to his solitude. He signs a few then hurries along. Clouds are moving in.

Neco Padaratz takes his board from the boot of a run-down station wagon in the dusty car park. He gets changed in the public bar instead of the surfers' area. He was banned from the tour in 2004 for taking steroids and has lost friends because of it. He kisses a baby on the forehead as if he's blessing it. Tattoos adorn his forearms and the back of his neck. Chunky gold rings are on his fingers. The man is a Brazillian hero. He feeds off the energy of the locals. He's banging his fist against his heart and saying *Brazillia*. A diminutive man is ten feet tall. His nose and right ear are pierced. He has a shaved head and a dark beard. His face is pale, gaunt and haunting. His eyes have a pale film over them like those of an albino. The family of his former wife have put a curse on him because they didn't want him doing the tour. He blows kisses to the crowd. 'One heat you're running down the beach and they're cheering for you,' Fanning says, 'then you go against Neco and you're like, "What did I do? Why does everyone hate me?"'

Padaratz starts busily. The wind has died away; the sea is an oily grey. Fanning waits anxiously. Every second is another reason to worry. Nothing comes. Fanning is showing commendable patience but it's fraught with danger. He might not get any waves. But then he gets two bombs and cuts them both to ribbons. He's needed a 6 and taken an 8 on a wave advertising nothing more valuable than a 7. Under the most excruciating pressure, with a beach full of Brazillians baying for his blood, he's done these inversions so severe they make a security guard drop a bottle of beer he's just confiscated. It smashes on the concrete. The 8.17: on paper, and over time, this ride will be lost to the memory. But it's immense. Fanning was on the brink. He had two waves to save himself. When push came to shove, he attacked with the commitment of a kamakaze pilot.

The ocean is rising. Padaratz speaks in disjointed English. 'When I see Mick this year, I see him and this is from the heart. Mick has had to fight in his life. We started on the tour together, we went off the tour together and we come back together. He is my friend. I have lost friends, but I did not lose Mick. He is my brother.' Neco Padaratz thumps his chest one last time.

Burrow sprints across the sand. His quarter-final is against Tom Whitaker. Whitaker is another mate to both Burrow and Fanning—and another Australian staying with Burrow. He's caught between a rock and an impossible place. 'What do you do?' Whitaker says. 'You can't go out there and lay down. No-one does that on this tour.'

Burrow botches his first wave. Whitaker creams his and ASP boss Brodie Carr takes the world championship trophy into a back room. It sits on a small wooden table, waiting.

Fanning watches Burrow fall from the viewing deck. He does not blink. DO NOT LET ANYTHING IN. Whitaker has been given a 6.8 for a big right. You swear you cannot tell the difference between a 6 and an 8. And you're not entirely sure the judges can, either. Fanning moves to the back of the room and stretches. He's doing his normal routine—but with one eye on Burrow and Whitaker. He presses his earphones close and flicks through his playlist. The last album he listens to before his semi-final against Joel Parkinson is *10 000 Days* by Tool. It is not for the faint of heart. There's the constant guttural pounding of bass guitars and drums and they sound like a religious chant. The themes are dark and the lyrics howl about tragedy and death and bug-eyed demons and vampires and the devil and prayers and mortality and love and hate and it's dark and full of aggro with the raw passion of a wounded animal.

Fanning mouths words about this being his time; about this being when he so desperately needs to be given his wings.

Slater is still in the room and he chats with Fanning's semi-final opponent: Parkinson. Having come to Brazil mainly in the hope he could be near Fanning if and when *it* happened, Parkinson is about to become a piece in the puzzle. He could conceivably knock out Fanning and then Burrow can take the race to Hawaii and win it and Joel Parkinson will have to live with the fact that he denied his mate a heart's desire. Parkinson grabs his wetsuit and puts it on like a six-year-old getting into his pyjamas when he's been told to go to bed—but doesn't want to. He can't win. Whatever he does, he cannot win.

Fanning's last words are spoken softly: 'Let's do this.'

He meditates once more on the sand. The crowd stands back and watches him in silence. There's the slightest of furrows on his brow. His fingers aren't touching this time. His elbows are on his thighs and his hands are limp. The fingers of his left hand are twitching. His singlet is yellow. After 45 seconds, his eyes jolt open as if he's woken from a nightmare. He jumps to his feet and walks to the water's edge. He looks to the sea and stands there a while. He moves slowly through the waist-high breakers while holding the nose of his board in his right hand. He doesn't paddle out, but allows the current to take him. He's floating. Thousands of people have filled the point and he ever-so-briefly looks their way. Parkinson follows him out. Parkinson is behind Mick Fanning. All year, Joel Parkinson has been behind Mick Fanning. It never used to be this way. Burrow is in trouble. This is real.

Word gets to Mark Occhilupo that Fanning is on the brink of becoming world champion. He runs through the corridors of the Praia Hotel and jumps in his car with Bruce Irons. Fuck the seat belt. He's fast becoming an emotional wreck. Occhilupo turns the ignition, puts his car into gear and rams his foot down. But he's put it in reverse. The car crashes straight into a tree so hard the back window smashes. Worse things can happen when your car hits a tree. A lot of bad things can happen when you least expect them to. Some of them will never make sense. Others, in hindsight, are the best things that ever happened to you.

'That's just what life is,' Fanning says of the injury which made this kind of achievement seem an impossibility. 'You just take the good with the bad. You go through ups and downs and even though I was hurt, it was probably the best six months of my life. I didn't have to worry about surfing. I had fun with my friends and at the end of it I found the girl that I love and want to marry so even though it was bad for my body, it was probably a million times better for my mind and heart.' Fanning reaches the line-up and Whitaker is grinning at him. They're so far out to sea that no-one can hear the scores because the wind has swung on-shore. Fanning is asking Whitaker for an update, pleading with him for at least a hint, but Whitaker keeps quiet. He knows he's beating Burrow but he just keeps grinning the way you do when you're carrying an especially valuable secret. And then they're joined by a dolphin.

'Every time I've had a heat today there's been a dolphin in the line-up, just chilling,' Fanning says. 'I don't know if it's my brother, or what. I saw some footage of Dave Rastovich trying to save the dolphins in Japan. I got so emotional watching that and then seeing that dolphin out there today.'

Later, he'll be asked if he genuinely believed the dolphin was Sean. Do not doubt the dolphin is out there. Parkinson and the water cameraman confirm it. They also vouch for the fact that throughout this final day, the dolphin disappears whenever Fanning isn't in the water. Straight after the heat, it vanishes. 'Yeah,' Fanning says. 'I do think it was Sean.' Fanning is about to become world champion, and he is sitting on his board ten feet from none other than Joel Parkinson. You couldn't make up this stuff if you tried.

'It was so cool to have Joel out there,' Fanning says. 'There have been a few times during the year when I haven't known how to be with Joel and all my mates. There have been times when I've felt a bit selfish and that I've maybe been neglecting my friends and family. I hope it hasn't been like that for them. I would have loved to ask Parko for his advice but I couldn't because we were competing. You're mates but when it comes to the tour it's every man for himself and that's one of the hardest things to get your head around. There have been a few times when I wondered if Parko understood. He's come all the way to Brazil because I might win it and he wanted to be here, and that's why he will always be a mate. I'd do the same for him.'

Burrow needs an 8.1 against Whitaker. He looks to the horizon, looks north, looks south and ultimately, looks down. There's nothing coming. Burrow is crest-fallen. Whitaker isn't exactly doing cartwheels. 'I'm really close with both those guys,' he says. 'I'm hugging Mick because he's a mate and it's the world title and it doesn't get any bigger than that. He's been a rock. Mick and Joel were super-stoked but then I looked back and saw Taj sitting there and he was devastated. He's had this massive campaign and it's all over. He paddled over and congratulated Mick and I felt for him. I'd effectively knocked one of my best mates out of the world-title race.'

Fanning watches the dolphin.

'So many things have happened in my life—good, bad, average,' he says. 'This will be one of the more amazing things.'

The dolphin keeps circling, dancing.

Some Day

'He was a funny bastard, Sean. He was a character—really funny and cheeky, but he had a lot of respect for people. He was one of those guys who was the leader of the pack. He wanted to make sure everyone was OK. He was a few years older than me and my mates. I looked up to him so much because he was a really good guy. You know when you're kind of fifteen and sixteen and you have that older guy you want to be like? I guess that was Sean to me. I just followed him around everywhere. Whatever he was doing, I wanted to do it with him. Whatever he said, went. He was my older brother so I just couldn't imagine there would ever be a time when he wasn't there. I didn't really understand it. We had some amazing times. Losing him was extremely difficult, and I don't want anyone to forget about him. He played such a big role in my life and the lives of everyone in my family. He would have made the tour—but just never got the chance. I didn't want to waste this year because who knows if I'll ever get into this position again.

'There have been a lot of times today when I've thought about him. I miss him, you know. I really do. I don't know if I'll ever get over that. I don't know if you're even supposed to. And I don't know if I want to. I like having him here. I still think about him a lot. I kind of feel like his spirit is around me. And his energy. I can feel that a lot. I guess it's become easier to deal with over the years because I've just gotten used to the way I think about him. It's almost like I've got this other brother now or . . . I don't know how to explain it. It's weird. I just feel like he's around me a lot. I'll just always miss him and there are times when all I want to do is see him again. It's like I keep expecting it to happen. I guess it's like if you have a friend you've grown up with, but then your friend moves to a different town. You've always done everything together, gone to all the same places together, but then your friend is living somewhere else and you don't get to see him anymore. You're still going to the same places and you can't help wishing your friend was still going with you. You keep imagining what it would be like if he was still around. Sometimes I dream about him every night for a whole week and that gets me so pumped. I feel amazing when I wake up in the morning because I feel like I've spent some time with him. Everyone has people like that in their lives—just talking to them on the phone can give them all this amazing energy. I see that happen all the time with people. It can feel very real. I'd do anything to be able to see him again, just one more time. Just for a couple of minutes.'

One second before Mick Fanning becomes world champion . . .

'I looked at Joel and said, "What do we do?"'

The moment—that very instant—when Mick Fanning becomes world champion . . .

Everything goes quiet.

'I woke up this morning and I just had a good feeling it was going to happen today,' he says. 'I'd put all this emotion into it, and it was building and building and I thought all this earth-shattering stuff was going to happen—but it didn't. It was like time stopped.

One second after Mick Fanning becomes world champion . . .

His first wave as the title holder is a joyous celebration. Fittingly, he's given a big right-hander. Fittingly, he slaughters it. 'I can never remember my best waves,' he says. 'Something happens and you stop thinking and everything just clicks and you go into this other world. You ride it without even really knowing what you're doing. And you get to the end and you're thinking, "What did I just do?" All you know is that it feels good.'

Some Day

Parkinson and Phil McDonald carry Fanning up the beach. 'I really wanted to be here for this,' Parkinson says. 'And I've ended up being the one sitting next to him when it happened. It's pretty ironic. We were a bit shocked for a minute. We didn't know what to do. Then we went a bit crazy. I tried to drown him. It didn't work. When we were young, all we wanted was to be pro surfers when we got older so to have this happen today, and to be there with him right when it happened, it couldn't have been written any better. We were speechless, actually. It was just me and Mick and a dolphin circling us for ages, doing laps. We were like, "Can you believe this is happening?" He was talking about how much he's been stressing over the last week. I don't know if you could make up a finish like that. It was like being in the last scene of a movie.'

Burrow has a shower. He watches Fanning beat Parkinson (and go on to win the final against Kai Otton) and conducts himself throughout with the greatest dignity and humility. A room full of his peers are celebrating Fanning's triumph and therefore, unintentionally, Burrow's demise. He joins in the revelry even though this is killing him. 'I'm kind of having a hard time smiling right now,' he says. 'But I'm stoked for Mick. I mean that. He's worked hard for this and he deserves it. Second is so close. I'm going to roll this into next year because I know I'm nearly there. But it's a bit hard for me right now.'

Occhilupo bursts into the room while simultaneously bursting into tears. He bear-hugs his mate. A grown man is crying. Occhilupo embraces Fanning as if tomorrow won't come. 'I'm a mess,' Occhilupo says. 'I wasn't going to come to the beach today but when I heard Mick was about to win it—I get goosebumps just thinking about it. It's been eight years and it's coming back to Australia. It's been too long. This will open the floodgates. Yeah, I smashed the car up a bit. Just a bit of a fender bender. Don't write that. Ah, go on, write it. I'm just so proud of him, but he doesn't quite get it yet. He doesn't know what he's done. We have an Australian world champion again and I think the world champion is going to be an Australian for a long time to come.'

Fanning remembers the day Occhilupo won. 'I went surfing really early. I ended up listening to the radio later on and they started saying Occy was the world champion and even back then, I was just so pumped. Look at all the kids around here. I was a kid when Occy won, and now I've won and there are kids watching me. They'll have their goals. It can seem like a long way away when you're younger, but it's not that far. You just have to believe you'll get there. To take the reins from Occy is incredible. He's a legend of the sport and such a cool guy. Everyone in Australia loves him. Even with Andy, I was there for his first world title and he's such a determined guy as well. And Kelly, I don't know what to say about him. I'm really proud that I've gotten to know him. He's the guy who has given inspiration to every kid who surfs today.'

Fanning buries his face into his own hands. 'Look at him,' Occhilupo says. 'It's sinking in.'

Slater is waiting for the presentation while Fanning is being badgered for photographs and interviews. 'Welcome to the real world, Mick Fanning,' Slater laughs. He's in an especially ebullient mood.

'It's been such a long journey,' Fanning says. 'Anyone who has helped me, anyone who has kicked me in the arse, it's all good.'

You ask Slater for one word—just one word—to describe the new world champion. He scratches his head, ums and ahs, puts words on the tip of his tongue only to pull them back.

'Got it,' he says. 'Dickhead.' He laughs so hard he nearly falls off the stage. He gives Fanning one of his boards and congratulates him again and have no doubt that Kelly Slater thinks Mick Fanning is a class act. He'll write him a letter telling him just that. 'Surfing is in good hands,' Slater says. 'Mick is a professional in every aspect and he'll be a great ambassador.' Slater leaves but you want him to come back. It's highly doubtful you will ever again enjoy a sporting contest as much as you have relished the battle between Mick Fanning, Kelly Slater and Taj Burrow. Of walking through airports and waking at dawn with the kind of excitement you wish you could feel every day. Slater will be competing in another contest in Florida by the end of the week to raise awareness about the dangers of skin cancer. In all honesty and sincerity, there can be few more fascinating creatures roaming the planet than Robert Kelly Slater. Only when he really does retire will people take a moment to reflect on his accomplishments and idiosyncracies and just his *way* and it will defy all comprehension. He's a god.

The best advice Fanning has received all year—Do It Your Way, Mate—has come from another god, Mark Richards. 'What Mick has done is bring an unprecedented focus to a campaign that has lasted pretty much ten months,' Superman says. 'Kelly and Andy have always had this incredible competitive determination and focus and drive and seething desire to win, but Mick has out-Kelly'd Kelly and out-Andy'd Andy. He's basically beaten them at their own games. He's taken their intensity and turned it up. He's been more driven than the two most driven guys we've ever seen and my hat goes off to him. In the past I think Australian surfers have been happy enough to win an event, not go so well in the next, do OK in the next then stuff up the next one. They didn't seem to have that year's worth of commitment but I think Mick just sat down with his family and his team and said, "You know, if I buckle down, I might just be able to win this".

'Snapper was such a tremendous springboard for his whole year. He was on the ropes against Josh Kerr; so far behind that he should have paddled in. Josh had two 9's—I would have paddled in and given up. I reckon all but three of the guys on the tour would have given up in that situation, but I think a little voice inside Mick's head said, "Kelly and Andy don't quit and I'm not going to quit, either". To come back from there must have made him feel invincible.

Then he had to hold his lead all year—and that's an ordeal. That made him a target. Everyone wanted to knock him off because even though Kelly was the defending world champion, Mick had the No.1 ranking straight after Snapper. Everyone tries that little bit harder against you when you're on top because they want to bridge the gap. You're the biggest scalp out there. They all wanted to get rid of him, but he fought them off. Kelly was right there, and Kelly is the master of the mind-fuck. If you're a competitive surfer on the tour, you don't want to go within two inches of him because he'll find a way to mess with your head. He takes the battle out of the water and onto the land and if he can gain a psychological advantage before you get in the water, he'll use it. He's the master tactician and that's why he's won eight world titles. He hasn't just out-surfed people, he's messed with them psychologically. Mick overcame all that because Kelly threw him a test at Trestles. He threw him the "Are you worthy?" test, pretty much standing in front of Mick and saying, "Are you REALLY worthy of being world champion?" Mick turned around and won the world title in France. In my view, that's where he won it. He could have wilted there. He could have pressured-out when Kelly lost and gone, my god, here's my chance. But it was like, all year, pressure didn't even exist for him.'

Fanning has pulled off what Superman calls 'the greatest world championship performance ever because I don't know if anyone has ever won it with that level of consistency. At the end of the day, it would have been a total injustice if he hadn't won. It's something you can't say in sport but if anyone ever deserved to win, it was Mick this year because of the way he surfed from his first heat until his last. No-one can ever question his title. There are no doubts and no what-ifs. He took on Kelly Slater and Andy Irons and he beat them both of them fair and square.'

Every man and his dog makes long-winded attempts at pinpointing why—HOW—Fanning has reached the summit, but Superman needs only three words to get to the heart of the matter. Superman is asked for one sentence, just one sentence, to sum up Mick Fanning's world title and he doesn't do a Slater and take his time, no procrastinating and hesitating, requiring just a split-second to say categorically and emphatically: 'Balls Of Steel.' Say no more.

Fanning is overwhelmed now. There have been times in his life when the sorrow was so great he ceased to exist. He didn't want to surf because the guy he surfed with was gone. He didn't want to do *anything* because the guy he did *everything* with was no longer by his side. The agony of 14 August 1998 will never completely fade for Mick Fanning, but that's OK. He's dealing with it. Perhaps you imagine this, perhaps it's real, but standing here on Praia da Vila, he no longer looks ten years older. He no longer looks like a wise old soul, and nor should he. In the middle of this cataclysm of celebrations, he looks to be exactly what he is—just an extraordinarily talented and tremendously courageous 26-year-old man with the world at his feet. The noise reaches an absolute crescendo and the power surge of atmosphere goes above and beyond anything Fanning expected, anything he could ever have imagined, and what a world this is. He runs the gauntlet one last time.

The end

You know when everything is so loud you can't hear? You know when you have so many thoughts you can't think? You know when you're so entranced by the beauty of a single moment that you are certain, already you are certain, you will replay this scene over and again in your mind for as long as you draw breath? You know when you're so enamoured by a group of people that all you want to do is march up to them, put their faces in your hands and tell them: 'You know what? This is fucking brilliant.' Ever feel like that?

You remember being eight. You remember finding that little red MR board under the Christmas tree. You remember standing on the shore and asking your big heroic dad: 'Come out with me?' You remember him pushing you onto waves. You remember his arms in the air when you rode them to shore. You remember the joy on his face. You remember him sitting on the bench at Merewether when you were old enough to surf by yourself. You remember that every time you caught a wave, the first thing you did was turn around to make sure he was watching. *Did you see, Dad? Did you see?* Thirty years later, every time you catch a wave, the first thing you do is turn around to make sure he's still watching. Maybe that's pathetic. Maybe that's beautiful. Maybe that just shows how much you love the old boy. Now you have children of your own, maybe that's why, when they start catching waves by themselves, you will always want to be there to see.

Far away from this madness, far away from Rip Curl caps and internet cameras and microphones and interviews and prize money and computer points and all the back-slapping he's getting from a swarm of virtual strangers, Mick Fanning will be left with the strongest emotions of all—his own. He will go off by himself for a short while. He will close his eyes and talk to his brother. Only they will ever know what is said. Only they will ever truly understand their bond. Mick will stand alone on the hill at Kirra. He will look at the small wooden cross dedicated to the memory of Sean Fanning, 1978–1998, and he will cry. He will tell his brother once more that he loves him. He will tell his brother again that he misses him. If the world really is a good and fair place, Sean will find a way to say it back. Mick Fanning is the champion of the world. Some day has arrived. He looks to the sky. *Did you see, Sean? Did you see?*